بری ء من
الأذى

Free

from

Harm

Free from Harm

ISBN 978-0-578-95362-5

Free Islamic resources:  arnabmubashir.com

بسم الله الرحمن الرحيم

# التبول

*Urination*

عن أبي هريرة قال قال رسول الله ﷺ أكثر عذاب القبر من البول

سنن إبن ماجه كتاب الطهارة وسننها

From Abu Huraira who said: The Messenger of Allah (SAW) said: Most of the torment of the grave is from urine.

*Sunan Ibn Majah, The book of purity and its sunnah*


عن إبن عباس قال مر رسول الله ﷺ بقبرين جديدين فقال إنهما ليعذّبان وما يعذبان في كبير أما احدهما فكان لا يستنزه من بوله وأما الأخر فكان يمشي بالنميمة

سنن إبن ماجه كتاب الطهارة وسننها

From Ibn 'Abbas, who said: The Messenger of Allah (SAW) passed by two new graves, and said: Indeed these two are being punished, although they are not being punished for something serious. One of them used to not be careful about his urine, and the other went around talking bad about people.

*Sunan Ibn Majah, The book of purity and its sunnah*


عائشة رضي الله عنها زوج النبي ﷺ قالت انما مرّ رسول الله ﷺ على يهودية يبكي عليها أهلها فقال إنهم ليبكون عليها وانها لتعذَّب في قبرها

صحيح البخاري كتاب الجنائز

'Aishah (may Allah be pleased with her), the wife of the Prophet (SAW), said: The Messenger of Allah (SAW) passed by a Jewish woman whose household was mourning over her, and He said: They weep for her, and indeed she is tormented in her grave.

*Sahih Al-Bukhari, The book of funerals*


عائشة رضي الله عنها قالت دخلت علي إمرأة من اليهود فقالت إن عذاب القبر من البول فقلتُ كذبتِ فقالت بلى إنّا لنقرض منه الجلد والثوب نخرج رسول الله ﷺ إلى الصلاة وقد ارتفعت أصواتنا فقال ما هذا فأخبرته بما قالت فقال صدقَت فما صلى بعد يومئذٍ صلاة إلا قال في دبر الصلاة رب الصلاة رب جبريل وميكائيل واسرافيل أعذني من حرّ النار وعذاب القبر

سنن النسائي كتاب السهو

'Aishah (may Allah be pleased with her) said: A woman of the Jews came in to see me and said: Indeed the torment of the grave is because of urine. I said: You lie. But she said: Indeed it's true; we cut back our skin and clothes from it. And the Messenger of Allah (SAW) went out to prayer, but our voices got loud and He said: What is this?! I told him what she had said. And He said: She's right. And from that day on He never prayed a prayer without saying at the end of it: "Lord of Jibril, Mika'il, and Israfil, give me refuge from the heat of hellfire and the torment of the grave."

*Sunan Al-Nasa'i, The book of inattentiveness*


عن عائشة قالت من حدثكم أن النبي ﷺ كان يبول قائماً فلا تصدقوه ما كان يبول إلا قاعداً

جامع الترمذي كتاب الطهارة

'Aishah said: Whoever tells you that the Prophet (SAW) urinated standing up, do not believe him; He only urinated sitting down.

*Sunan Al-Tirmidhi, The book of purity*


عن جابر عن رسول الله ﷺ أنه نهى أن يبال في الماء الراكد

صحيح مسلم كتاب الطهارة

Jabir related from the Messenger of Allah (SAW) that He forbade one to urinate into stagnant water.

*Sahih Muslim, The book of purity*


عن ابي هريرة عن النبي ﷺ قال لا يبولنّ أحدكم في الماء الدائم ثم يغتسل منه

صحيح مسلم كتاب الطهارة

Abu Huraira related from the Prophet (SAW), who said: Let none of you ever urinate into stagnant water and then bathe with it.

*Sahih Muslim, The book of purity*


عن حكيمة بنت أميمة بنت رقيقة عن أمها قالت انها كان للنبي ﷺ قدح من عيدان تحت سريره يبول فيه بالليل

سنن ابي داود كتاب الطهارة

Hukaimah bint Umaimah bint Ruqaiqa related that her mother said: The Prophet (SAW) had a wooden cup under his bed that He urinated into at night.

*Sunan Abu Dawud, The book of purity*

عن حكيمة بنت أميمة عن أمها أميمة قالت كان للنبي ﷺ قدح من عيدان يبول فيه ويضعه تحت سريره فقام فطلب فلم يجده فسأل فقال أين القدح قالوا شربته برة خادم أم سلمة التي قدمت معها من أرض الحبشة فقال النبي ﷺ لقد إحتظرت من النار بحظار

المعجم الكبير للطبراني باب الباء

Hukaimah bint Umaimah related that her mother Umaimah said: The Prophet (SAW) had a wooden bowl that He would urinate into and put under his bed. One time He got up and looked for it, but did not find it; so He asked and said: Where is the bowl? They said: Barrah the servant of Umm Salamah, the one who came with her from the land of the Ethiopians, drank it. And the Prophet (SAW) said: She has shielded herself from hellfire with a sure shield.

*Al-Tabarani, Al-mu'jam Al-kabir, Section: Coitus*

عن حكيمة بنت أميمة عن أمها أميمة بنت رقيقة قالت كان للنبي ﷺ قدحٌ من عيدان يبول فيه يضعه تحت السرير فجاءت إمرأة اسمها بركة فشربته فطلبه فلم يجده فقيل شربته بركة فقال لقد احتظرتَ من النار بحظارٍ قال الحافظ أبو الحسن بن الأثير وقيل إن التي شربت بوله عليه الصلاة والسلام انما هي بركة الحبشية التي قدمت مع أم حبيبة من الحبشة وفرق بينهما فالله أعلم

البداية والنهاية لإبن كثير سنة إحدى عشرة من الهجرة باب ذكر عبده ﷺ اماؤه عليه الصلاة والسلام

Hakimah bint Umaimah related from her mother Umaimah bint Ruqaiqah, who said: The Prophet (SAW) had a wooden bowl to urinate in, and He would put it under the bed. And a woman named Barakah came and drank it. He searched for it but did not find it. Someone said: Barakah drank it. And He said: She has shielded herself from hellfire with a sure shield. Al-Hafidh Abu Al-Hasan Al-Athir said: Someone said that the one who drank his (prayers and peace upon him) urine was indeed Barakah the Ethiopian, the one that came over with Umm Habibah from Ethopia; he made a distinction between the two of them. But Allah knows better.

*Ibn Kathir, Al-bidaya wa Al-nihaya, Year eleven after the Hijra; Section: Mention of His (SAW) servants; His (prayers and peace upon him) female servants*

عن أم أيمن قالت قام رسول الله ﷺ من الليل إلى نخارة في جانب البيت فبال فيها فقمت من الليل وأنا عطشانة فشربت ما فيها وأنا لا أشعر فلما أصبح النبي ﷺ قال يا أم أيمن قومي فأهريقي ما في تلك الفخارة قلت قد والله شربت ما فيها قالت فضحك رسول الله ﷺ حتى بدت نواجذه ثم قال أما انك لا تجعين بطنك أبداً

المعجم الكبير للطبراني ما اسندت أم أيمن

From Umm Ayman, who said: The Messenger of Allah (SAW) got up during the night to go to a jar on the side of the house, and urinated in it. I got up during the night, and I was thirsty, so I drank what was in it, but I wasn't aware of anything. And when the Prophet (SAW) arose in the morning, He said: Oh Umm Ayman, get up and pour out what is that jar. She said: I ... I swear by Allah I drank what was in it. And the Messenger of Allah (SAW) laughed until his molars showed, then said: Indeed you will never suffer stomach pain.

*Al-Tabarani, Al-mu'jam Al-kabir, Section: Narrations from Umm Ayman*

عن عبدالله رضي الله عنه قال ذُكر عند النبي ﷺ رجلٌ فقيل مازال نائماً حتى أصبح ما قام إلى الصلاة فقال بال الشيطان في أذنه

صحيح البخاري كتاب التهجد

'Abdullah (may Allah be pleased with him) said: A certain man was mentioned to the Prophet (SAW), who was told that he had remained asleep until morning and had not gotten up for prayer. And He said: Satan has urinated in his ear.

*Sahih Al-Bukhari, The book of night prayer [tahajjud]*

عن عيسى بن يزداد اليماني عن أبيه قال قال رسول الله ﷺ إذا بال أحدكم فلينتر ذكره ثلاث مرات

سنن ابن ماجه كتاب الطهارة وسننها

'Isa ibn Yazdad Al-Yamani related from his father who said: The Messenger of Allah (SAW) said: Whenever any of you urinates, he should yank [yantur] his penis three times.

*Sunan Ibn Majah, The book of purity and its sunnah*

عن عيسى بن يزداد عن أبيه أنه قال قال رسول الله ﷺ إذا بال أحدكم فلينثر ذكره ثلاثاً قال زمعة فإن ذلك يجزئ عنه

المصنف لإبن أبي شيبة كتاب الطهارة

'Isa ibn Yazdad related from his father, who said: The Messenger of Allah (SAW) said: Whenever any of you urinates, he should shake out [yanthir] his penis three times. Zam'a added: Indeed that is profitable for him.

*Ibn Abi Shayba, Al-musannaf, The book of purity*

عن عبدالله بن أبي قتادة عن أبيه قال قال رسول الله ﷺ لا يمسكنَّ أحدكم ذكره بيمينه وهو يبول ولا يتمسّح
من الخلاء بيمينه ولا يتنفس في الإناء

صحيح مسلم كتاب الطهارة

'Abdullah ibn Abi Qatada related from his father, who said: The Messenger of Allah
(SAW) said: Let none of you ever take hold of his penis with his right hand as he is
urinating, and let him not wipe in the toilet with his right hand, and let him not
breathe in and out of a [drinking] vessel.

*Sahih Muslim, The book of purity*

عن جابر بن عبدالله قال نهى نبي الله ﷺ أن نستقبل القبلة ببول فرأيته قبل أن يُقبض بعام يستقبلها

سنن أبي داود كتاب الطهارة

From Jabir ibn Abdullah, who said: The Prophet of Allah (SAW) forbade us to face
the *qiblah* to urinate, but I saw him, a year before he was taken, facing it.

*Sunan Abi Dawud, The book of purity*

عن عبدالله بن سرجس أن رسول الله ﷺ نهى أن يبال في الجحر قال قالوا لقتادة ما يُكره من البول في الجحر
قال كان يقال إنها مساكن الجن

سنن أبي داود كتاب الطهارة

'Abdullah ibn Sarjis related that the Messenger of Allah (SAW) prohibited one to
urinate in animal burrows. Some people said to Qatada: What is disliked about
urinating into animal burrows? He said: It was said that they are where genies live.

*Sunan Abu Dawud, The book of purity*

قال يحيى وسئل مالك عن غسل الفرج من البول والغائط هل جاء فيه أثر فقال بلغني أن بعض من مضى
كانوا يتوضؤن من الغائط وأنا أحب أن اغسل الفرج من البول

موطأ مالك كتاب الطهارة

Yahya said: Malik was asked about washing the crotch from urine and feces; had any
hadith been related regarding this? He said: It came to my knowledge that some of
those who have since passed used to perform ablution from having defecated; myself
I like to wash the urine off my crotch.

*Muwatta' Malik, The book of purity*

عن يحيى بن سعيد أنه قال دخل أعرابي المسجد فكشف عن فرجه ليبول فصاح الناس به حتى علا الصوت
فقال رسول الله ﷺ اتركوه فتركوه فبال ثم أمر رسول الله ﷺ بذنوب من ماءٍ فصبّ على ذلك المكان

موطأ مالك كتاب الطهارة

Yahya ibn Sa'id related that he said: A certain Bedouin man entered the mosque and uncovered his crotch to urinate. And the people made an uproar about it to the point that the noise got loud. But the Messenger of Allah (SAW) said: Leave him alone. So they left him alone, and he urinated. Then the Messenger of Allah (SAW) called for a bucket of water, and it was poured over the location.

*Muwatta' Malik, The book of purity*

عن ابي وائل قال كان أبو موسى يشدّد في البول ويبول في قارورة ويقول إن بني إسرائيل كان إذا أصاب
جلد أحدهم بول قرضه بالمقاريض فقال حذيفة لوددت أن صاحبكم لا يشدد هذا التشديد فلقد رأيتني أنا
ورسول الله ﷺ نتماشى فأتى سباطة خلف حائط فقام كما يقوم أحدكم فبال فانتبذتُ منه فأشار إلي فجئتُ
فقمت عند عقبه حتى فرغ

صحيح مسلم كتاب الطهارة

From Abu Wa'il who said: Abu Musa would exert heavily when he urinated, and would urinate in a bottle, and he would say: Indeed the children of Israel, whenever urine got on the skin of any of them, would cut it off with a pair of shears. And Hudhaifa said: I wish that your companion would not exert so intensely. I found myself and the Messenger of Allah (SAW) walking together, and He came to a garbage dump behind a wall. He got up as any of you would get up, and urinated. I stepped away from Him, but He gestured to me, so I came and stood behind Him until He finished.

*Sahih Muslim, The book of purity*

عن إبن عمر أن رجلاً سلم على النبي ﷺ وهو يبول فلم يرد عليه

سنن الترمذي كتاب الطهارة

Ibn 'Umar related that a man greeted the Prophet (SAW) while He was urinating, but He did not respond to him.

*Sunan Al-Tirmidhi, The book of purity*

عن جابر بن عبدالله أن رجلاً مرّ على النبي ﷺ وهو يبول فسلم عليه فقال له رسول الله ﷺ إذا رأيتني على مثل هذه الحالة فلا تسلم عليّ فإنك إن فعلت ذلك لم أرد عليك

سنن إبن ماجه كتاب الطهارة والسنه

Jabir ibn Abdullah related that a certain man passed by the Prophet (SAW) while He was urinating, and greeted him. But the Messenger of Allah (SAW) said to him: Whenever you see me like this, do not greet me, for indeed if you do that I will not answer you.

*Sunan Ibn Majah, The book of purity and sunnah*

عن عائشة أن النبي ﷺ وضع صبياً في حجره يحنّكه فبال عليه فدعا بماءٍ فأتبعه

صحيح البخاري كتاب الأدب

'Aishah related that the Prophet (SAW) placed a boy in His lap to pass pre-chewed dates into his mouth [*tahneek*], and he urinated on Him, so He called for some water and followed up where the urine was.

*Sahih Al-Bukhari, The book of manners*

عن حذيفة قال أتى رسول الله ﷺ سباطة قوم فبال قائماً ثم دعا بماءٍ فمسح على خفّيه

سنن ابي داود كتاب الطهارة

From Hudhaifa who said: The Messenger of Allah (SAW) came to some people's garbage heap, and urinated standing up, then called for some water and wiped over his socks.

*Sunan Abu Dawud, The book of purity*

عن عبدالله بن عمر قال كانت الصلاة خمسين والغسل من الجنابة سبع مرار وغسل البول من الثوب سبع مرار فلم يزل رسول الله ﷺ يسأل حتى جُعلت الصلاة خمساً والغسل من الجنابة مرة وغسل البول من الثوب مرة

سنن ابي داود كتاب الطهارة

From Abdullah ibn 'Umar who said: Prayer used to be fifty, and washing from sexual impurity seven times, and washing urine off of garments seven times, but the Messenger of Allah (SAW) did not cease to appeal until prayer was made five, and washing from sexual impurity one time, and washing urine off of garments one time.

*Sunan Abi Dawud, The book of purity*

عن عبد الرحمن بن حسنة قال انطلقت أنا وعمرو بن العاص إلى النبي ﷺ نخرج ومعه درقةٌ ثم إستتر بها ثم
بال فقلنا انظروا إليه يبول كَما تبول المرأة فسمع ذلك فقال ألم تعلموا ما لقيَ صاحب بني إسرائيل كانوا إذا
أصابهم البول قطعوا ما أصابه البول منهم فنهاهم فعُذّب في قبره

سنن أبي داود كتاب الطهارة

From 'Abd Al-Rahman ibn Hasana, who said: I set out, me and 'Amr ibn Al-'As, to
see the Prophet (SAW). He came out holding a leather shield with him, shielded
himself with it, and urinated. We said: Look at him! He's urinating like a woman!
And He heard this and said: Have you all not heard what happened to a certain
companion of the Children of Israel? Whenever urine got on them, they used to cut
off where the urine got on them, but this man forbade them to do so, and was
punished in his grave.

*Sunan Abu Dawud, The book of purity*

عن علي أن النبي ﷺ قال في بول الرضيع يُنضح بول الغلام ويُغسل بول الجارية قال أبو الحسن بن سلمة
حدثنا أحمد بن موسى بن معقل حدثنا أبو اليمان المصري قال سألتُ الشافعي عن حديث النبي ﷺ يُرشّ من
بول الغلام ويغسل من بول الجارية والماءان جميعاً واحد قال لأن بول الغلام من الماء والطين وبول الجارية
من اللحم والدم ثم قال لي فهمتَ أو قال لقنت قال قلت لا قال إن الله تعالى لما خلق آدم خُلقت حواء من
ضلَعه القصير فصار بول الغلام من الماء والطين وصار بول الجارية من اللحم والدم قال قال لي فهمت قلت
نعم قال لي نفعك الله به

سنن إبن ماجه كتاب الطهارة وسننها

'Ali related that the Prophet (SAW) said regarding the urine of nursing children: a
boy's urine is to be moistened, and a girl's urine is to be washed. Abu Al-Hasan ibn
Salama said: Ahmad ibn Musa ibn Ma'qil related to us that Abu Al-Yaman Al-Misri
said: I asked Al-Shafi'i about the hadith of the Prophet (SAW) – water should be
sprinkled on a boy's urine, and a girl's urine should be washed – but both of these
urines are the same. He replied: This is because a boy's urine is from water and clay,
while a girl's urine is from flesh and blood. Then he asked me: Do you understand?
(Or maybe he said: Have you grasped it?) I said: No. He said: Indeed Allah Most
High, when He created Adam, Eve was created from his short rib, and so a boy's urine
became of water and clay, and a girl's urine became of flesh and blood. He said to me:
Do you understand? I said: Yes. He said to me: May Allah make this of use to you.

*Sunan Ibn Majah, The book of purity and its sunnah*

عن ابي هريرة أن رسول الله ﷺ قال لتُتركنَّ المدينة على أحسن ما كانت حتى يدخل الكلب أو الذئب فيغذِّي على بعض سواري المسجد أو على المنبر فقالوا يا رسول الله فلِمن تكون الثمار ذلك الزمان قال للعوافي الطير والسِباع

موطأ مالك كتاب المدينة

Abu Huraira related that the Messenger of Allah (SAW) said: Truly Medina will be left the best it ever was until dogs or wolves enter and spray on one of the pillars of the mosque or on the pulpit. And the people said: Oh Messenger of Allah, who will reap the benefit at that time? He said: Night-hunting animals, birds, and beasts of prey.

*Muwatta' Malik, The book of Medina*


عن إبن التيمي عن أبيه أن حذيفة بن اليمان وزيد بن ثابت والحسن وعطاء كانوا لا يرون بأساً بالبلل يجده الرجل في الصلاة ما لم يقطُر

المصنف لعبد الرزاق كتاب الطهارة

Ibn Al-Taymi related from his father that Hudhaifa ibn Al-Yaman, Zaid ibn Thabit, Al-Hasan, and 'Ataa did not have any issue with a man feeling wetness during prayer, as long as it was not dripping.

*'Abd Al-Razzaq, the Musannaf, The book of purity*


عن أنس أن ناساً من عرينة قدموا المدينة فإجتووها فبعثهم رسول الله ﷺ في ابل الصدقة وقال اشربوا من البانها وأبوالها

جامع الترمذي كتاب الطب

Anas related that some people from 'Uraiba came to Medina, but they found staying there disagreeable, and so the Messenger of Allah (SAW) sent them some camels as charity, and He said: Drink their milk and their urine.

*Sunan Al-Tirmidhi, The book of medicine*


عن يسار بن نمير قال كان عمر إذا بال مسح ذكره بحائطٍ أو بحجر ولم يمسه ماءً

المصنف لإبن ابي شيبة كتاب الطهارة

From Yasar ibn Numair, who said: 'Umar, whenever he urinated, would wipe his penis on a wall or with a stone, but did not use any water on it.

*Ibn Abi Shayba, Al-musannaf, The book of purity*

عن منصور عن ابراهيم قال بال ثم أخذ ماءً فأدخل يده في ثيابه فمسح ذكره

المصنف لإبن ابي شيبة كتاب الطهارة

Mansur related from Ibrahim that he urinated, then took some water, slipped his hand inside his garment, and wiped his penis.

*Ibn Abi Shayba, Al-musannaf, The book of purity*

عن مجاهد أن عمر كان إذا بال يتيمم قال أتيم حتى يحل لي التسبيح

المصنف لإبن ابي شيبة كتاب الطهارة

Mujahid related that 'Umar, whenever he urinated, would wipe with dust [*tayammum*]; he said: I wipe with dust until a shout of praise comes over me [*tasbih*, "*Subhana Allah!*"].

*Ibn Abi Shayba, Al-musannaf, The book of purity*

عن عطاء أنه سئل عن بول البعير يصيب ثوب الرجل فقال وما عليك لو أصابك وقال حماد إني لاغسل البول كله

المصنف لإبن ابي شيبة كتاب الطهارة

'Ataa related that he was asked about camel urine getting on a man's garment; and he said: There is nothing for you to worry about if it gets on you. But Hammad said: Indeed I wash off all urine.

*Ibn Abi Shayba, Al-musannaf, The book of purity*

عن ابي جعفر وعن ليث عن عطاء في الرجل يصيب ثوبه البول فلا يدري أين هو قالا يغسل الثوب كله

المصنف لإبن ابي شيبة كتاب الطهارة

Abu Ja'far and Layth related from 'Ataa regarding a man who gets urine on his garment but does not know where it is; they said: He should wash the entire garment.

*Ibn Abi Shayba, Al-musannaf, The book of purity*

عن ابراهيم في الرجل يبول فينضَح على نخِذيه وساقيه قال ينضحه بالماء

المصنف لإبن ابي شيبة كتاب الطهارة

From Ibrahim, regarding a man who urinates and dribbles down his thighs and legs; he said: He should sprinkle it with water.

*Ibn Abi Shayba, Al-musannaf, The book of purity*

عن الحسن قال كان النبي ﷺ إذا بال تفاجّ حتى يُرثى له

المصنف لإبن ابي شيبة كتاب الطهارة

From Al-Hasan, who said: Whenever the Prophet (SAW) urinated, He would spread his legs until people felt sorry for him.

*Ibn Abi Shayba, Al-musannaf, The book of purity*

عن أنس قالكان رسول الله ﷺ يصلي فيطيل القيام وإن النبي ﷺ بال في بئر في داره قال فلم يكن في المدينة بئراً أعذب منها قال وكانوا إذا حضروا استعذب لهم منها وكانت تسمى في الجاهلية البرود

دلائل النبوة لابي نعيم الأصفهاني ألفصل الثالث والعشرون

Anas related: The Messenger of Allah (SAW) used to pray, and would prolong getting up from praying; and indeed the Prophet (SAW) once urinated into a well that was in his house. He [Anas] said: There was no well in Medina with fresher water than this one. He said: And whenever people came over, what came up from it was pleasant to them. In the age of ignorance it was called "*Al-burud*" ["The cool well"].

*Abu Na'im Al-Asfahani, Dala'il Al-nubuwa, Chapter 23*

عن عائشة قالت كنت مسنداً النبي ﷺ إلى صدري أو قالت إلى حجري فدعا بطَست ليبول فيه ثم بال فمات

الشمائل المحمدية للترمذي ما جاء في وفاة رسول الله ﷺ

From 'Aishah who said: I had the Prophet (SAW) propped up against my chest – or she said on my lap – and He asked for a washbasin to urinate in; then He urinated, and died.

*Al-Tirmidhi, Al-shama'il al-Muhammadiya, The section concerning the Messenger of Allah's (SAW) passing*

عن عائشة قالت يقولون إن رسول الله ﷺ أوصى إلى علي رضي الله عنه لقد دعا بالطَّست ليبول فيها فإنخنثَت نفسُه ﷺ وما أَشعُر فإلى مَن أوصى

سنن النسائي كِتَاب الوصايا

From 'Aishah, who said: They say that the Messenger of Allah (SAW) made 'Ali (may Allah be pleased with him) executor of his will. He asked for a washbasin to urinate in, and then His (SAW) soul fell limp without me feeling anything – so then who did He make his executor?

*Sunan Al-Nasa'i, The book of wills*

التعوط

Defecation

عن سلمان قال قيل له قد علّمكم نبيّكم ﷺ كل شيء حتى الخراءة قال فقال أجل لقد نهانا أن نستقبل القبلة
لغائط أو بول أو أن نستنجي باليمين أو أن نستنجي بأقل من ثلاثة أحجار أو أن نستنجي برجيع أو بعظم

صحيح مسلم كتاب الطهارة

From Salman, who said that someone told him: Your Prophet (SAW) has taught you all everything, even how to go out to defecate [al-khira'a]. He said: Yes indeed; He forbade us to face the *qiblah* for defecating or urinating, or to wipe with our right hand or to wipe with less than three stones, or to wipe with dung or with bones.

*Sahih Muslim, The book of purity*

عن ابي هريرة قال قال رسول الله ﷺ انما أنا لكم مثل الوالد لولده أعلّمكم إذا أتيتم الغائط فلا تستقبلوا القبلة
ولا تستدبروها وأمر بثلاثة أحجار ونهى عن الروث والرِّمّة ونهى أن يستطيب الرجل بيمينه

سنن إبن ماجه كتاب الطهارة وسننها

From Abu Huraira, who said: The Messenger of Allah (SAW) said: Truly I am to you all like a father to his son, I teach you all; whenever you go out to defecate, do not face the *qiblah* and do not turn your backs to it. And He ordered them to use three stones, and forbade them to use dung or worn-out bones (or other decomposing body part; *rimmah*), and forbade anyone to wipe with their right hand.

*Sunan Ibn Majah, The book of purity and its sunnah*

عن ابي أيوب الأنصاري قال قال رسول الله ﷺ إذا أتى أحدكم الغائط فلا يستقبل القبلة ولا يولّها ظهره
شرّقوا أو غرّبوا

صحيح البخاري كتاب الوضوء

From Abu Ayub Al-Ansari who said: The Messenger of Allah (SAW) said: If any of you goes out to defecate he should not face the *qiblah* or turn his back towards it; he should face the east or the west.

*Sahih Al-Bukhari, The book of ablution*

عن عبدالله بن عمر قال لقد ارتقيت على ظهر البيت فرأيت رسول الله ﷺ على لِبَنتين مستقبل بيت المقدس لحاجته

سنن ابي داود كتاب الطهارة

From Abdullah ibn 'Umar, who said: I went up to the roof of the house and I saw the Messenger of Allah (SAW) on top of two bricks, facing Bait Al-Maqdis [Jerusalem] relieving his need.

*Sunan Abu Dawud, The book of purity*

عن إبن عمر قال رأيت النبي ﷺ جالساً يقضي حاجته متوجّهاً نحو القبلة

المصنف لإبن ابي شيبة كتاب الطهارة

From Ibn 'Umar, who said: I saw the Prophet (SAW) sitting down to fulfill his need, facing towards the *qiblah*.

*Ibn Abi Shayba, Al-musannaf, The book of purity*

حبيب بن صالح قال كان رسول الله ﷺ إذا دخل الخلاء لبس حذاءه وغطى رأسه

السنن الكبرى للبيهقي كتاب الطهارة

Habib ibn Salih said: Whenever the Messenger of Allah (SAW) went to relieve himself, He put on his shoes and covered his head.

*Al-Bayhaqi, Al-sunan Al-kubra, The book of purity*

عن أنس بن مالك قال كان النبي ﷺ إذا دخل الخلاء قال اللهم اني أعوذ بك من الخبث والخبائث

صحيح البخاري كتاب الدعوات

Anas Ibn Malik said: Whenever the Prophet (SAW) went out to relieve himself He said: Oh Allah! I seek refuge in you from harmful and repulsive things [or, male and female devils; *kubuth* and *kaba'ith*].

*Sahih Al-Bukhari, The book of supplications*

عن أنس أن رسول الله ﷺ كان إذا دخل الخلاء نزع خاتمه

سنن النسائي كتاب الزينة والسنن

Anas related that the Messenger of Allah (SAW), when He entered to relieve himself [*khalaa*; i.e. the vacant area], he removed his signet.

*Sunan Al-Nasa'i, The book of adornment and lifestyle*

وقد حكى بعض المعتنين باخباره وشمائله ﷺ أنه كان إذا أراد أن يتغوّط انشقّت الأرض فابتلعت غائطه وبوله
وفاحت لذلك رائحة طيبة

الشفا للقاضي عياض اليحصبي القسم الأول في تعظيم العلي الأعلى لقدر النبي المصطفى ﷺ قولاً وفعلاً

Some of those concerned with His (SAW) accounts and His attributes narrated that whenever He wished to defecate, the earth would split open and swallow his defecation and his urine, and then exude a pleasant aroma over it.

*Al-qadi 'Iyad Al-Yahsubi, Al-shifa, Part One: Regarding the exaltation of the High and Most High to the eminence of the chosen Prophet (SAW) in word and in deed*

عن ابي هريرة أن رجلاً كان يأكل أكلاً كثيراً فأسلم فكان يأكل أكلاً قليلاً فذُكر ذلك للنبي ﷺ فقال إن المؤمن يأكل في مِعًى واحد والكافر يأكل في سبعة أمعاءٍ

صحيح البخاري كتاب الأطعمة

Abu Huraira related that a certain man used to be a big eater; then he became a Muslim and would eat meagerly. This was mentioned to the Prophet (SAW), and He said: Indeed a Believer eats in one intestine, but a disbeliever eats in seven intestines.

*Sahih Al-Bukhari, The book of foods*


عن يوسف بن ابي بردة عن أبيه حدثتني عائشة أن النبي ﷺ كان إذا خرج من الغائط قال غفرانك

سنن ابي داود كتاب الطهارة

Yusuf ibn Abu Burda related that his father said: 'Aishah told us that when the Prophet (SAW) came out from defecating, He would say: "Your forgiveness" ["*Ghufranak*"].

*Sunan Abu Dawud, The book of purity*


عن طاوس قال قال رسول الله ﷺ إذا خرج أحدكم من الخلاء فليقل الحمد لله الذي اذهب عني ما يؤذيني وأمسكَ علي ما ينفعني

المصنف لإبن ابي شيبة كتاب الطهارة

From Tawus, who said: The Messenger of Allah (SAW) said: Whenever any of you comes out from relieving himself, let him say "Praise be to Allah who has removed from me what harms me, and has kept for me what is beneficial to me" ["*Al-hamdu Lillah alladhi adhhaba 'anni ma yu'dheeni, wa amsaka 'alaya ma yanfa'uni*"].

*Ibn Abi Shayba, Al-musannaf, The book of purity*


عن عائشة أن رسول الله ﷺ قال إذا ذهب أحدكم إلى الغائط فليذهب معه بثلاثة أحجار يستطيب بهن فانها تجزئ عنه

سنن ابي داود كتاب الطهارة

'Aishah related that the Messenger of Allah (SAW) said: When any of you goes to defecate let him take three stones with him to wipe with, for that will avail him.

*Sunan Abu Dawud, The book of purity*

بسم الله فيه أبداً لمسجد أُسِّس على التقوى من أول يوم أحق أن تقوم فيه فيه رجال يحبون أن يتطهروا
والله يحب المطهرين ۞ التوبة ١٠٨

{ *Do not ever go there; indeed a mosque founded on piety from the first* }
{ *day is more worthwile for you to enter; in it there are men who love* }
{ *to purify themselves; and Allah loves those who purify themselves* }
*Al-tawba* 108


عن ابي هريرة عن النبي ﷺ قال نزلت هذه الآية في أهل قباء ﴿ فيه رجال يحبون أن يتطهَّروا ﴾ قال كانوا
يستنجون بالماء فنزلت فيهم هذه الآية

سنن ابي داود كتاب الطهارة

Abu Huraira related that the Prophet (SAW) said: This verse { In it there are men
who love to purify themselves } came down regarding the people of Qubaa; he said:
They would clean themselves up with water. So this verse came down regarding them.

*Sunan Abu Dawud, The book of purity*


عن مجمع بن يعقوب بن مجمع أن رسول الله ﷺ قال لعويم بن ساعدة ما هذا الطهور الذي أثنى الله عليكم قالوا
نغسل الأدبار

المصنف لإبن ابي شيبة كتاب الطهارة

Mujammi' ibn Ya'qub ibn Mujammi' related that the Messenger of Allah (SAW) asked
'Uwaim ibn Sa'ida: What is this purification that Allah has praised you all for? They said:
We wash our rears.

*Ibn Abi Shayba, Al-musannaf, The book of purity*


روى إبن خزيمة في صحيحه عن عويم بن ساعدة أنه ﷺ أتاهم في مسجد قباء فقال إن الله تعالى قد أحسن
عليكم الثناء في الطهور في قصة مسجدكم فما هذا الطهور الذي تطهَّرون به قالوا والله يا رسول الله ما نعلم شيئاً
إلا أنه كان لنا جيران من اليهود وكانوا يغسلون أدبارهم من الغائط فغسلنا كما غسلوا وفي حديث رواه البزار
فقالوا نُتبع الحجارة بالماء فقال هو ذاك فعليكموه

تفسير الجلالين

Ibn Khuzaima narrated in his *Sahih*, from 'Uwaim ibn Sa'ida, that He (SAW) came to
them in the mosque at Qubaa, and said: Indeed Allah Most High has highly praised
you all for the purification in the story of your mosque, so what is this purification

that you purify yourselves with? They said: We swear by Allah, oh Messenger of Allah, we know nothing except that we had some Jewish neighbors, and they would wash their rears after defecating, so we washed as they washed. In a hadith narrated by Al-Bazzar, they said: We used stones followed by water. And He said: That's the way; do it like that.

*Tafsir Al-Jalalain*

وقيل هو عام في التطهر من النجاسات كلها وقيل كانوا لا ينامون الليل على الجنابة ويتبعون الماء أثر البول

تفسير الزمخشري

It is said that this is about purification in general from all kinds of filthiness. And it is said that they would not sleep a night in a state of sexual impurity, and that they would follow up any traces of urine with water.

*Tafsir Al-Zamakhshari*

عن شهر بن حوشب قال لما نزل ﴿ فيه رجال يحبون أن يتطهّروا ﴾ قال رسول الله ﷺ ما الطهور الذي أثنى الله عليكم قالوا يا رسول الله نغسل أثر الغائط ... عن قتادة قال لما نزلت ﴿ فيه رجال يحبون أن يتطهروا ﴾ قال النبي ﷺ يا معشر الأنصار ما هذا الطهور الذي أثنى الله عليكم فيه قالوا إنا نستطيب بالماء إذ جئنا من الغائط ... عن عطية قال لما نزلت هذه الآية ﴿ فيه رجال يحبون أن يتطهروا ﴾ سألهم رسول الله ﷺ ما طهوركم هذا الذي ذكر الله قالوا يا رسول الله كنا نستنجي بالماء في الجاهلية فلما جاء الاسلام لم ندعه قال فلا تدعوه

تفسير الطبري

From Shahr ibn Hawshab, who said: When { In it there are men who love to purify themselves } was sent down, the Messenger of Allah (SAW) said: What is the purification that Allah has praised you all for? They said: Oh Messenger of Allah, we wash off the traces of feces. ... From Qatada, who said: When { In it there are men who love to purify themselves } came down, the Prophet (SAW) said: Oh Ansar folk! What is this purification that Allah has praised you all about? They said: Indeed we free ourselves of filth with water when we come back from defecating. ... From 'Atiyya who said: When this verse came down { In it there are men who love to purify themselves } , the Messenger of Allah (SAW) asked them: What is this purification you all do that Allah has mentioned? They said: Oh Messenger of Allah, in the age of ignorance [*jahiliya*] we used to clean up with water, and when Islam came, we did not stop doing this. He said: Don't stop doing it.

*Tafsir Al-Tabari*

فدل هذا على أن إكمال الطهارة يُسهّل القيام في العبادة ويُعين على اتمامها واكمالها والقيام بمشروعاتها

تفسير إبن كثير

And this proves that perfection in purification facilitates the act of worship and aids in its fulfillment, completion, and carrying out all that is prescribed in it.

*Tafsir Ibn Kathir*

•     •     •

عن ابي هريرة عن النبي ﷺ قال ... من أتى الغائط فليستتر فإن لم يجد إلا أن يجمع كثيباً من رملٍ فليستدبره فانّ الشيطان يلعب بمقاعد بني آدم من فعل فقد أحسن ومن لا فلا حرج

سنن ابي داود كتاب الطهارة

Abu Huraira related from the Prophet (SAW) who said: ... Whoever goes to defecate should remain discreetly concealed, and even if he only finds enough to gather a pile of sand he should get with his back against it, for indeed Satan plays with people's backsides. Whoever does this has done well, but whoever does not, there is no blame.

*Sunan Abu Dawud, The book of purity*

عن علي بن ابي طالب رضي الله عنه أن رسول الله ﷺ قال  ستر ما بين أعين الجن وعورات بني آدم إذا دخل احدهم الخلاء أن يقول بسم الله

جامع الترمذي أبواب السفر

'Ali ibn Abi Talib (may Allah be pleased with him) related that the Messenger of Allah (SAW) said: The screen between the eyes of the genies [*jinn*] and the nakedness of men, whenever any of them enters to relieve himself, is that he says "*Bismillah...*"

*Sunan Al-Tirmidhi, The section on travelling*

عن عائشة أن أزواج النبي ﷺ كن يخرجن بالليل إذا تبرزن إلى المناصع وهو صعيد أفيح فكان عمر يقول للنبي
ﷺ احجب نساءك فلم يكن رسول الله ﷺ يفعل فخرجت سودة بنت زمعة زوج النبي ﷺ ليلة من الليالي عشاءً
وكانت إمرأة طويلة فناداها عمر ألا قد عرفناك يا سودة حرصاً على أن ينزل الحجاب فأنزل الله آية الحجاب
صحيح البخاري كتاب الوضوء

'Aishah related that the Prophet's (SAW) wives would go out at night, whenever they
needed to relieve themselves, to Al-Manasi', a wide-open plain. And 'Umar used to say
to the Prophet (SAW): Veil your women. But the Messenger of Allah (SAW) did not do
it. Early one night, Sawdah bint Zam'a, the wife of the Prophet (SAW), went out; she
was a tall woman. 'Umar called to her: "Indeed we've seen you, Oh Sawdah!", hoping
that the issue of the *hijab* would be revealed. And so Allah sent down the *hijab* verse.

*Sahih Al-Bukhari, The book of ablution*


جابر يقول نهى رسول الله ﷺ أن يُتمسّح بعظمٍ أو بِبَعر
صحيح مسلم كتاب الطهارة

Jabir said: The Messenger of Allah (SAW) forbade one to wipe himself with bones or
dung [*ba'r*, i.e. of hooved animals].

*Sahih Muslim, The book of purity*


عبدالله يقول أتى النبي ﷺ الغائط فأمرني أن آتيه بثلاثة أحجار فوجدت حجرين والتمست الثالث فلم أجده
فأخذت روثةً فأتيته بها فأخذ الحجرين وألقى الروثة وقال هذا ركسٌ
صحيح البخاري كتاب الوضوء

'Abdullah said: The Prophet (SAW) went out to defecate, and He ordered me to bring
him three stones. I found two stones and looked around diligently for a third, but I
could not find one, so I grabbed a piece of dung and brought it to him. He took the
two stones but tossed the piece of dung, and He said: This is filthy!

*Sahih Al-Bukhari, The book of ablution* [*wudu'*]


عن ابي هريرة أن رسول الله ﷺ قال من توضأ فليستنثر ومن استجمر فليوتر
صحيح مسلم كتاب الطهارة

Abu Huraira related that the Messenger of Allah (SAW) said: Whoever performs
ablution, let him rinse out his nose [*istinthar*]; and whoever wipes with stones, let him
use an odd number.

*Sahih Muslim, The book of purity*

عن جابر قال قال رسول الله ﷺ الإستجمار تو ورمي الجمار تو والسعي بين الصفا والمروة تو والطواف تو وإذا استجمر أحدكم فليستجمر بتوٍ

صحيح مسلم كتاب الحج

From Jabir, who said: The Messenger of Allah (SAW) said: Wiping with stones [istijmar] is to be done with an odd number, the casting of the stones is to be done with an odd number, the ritual walk between Safa and Marwa is an odd number of times, the circumambulation is an odd number of times; and whenever any of you wipes himself with stones, he should wipe with an odd number.

*Sahih Muslim, The book of hajj*

عن هشام بن عروة عن أبيه أن رسول الله ﷺ سئل عن الاستطابة فقال أولا يجد أحدكم ثلاثة أحجار

موطأ مالك كتاب الطهارة

Hisham ibn 'Urwa related from his father that the Messenger of Allah (SAW) was asked about wiping; and He said: Can't any of you find three stones?

*Muwatta Malik, The book of purity*

عن جابر قال خرجت مع رسول الله ﷺ في سفرٍ وكان رسول الله ﷺ لا يأتي البَراز حتى يتغيَّب فلا يُرى

المصنف لإبن أبي شيبة كتاب الطهارة

From Jabir, who said: I went out with the Messenger of Allah (SAW) on a journey, and the Messenger of Allah (SAW) would not go to out defecate until concealing himself so that He would not be seen.

*Ibn Abi Shayba, Al-musannaf, The book of purity*

عن عائشة قالت ما رأيت رسول الله ﷺ خرج من غائطٍ قط إلا مسّ ماءً

سنن إبن ماجه كتاب الطهارة وسننها

From 'Aishah who said: I never saw the Messenger of Allah (SAW) ever come out from defecating without using some water.

*Sunan Ibn Majah, The book of purity and its sunnah*

﷽ يَا أَيُّهَا الَّذِينَ آمَنُوا لَا تَقْرَبُوا الصَّلَاةَ وَأَنْتُمْ سُكَارَى حَتَّى تَعْلَمُوا مَا تَقُولُونَ وَلَا جُنُبًا إِلَّا عَابِرِي سَبِيلٍ
حَتَّى تَغْتَسِلُوا وَإِنْ كُنْتُمْ مَرْضَى أَوْ عَلَى سَفَرٍ أَوْ جَاءَ أَحَدٌ مِنْكُمْ مِنَ الْغَائِطِ أَوْ لَامَسْتُمُ النِّسَاءَ فَلَمْ تَجِدُوا مَاءً فَتَيَمَّمُوا
صَعِيدًا طَيِّبًا فَامْسَحُوا بِوُجُوهِكُمْ وَأَيْدِيكُمْ إِنَّ اللَّهَ كَانَ عَفُوًّا غَفُورًا ﴿ النساء ٤٣

{ *Oh you who have believed! Do not come for prayer when you are drunk, until you are aware of what you are saying, nor being sexually impure, unless you are on your way along a road, until you have bathed; and if you are sick or on a journey, or any of you has come from defecating [gha'it], or you have touched women, and you can not find any water, then dry wipe with clean earth, and wipe your faces and your hands. Indeed Allah is forbearing, forgiving.* } *Al-nisaa 43*

﷽ يَا أَيُّهَا الَّذِينَ آمَنُوا إِذَا قُمْتُمْ إِلَى الصَّلَاةِ فَاغْسِلُوا وُجُوهَكُمْ وَأَيْدِيَكُمْ إِلَى الْمَرَافِقِ وَامْسَحُوا بِرُءُوسِكُمْ
وَأَرْجُلَكُمْ إِلَى الْكَعْبَيْنِ وَإِنْ كُنْتُمْ جُنُبًا فَاطَّهَّرُوا وَإِنْ كُنْتُمْ مَرْضَى أَوْ عَلَى سَفَرٍ أَوْ جَاءَ أَحَدٌ مِنْكُمْ مِنَ الْغَائِطِ أَوْ لَامَسْتُمُ
النِّسَاءَ فَلَمْ تَجِدُوا مَاءً فَتَيَمَّمُوا صَعِيدًا طَيِّبًا فَامْسَحُوا بِوُجُوهِكُمْ وَأَيْدِيكُمْ مِنْهُ مَا يُرِيدُ اللَّهُ لِيَجْعَلَ عَلَيْكُمْ مِنْ حَرَجٍ
وَلَكِنْ يُرِيدُ لِيُطَهِّرَكُمْ وَلِيُتِمَّ نِعْمَتَهُ عَلَيْكُمْ لَعَلَّكُمْ تَشْكُرُونَ ﴿ المائدة ٦

{ *Oh you who have believed! Whenever you all get up to go to prayer, wash your faces and your hands up to the elbows, and wipe your heads and your feet up to the ankles; if you are sexually impure, then purify yourselves, and if you are ill, or on a journey, or any of you have come back from defecating [gha'it], or you have touched women, and you can not find any water, then dry wipe with clean earth, and wipe your faces and your hands with it; Allah does not wish to make things awkward for you, but wishes to purify you and to perfect his grace upon you so that perhaps you might give thanks.* } *Al-ma'ida 6*

والغائط إسم للمطمئن من الأرض وكانت عادة العرب إتيان الغائط للحدث فكُنّي عن الحدث بالغائط

تفسير البغوي

*"Gha'it"* is a name for a calm and secure area of land; it was the customary practice of the Arabs to go out to a *gha'it* for bodily needs, and so bodily needs were alluded to as *"gha'it"*.

Tafsir Al-Baghawi (Al-nisaa 43)

﴿ أو جاء منكم من الغائط ﴾ يقول أو جاء أحد منكم من الغائط قد قضى حاجته وهو مسافر فليتيمم صعيداً طيباً والغائط ما إتّسع من الأودية وتصوّب وجعل كناية عن قضاء حاجة الانسان لأن العرب كانت تختار قضاء حاجتها في الغيطان

تفسير الطبري

{ Or any of you has come from defecating } : having fulfilled his need, being a legitimate traveller, then let him dry wipe [*tayammum*] with clean earth. And "defecating" [*gha'it*] refers to the wide open and straight parts of valleys; this became an allusion for fulfilling one's need, because the Arabs would prefer to fulfill their needs in *gha'its*.

Tafsir Al-Tabari (Al-nisaa 43)

﴿ أو جاء أحد منكم من الغائط ﴾ الغائط أصله ما إنخفض من الأرض والجمع الغيطان أو الأغواط وبه سُمّيَ غوطة دمشق وكانت العرب تقصد هذا الصنف من المواضع لقضاء حاجتها تَسَتُّراً عن أعين الناس ثم سمي الحدث الخارج من الانسان غائطاً للمقارنة ... إن كنتم مرضى أو على سفر وجاء أحد منكم من الغائط فتيمموا فالسبب الموجب للتيمم على هذا هو الحدث لا المرض والسفر فدلّ على جواز التيمم في الحضر كما بيناه ... لفظ غائط يجمع بالمعنى جميع الأحداث الناقضة للطهارة الصغرى

تفسير القرطبي

{ Or any of you has come from defecating } : "Defecating" [*gha'it*]; *gha'it* originally refers to depressions in the landscape (plural *ghitan* or *aghwat*); the Ghouta region in Damascus was named accordingly. The Arabs would seek out these types of locations to fulfill their need, shielded from the eyes of people. Then the bodily occurrences that come out from people were called *gha'it* due to the connection. ... { If you are sick or on a journey, or any of you has come from defecating ... then dry wipe } : what makes *tayammum* obligatory in this case is the bodily occurrence, not the sickness or the journey; and this is evidence that *tayammum* is permissible in populated areas, as we have demonstrated. ... The term *gha'it* encompasses in meaning all bodily occurrences that invalidate minor purification [*al-tahara al-sughra*; i.e. for some but not all of the body].

Tafsir Al-Qurtubi (Al-nisaa 43)

﴿ أو جاء أحد منكم من الغائط ﴾ يقول أو جاء أحدكم من الغائط بعد قضاء حاجته فيه وهو مسافر وإنما عنى
بذكر مجيئه منه قضاء حاجته فيه

تفسير الطبري

{ Or any of you has come from defecating } ; He is saying: Or any of you has come from the *gha'it* after having fulfilled his need there, him being on a journey; indeed by mentioning his coming from there, he is referring to the fulfillment of his need there.

*Tafsir Al-Tabari* (Al-ma'ida 6)

أوجب التيمم على المتغوط والمجامع إذا لم يجد الماء

تفسير الرازي

*Tayammum* [dry wiping with dust] is obligatory for anyone who has defecated or had sex whenever they can not find any water.

*Tafsir Al-Razi* (Al-ma'ida 6)

•    •    •

أبو سعيد قال سمعت رسول الله ﷺ يقول لا يخرج الرجلان يضربان الغائط كاشفين عن عورتهما يتحدثان فإن الله عز وجل يمقت على ذلك

سنن ابي داود كتاب الطهارة

Abu Sa'id said: I heard the Messenger of Allah (SAW) say: Two men should not go out to defecate, exposing their nakedness and talking together; Allah Mighty and Sublime abhors this.

*Sunan Abi Dawud, The book of purity*


عن مالك عن نافع وعبدالله بن دينار أنهما أخبراه أن عبدالله بن عمر قدم الكوفة على سعد بن ابي وقاص وهو أميرها فرآه عبدالله بن عمر يمسح على الخفَّين فأنكر ذلك عليه فقال له سعد سلْ أباك إذا قدمت عليه فقدم عبدالله فنسي أن يسأل عمر عن ذلك حتى قدم سعد فقال أسألت أباك فقال لا فسأله عبدالله فقال عمر إذا أدخلت رجليك في الخفين وهما طاهرتان فامسح عليهما قال عبدالله وإن جاء أحدنا من الغائط قال عمر نعم وإن جاء أحدكم من الغائط

موطأ مالك كتاب الطهارة

Malik related from Nafi' and 'Abdullah ibn Dinar that the two of them told him that 'Abdullah ibn 'Umar went to Kufa to see Sa'd ibn Abi Waqqas, the Amir of Kufa. And 'Abdullah ibn 'Umar saw him wiping over his socks and disapproved of that. And Sa'd said to him: Ask your father when you go back to see him. And 'Abdullah went back but forgot to ask 'Umar about it, until Sa'd met up with him and said: Have you asked your father? And he said: No. Then 'Abdullah asked him. And 'Umar said: Whenever you put on your socks when your feet are pure, then just wipe over them. 'Abdullah said: Even if we have just come back from defecating? And 'Umar said: Yes, even if you have just come back from defecating.

*Muwatta Malik, The book of purity*


عن يحيى بن سعيد أنه سمع سعيد بن المسيب يسأل عن الوضوء من الغائط بالماء فقال سعيد إنما ذلك وضوء النساء

موطأ مالك كتاب الطهارة

Yahya ibn Sa'id related that he heard Sa'id ibn Al-Musayyib being asked about ablution [*wudu'*] with water after defecating, and Sa'id said: Indeed that is how women do *wudu'*.

*Muwatta Malik, The book of purity*

عن محمد بن يحيى عن عمه واسع بن حبان قال كنت أصلي في المسجد وعبدالله بن عمر مسند ظهره إلى القبلة فلما قضيت صلاتي انصرفت إليه من شقي فقال عبدالله يقول ناس إذا قعدت للحاجة تكون لك فلا تقعد مستقبل القبلة ولا بيت المقدس قال عبدالله ولقد رقيت على ظهر بيتٍ فرأيت رسول الله ﷺ قاعداً على لبنتين مستقبلاً بيت المقدس لحاجته

صحيح مسلم كتاب الطهارة

Muhammad ibn Yahya related from his uncle Wasi' ibn Habban, who said: I was praying in the mosque and 'Abdullah ibn 'Umar was reclining his back towards the *qiblah*, and when I finished my prayer, I went over to him from the side. And 'Abdullah said: People say that whenever you sit down to fulfill a need that you have, you should not sit facing the *qibla* and not facing *Bait Al-maqdis* [Jerusalem]. 'Abdullah said: I went up to the top of a house one time, and I saw the Messenger of Allah (SAW) sitting on two bricks, facing *Bait Al-maqdis*, to fulfill His need.

*Sahih Muslim, The book of purity*

إبن عباس يقول كنا عند النبي ﷺ بجاء من الغائط وأتي بطعام فقيل له ألا تتوضأ فقال لمَ أأصلي فأتوضأ

صحيح مسلم كتاب الحيض

Ibn 'Abbas said: We were with the Prophet (SAW), and He came back from defecating when food was being brought. Someone said to Him: Are you not going to perform ablution [*wudu'*]? He said: Why? Am I about to pray, that I need to perform ablution?

*Sahih Muslim, The book of menstruation*

عن إبن عمر قال أقبل رسول الله ﷺ من الغائط فلقيه رجلٌ عند بئر جمل فسلّم عليه فلم يرد عليه رسول الله ﷺ حتى أقبل على الحائط فوضع يده على الحائط ثم مسح وجهه ويديه ثم رد رسول الله ﷺ على الرجل السلام

سنن أبي داود كتاب الطهارة

From Ibn 'Umar who said: The Messenger of Allah (SAW) came back from defecating; and a man met Him at Bi'r Jamal and greeted Him, but the Messenger of Allah (SAW) did not respond to him until He came to the wall. He put his hand on the wall and then wiped his face and his hands, and then the Messenger of Allah (SAW) returned the greeting to the man.

*Sunan Abu Dawud, The book of purity*

عن ابي سعيد قال جاء رجل إلى النبي ﷺ فقال إن أخي إستطلق بطنه فقال اسقه عسلاً فسقاه فقال إني
سقيته فلم يزده إلا استطلاقاً فقال صَدَقَ الله وكذب بطن أخيك

صحيح البخاري كتاب الطب

From Abu Sa'id, who said: A certain man came to the Prophet (SAW) and said: Indeed
my brother has runny bowels. He said: Give him honey to drink. So he gave him
honey. Then he said: Indeed I have given him honey to drink, but he has only gotten
runnier. And He said: Allah has told the truth but your brother's bowels have lied.

*Sahih Al-Bukhari, The book of medicine*

عن يعلى بن مرة عن أبيه قال كنت مع النبي ﷺ في سفر فأراد أن يقضي حاجته فقال لي ائتِ تلك الأشاءتين
قال وكيعٌ يعني النخل الصغار قال أبو بكر القصار فقل لهما إن رسول الله ﷺ يأمركما أن تجتمعا فاجتمعتا
فإستتر بهما فقضى حاجته ثم قال لي ائتهما فقل لهما لترجع كل واحدة منكما إلى مكانها فقلت لهما فرجعتا

سنن إبن ماجه كتاب الطهارة وسننها

Ya'la ibn Murra related from his father, who said: I was with the Prophet (SAW) on
a journey, and He wished to fulfill his need, so He said to me: Go over to those two
small palm trees (Waki' said he meant the small date palms; Abu Bakr said the short
ones) and tell them: Indeed the Messenger of Allah (SAW) orders both of you to come
close together. So the two of them came together, and He concealed himself with them
and fulfilled his need. Then He said to me: Go over to them and tell them: Each one
of you go back to your place. And so I told them, and they went back.

*Sunan Ibn Majah, The book of purity and its sunnah*

ومن أراد دخول الخلاء نحّى ما معه مما فيه ذكر الله تعالى كالخاتم وغيره ويقدم رجله اليسرى في الدخول
ويقول عند دخوله بسم الله أعوذ بالله من الخبث والخبائث ومن الرجس النجس الشيطان الرجيم ولا يرفع
ثوبه حتى يدنو من الأرض ولا يستقبل القبلة ولا يستدبرها ولا يستقبل الشمس ولا القمر ولا يبول في شق
ولا سرب ولا تحت شجرة مثمرة ولا في ظل حائط ولا قارعة طريق ولا يقعد فوق ما يحتاج إليه ولا دونه
ولا يتكلم فإن عطس حمد الله تعالى بقلبه فإذا فرغ تحول من موضعه لأجل الاستنجاء إلى موضع آخر
والاستنجاء واجب لكل ما يخرج من السبيلين إلا الريح ومتى لم يتعد الخارج أجزأ فيه الاستجمار وصفة ما
يستجمر به أن يكون جامداً طاهراً غير مطعوم لا حرمة له ولا متصلاً بحيوان وهذا يدخل فيه الحجر والخشب
والخزف والتراب وما أشبه ذلك ويخرج منه المأكولات والروث والرمة لأنها ما طعام الجن ويجزي الحجر
الذي له ثلاث شعب واختلف أصحابنا في صفة الاستجمار فقال الأكثرون يأخذ الحجر الأول بيده اليسرى
ويبدأ به من مقدم صفحته اليمنى ويجره إلى مؤخرتها ثم يعيده إلى الموضع الذي منه بدأ ثم يأخذ الحجر الثاني
ويبدأ به من مقدم الصفحة اليسرى ويجره إلى مؤخرتها ثم يعيده إلى الموضع الذي منه بدأ ثم يأخذ الحجر الثالث
فيديره حول الحلقة ويعيده على الوسط وذهب الشريف أبو جعفر وابن عقيل إلى أنه يعمم بكل حجر جميع
المحل لأنه إذا لم يعمم به كان تلفيقاً لا تكراراً ومتى لم تزل العين بثلاثة أحجار زاد حتى ينقى والمستحب للرجل
أن يبدأ بقُبله لئلا تتنجس يده إذا بدأ بالدبر فأما المرأة فهي مخيرة في ذلك والأفضل الجمع بين الأحجار
والماء فإن أراد الاقتصار على أحدها فالماء أفضل وإذا كانت المرأة بكراً فإن شاءت مسحت موضع البول
بالجامد الذي سبق وصفه وإن شاءت غسلته ومتى تعدى الخارج المخرج لم يجز إلا الماء وإن كانت ثيباً فإذا
خرج البول بحده ولم يسترسل لم يجب سوى الإستنجاء في موضع خروج البول وإن استرسل فدخل منه شيء
في الفرج وجب غسله فإن لم تعلم أوصل البول إلى الفرج أم لا استحب غسله وكتمان هذا عن المرأة غلول
للعلم لأنه إذا وجب غسل نجاسة فلم تغسل قدحت في صحة الصلاة وقد ظن جماعة من النساء أنهن إذا غسل
ما وصل إليه البول من باطن الفرج أن ذلك يقدح في الصوم وليس كذلك فإنه لا ينفذ إلى المعدة من البول
وأحب إدخال الإصبع لغسله ولا يفسد الصوم وإنما هو كالفم بخلاف الدبر فإنه ينفذ إلى المعدة وإذا خرج
الأنسان من الخلاء قدّم رجله اليمنى في الخروج وقال غفرانك الحمد لله الذي اذهب عني الأذى وعافاني

أحكام النساء لإبن الجوزي الباب السابع في ذكر اذاب الخلاء وصفة الاستجمار

Whoever wishes to go to relieve himself must remove anything he has that has remembrance of Allah Most High on it, such as a signet ring or anything else. Then he proceeds to enter with his left foot, saying as he enters: In the name of Allah, I seek refuge with Allah from harmful and repulsive things, and from filthy uncleanliness, the accursed Satan ["*Bismillah A'udhu billah min al-khubuth wa al-khaba'ith wa min al-rijs al-najas al-shaytan al-rajim*"]. He is not to lift up his garment until he has gotten down near the ground; he is not to face the *qiblah* or turn his back towards it; he is not to face the sun or the moon; he is not to urinate in a crack in the ground nor in an animal hole, nor under a fruit tree, nor in the shadow of a wall, nor in the middle of the road; and he is not to sit above something he needs, nor underneath it; and he is not to talk. If he sneezes, he is to pronounce praise to Allah ["*Al-hamdu Lillah*"] in his heart, and when he finishes he is to move away from where he is in order to cleanse himself in another location. Cleansing [*istinjaa*] is obligatory for anything that comes out of the two passages [i.e. the front and the rear], except for gas; if he remains uncertain whether or not anything has come out, it is fine for him to wipe with stones [*istijmar*]. The characteristics of something used to wipe is that it be solid, pure, not something that can be eaten, not something that is forbidden, and not attached to an animal. This includes stones, wood, pottery, dirt, and things similar to these. It does not include food items, dung, or decomposing bones, because these are food for the genies [*jinn*]. A stone with three corners is fine. Our companions disagree on the manner of performing *istijmar*; most of them say that one is to take the first stone in his left hand and begin with this from the front of his right side, dragging it backwards; then he repeats this towards the place from which he began. Then he takes the second stone and begins with it from the front of the left side, dragging it backwards; then he repeats this towards the place from which he began. Then he takes the third stone and moves it in a circle around the hole, and repeats this in the center. Al-Sharif Abu Ja'far and Ibn 'Aqil held that he is to include the whole area with each stone, since if he did not include the whole area, it would be something pieced together, not repetition. In case the stuff can not be removed with three stones, he is to use more until he is clean. It is desirable for a man to begin with his front parts, lest his hand become impure from his front parts if he begins from the rear. However a woman is free to chose in this regard, although it is best to use stones and water together; if she wants to limit it to one of these, water is best. If a woman is a virgin, then if she likes she can wipe the location of urine with the solid object described above, or if she likes she can wash it. When what is coming out reaches past the place where it comes out, nothing is permitted but water. If she is a previously married woman, then whenever urine comes out to the brink but does not freely flow, only wiping the place where urine came out is required. If it flows freely and some of it enters the vagina, washing it is required. If she does not know – has urine gotten into the vagina or not? – it is desirable to wash it. And withholding this knowledge from women is spiteful, since if washing from impurity is required, and she does not wash, then she has harmed the acceptability of her prayer. Some women think that if they wash wherever urine has gotten on the inside of the vagina, that this harms the fast, but it is not so. For indeed the urine is not connected to the stomach, and it is more desirable to insert a finger to wash it; this does not invalidate the fast, as it is similar to the mouth, in contrast to the rear, which is indeed connected to the stomach. And whenever anyone comes out from relieving himself, he is to proceed with his right foot first upon leaving, and he is to say: Your forgiveness; praise be to Allah who has removed the harm from me and has restored me to health ["*Ghufranak; al-hamdu lillah aladhi adhhab 'anni al-adha wa-'afani*"].

*Ibn Al-Jawzi, Ahkam Al-nisaa, Chapter seven: mention of manners in the toilet and description of cleansing oneself with stones*

عن عبدالله بن أرقم قال قال رسول الله ﷺ إذا أراد أحدكم الغائط وأُقيمت الصلاة فليبدأ به

سنن إبن ماجه كتاب الطهارة وسننها

From 'Abdullah ibn Arqam who said: The Messenger of Allah (SAW) said: Whenever any of you needs to defecate when the call to prayer has been given, let him do that first.

*Sunan Ibn Majah, The book of purity and its sunnah*


عن هشام بن عروة عن أبيه أن عبدالله بن الأرقم كان يؤُمّ أصحابه فحضرت الصلاة يوماً فذهب لحاجته ثم رجع فقال إني سمعت رسول الله ﷺ يقول إذا أراد أحدكم الغائط فليبدأ به قبل الصلاة

موطأ مالك كتاب قصر الصلاة في السفر

Hisham ibn 'Urwa related from his father that 'Abdullah ibn Al-Arqam served as *imam* to his companions. The time for prayer came one day, and he went to fulfill his need and then returned; he said: Indeed I heard the Messenger of Allah (SAW) say: Whenever any of you needs to defecate, he should do this first before prayer.

*Muwatta Malik, The book of shortening prayer during travel*


عن ابي أمامة أن رسول الله ﷺ نهى أن يصلى الرجل وهو حاقن

سنن إبن ماجه كتاب الطهارة وسننها

Abu Umama related that the Messenger of Allah (SAW) forbade anyone to pray if he was holding back the urge.

*Sunan Ibn Majah, The book of purity and its sunnah*


عن محمد سئل عن الرجل يعطس في الخلاء قال لا أعلم بأساً بذكر الله

المصنف لإبن ابي شيبة كتاب الطهارة

Muhammad related that he was asked about someone who sneezes in the latrine; he said: I don't know of any problem with making remembrance [*dhikr*] of Allah.

*Ibn Abi Shayba, Al-musannaf, The book of purity*

عن ابي إسحاق في الرجل يعطس في الخلاء قال قال أبو ميسرة ما أحب أن أذكر الله إلا في مكان طيب قال
قال منصور قال ابراهيم يحمد الله

المصنف لإبن ابي شيبة كتاب الطهارة

Abu Ishaq related regarding someone who sneezes in the latrine; he said: Abu Maysara
said: I don't like to make remembrance of Allah except in clean places. He also said:
Mansur said that Ibrahim said: He should give praise to Allah ["*Al-hamdu Lillah*"].

*Ibn Abi Shayba, Al-musannaf, The book of purity*

لا يجامعنّ أحدكم وبه حقن من خلاء فإنه يكون منه البواسير ولا يجامعن أحدكم وبه حقن من بول فإنه يكون
النواصير إبن النجار عن أنس

كنز العمال للهندي كتاب النكاح محظورات المباشرة

"Let none of you ever have sex when he is holding back a need to relieve himself, for
indeed this leads to hemmorhoids; and let none of you ever have sex holding back a
need to urinate, for indeed this leads to fistulas." (Transmitted by Ibn Al-Najjar as
related by Anas)

*Al-Hindi, Kanz Al-'Ummal, The book of marital relations, restrictions in intimate contact*

وفي الشفاء لإبن سبع عن بعض الصحابة قال صحبته ﷺ في سفر فلما أراد قضاء الحاجة تأملته وقد دخل
مكاناً فقضى حاجته فدخلت الموضع الذي خرج منه فلم ير له أثر غائط ولا بول ورأيت في ذلك الموضع ثلاثة
أحجار فأخذتهن فوجدت لهن رائحة طيبة وعطراً

المواهب للقسطلاني طيب ريحه ﷺ وعرقه ودمه

It is related in the *Shifa'* [*Shifa' Al-Sudur*] by Ibn Sabu', from one of the Companions,
who said: I accompanied Him (SAW) on a journey, and when He wanted to fulfill a
need, I observed carefully when He went in to a certain place. And He fulfilled His
need, and I went in to the place He had come out of, and no trace of defecation or
urine could be seen from Him. I saw three stones in that location, so I took them, and
I found that they had a pleasant aroma and were perfumed.

*Al-Qastalani, Al-mawahib, Section: The fragrance of His (SAW) wind, His sweat, and His blood*

عن عائشة قالت كان النبي ﷺ إذا دخل الغائط دخلت في أثره فلا أرى شيئاً إلا أني كنت أشم رائحة
الطيب فذكرت ذلك له فقال أما علمت يا عائشة أن أجسادنا تنبت على أرواح أهل الجنة وما خرج منها ابتلعته
الأرض

المواهب للقسطلاني طيب ريحه ﷺ وعرقه ودمه

From 'Aishah, who said: Whenever the Prophet (SAW) went out to defecate, I went in behind Him, but I didn't see anything, except that I would smell the scent of perfume. I mentioned this to Him, and He said: Oh 'Aishah! Did you not know that our bodies grow forth from the spirits of the people of *Jannah*, and whatever comes out of them, the earth swallows it up.

*Al-Qastalani, Al-mawahib, Section: The fragrance of His (SAW) wind, His sweat, and His blood*

عن أبي هريرة عن النبي ﷺ قال المبطون شهيد والمطعون شهيد

صحيح البخاري كتاب الطب

وأما المبطون فهو صاحب داء البطن وهو الإسهال  قال القاضي وقيل هو الذي به الاستسقاء وانتفاخ البطن
وقيل هو الذي تشتكي بطنه وقيل هو الذي يموت بداء بطنه مطلقاً

المنهاج في شرح صحيح مسلم للنووي كتاب الامارة باب بيان الشهداء

Abu Huraira related from the Prophet (SAW) who said: Anyone who is stricken by abdominal sickness [*mabtoun*] is a martyr, and one who is stricken by plague is a martyr.

*Sahih Al-Bukhari, The book of medicine*

Now then, *mabtoun* is someone who has abdominal sickness, this being diarrhea; Al-Qadi said: This is someone with swelling and a bloated abdomen. It is also said: This is someone with abdominal pains; and it is said that this is anyone who dies from abdominal sickness in general.

*Al-Nawawi, Al-minhaj fi Sharh Sahih Muslim [Open Path in Exposition of Sahih Muslim], The book of position of authority (emirate), Section: declaration of who are martyrs*

الريح

*Flatulence*

عن همام بن مُنبِّه أنه سمع أبا هريرة يقول قال رسول الله ﷺ لا تُقبل صلاة من أحدث حتى يتوضأ قال
رجل من حضرموت ما الحدث يا أبا هريرة قال فساء أو ضراط

صحيح البخاري كتاب الوضوء

Hammam ibn Munabbih related that he heard Abu Huraira say: The Messenger of
Allah (SAW) said: Prayer is not accepted from anyone who has had an occurrence
[hadath], until he performs ablution. A man from Hadramut said: What is hadath, oh
Abu Huraira? He said: Passing gas [fusaa, no sound] or farting [durat, with sound].

*Sahih Al-Bukhari, The book of ablution*

عن ابي هريرة عن النبي ﷺ قال لا يقبل الله صلاة أحدكم إذا أحدث حتى يتوضأ

صحيح البخاري كتاب الحيل

Abu Huraira related from the Prophet (SAW) that He said: Allah does not accept the
prayer of any of you if he has an occurrence, until he performs ablution [wudu'].

*Sahih Al-Bukhari, The book of guiles*

عن ابي هريرة أن رسول الله ﷺ قال الملائكة تصلي على أحدكم ما دام في مصلّاه الذي صلى فيه ما لم يُحدث
تقول اللهم إغفر له اللهم ارحمه

صحيح البخاري كتاب الصلاة

Abu Huraira related that the Messenger of Allah (SAW) said: The angels pray over
any of you while he remains in the place of prayer he prays in, as long as he does not
have an occurrence; they say: "Oh Allah, forgive him; Oh Allah, have mercy on him".

*Sahih Al-Bukhari, The book of prayer*

عن ابي هريرة أن رسول الله ﷺ قال إذا كان أحدكم في الصلاة فوجد حركة في دبره أحدث أو لم يحدث
فأشكل عليه فلا ينصرف حتى يسمع صوتاً أو يجد ريحاً

سنن ابي داود كتاب الطهارة

Abu Huraira related that the Messenger of Allah (SAW) said: If any of you is in prayer
and feels a movement in his rear and is uncertain whether or not he has had an
occurrence, he should not leave prayer until he hears a sound or perceives a smell.

*Sunan Abu Dawud, The book of purity*

عن ابي هريرة أن رسول الله ﷺ قال إذا كان أحدكم في المسجد فوجد ريحاً بين الْيَتَيه فلا يخرج حتى يسمع
صوتاً أو يجد ريحاً

جامع الترمذي كتاب الطهارة

Abu Huraira related that the Messenger of Allah (SAW) said: Whenever any of you is
in the mosque, and feels some gas between his two buttocks, he should not leave until
he hears a sound or perceives a smell.

*Sunan Al-Tirmidhi, The book of purity*

عن علي بن طلق أن رجلاً قال يا رسول الله إنه يخرج من أحدنا الرويْحة قال إذا فسا أحدكم فليتوضأ ولا تأتوا
النساء في أعجازهن

صحيح إبن حبان كتاب النكاح باب النهي عن إتيان النساء في أعجازهن

'Ali ibn Talq related that a certain man said: Oh Messenger of Allah, indeed sometimes
a little puff of wind [*ruwaiha*] comes out of one of us. He said: Whenever any of you
passes gas he should perform ablution; and do not come to women in their backsides.

*Sahih Ibn Hibban, The book of marital relations, Section: the prohibition of coming to women in their rears*

عن علي بن طلق قال أتى أعرابي النبي ﷺ فقال يا رسول الله الرجل منا يكون في الفلاة فتكون منه الرُويْحة
ويكون في الماء قِلَّة فقال رسول الله ﷺ إذا فسا أحدكم فليتوضأ ولا تأتوا النساء في أعجازهن فإنّ الله لا
يستحيي من الحق

جامع الترمذي كتاب الرضاع

From 'Ali ibn Talq who said: A Bedouin came to the Prophet (SAW) and said: Oh
Messenger of Allah, What if one of us is in the desert and a little puff of wind comes
out of him but water is scarce? And the Messenger of Allah (SAW) said: Whenever
any of you passes gas he should perform ablution [*wudu'*], and do not come to women
in their backsides, for indeed Allah is not ashamed of the truth.

*Sunan Al-Tirmidhi, The book of suckling*

عن ابي هريرة أن رسول الله ﷺ قال لا وضوء إلا من صوت أو ريح

جامع الترمذي كتاب الطهارة

Abu Huraira related that the Messenger of Allah (SAW) said: No ablution is necessary
except in the case of a sound or a smell.

*Sunan Al-Tirmidhi, The book of purity*

عن عائشة عن النبي ﷺ قال إذا صلى أحدكم فأحدث فليمسك على أنفه ثم لينصرف

سنن إبن ماجه كتاب إقامة الصلاة وألسنة فيها

'Aishah related from the Prophet (SAW) who said: Whenever any of you is praying and has an occurrence [hadath], he should grab his nose and leave.

*Sunan Ibn Majah, The book of calling to prayer and the sunnah regarding it*

عن ابي سعيد الخدري أن رسول الله ﷺ قال إن الشيطان يأتي أحدكم وهو في صلاته فيأخذ شعرة من دبره فيمدها فيرى أنه قد أحدث فلا ينصرف حتى يسمع صوتاً أو يجد ريحاً

المسند للإمام أحمد مسند ابي سعيد الخدري رضي الله تعالى عنه

Abu Sa'id Al-Khudri related that the Messenger of Allah (SAW) said: Indeed Satan may come upon any of you as he is in prayer, and will take hold of a hair from his rear and stretch it out, to see if he has had an occurrence, but he should not leave unless he hears a sound or perceives a smell.

*Musnad Ahmad, Section: The hadith of Abu Sa'id Al-Khudri – May Allah most high be pleased with him*

(فيرى) أي يظن المصلي (أنه أحدث) بخروج ريح من دبره فإذا وقع ذلك (فلا ينصرف) من صلاته أي لا يتركها ليتطهر ويستأنف (حتى يسمع صوتاً) أي صوت ريح يخرج منه (أو يجد ريحاً) أو يشم رائحة خرجت منه وهذا مجاز عن تيقن الحدث لأنها سبب للعلم به

فيض القدير شرح الجامع الصغير للعلام المناوي حرف الهمزة

(to see if) : that is, the person praying thinks (he has had an occurrence) from the passing of gas from his rear; and if this occurs (he should not leave) his prayer, that is, he should not abandon it to purify himself and resume again, (unless he hears a sound), that is, the sound of gas exiting him, (or perceives a smell), that is, he smells an odor coming from him. This is a figure of speech expressing the certainty of having had an occurrence, since this is how one becomes aware of it.

*Al-Munawi, Faid Al-Qadir, Section: the letter "hamza"*

عن إبن عباس رضي الله عنهما أن رسول الله ﷺ قال يأتي أحدكم الشيطان في صلاته فينفخ في مقعده فيخيَّل إليه أنه أحدث ولم يحدث فإذا وجد ذلك فلا ينصرف حتى يسمع صوتاً أو يجد ريحاً

بلوغ المرام لإبن الإبن حجر كتاب الطهارة

Ibn 'Abbas (may Allah be pleased with him) related that the Messenger of Allah (SAW) said: Satan can come upon any of you during his prayer and blow in his buttocks, and you will imagine that you have had an occurrence, when you have not; so you should not leave unless you hear a sound or perceive a smell.

*Ibn Hajar, Bulugh Al-maram, The book of purity*

عن شهر بن حوشب قال إن الشيطان ليأتي أحدكم فيدخل خطمه في دبره فيحركه ويحرك إحليله ليشرّ فلا ينصرفن حتى يسمع صوتاً أو يجد ريحاً
المصنف لإبن ابي شيبة كتاب الصلاة

From Shahr ibn Hawshab, who said: Indeed Satan may come upon any of you, and put his snout into your rear end, move it around, and move your shaft around, to be malicious, but you should in no instance leave unless you hear a sound or perceive a smell.

*Ibn Abi Shayba, Al-musannaf, The book of prayer*

عن علي بن ابي طالب رضي الله عنه قال قال رسول الله ﷺ وكاء السَّه العينان فمن نام فليتوضأ
سنن ابي داود كتاب الطهارة

From 'Ali ibn Abi Talib (may Allah be pleased with him), who said: The Messenger of Allah (SAW) said: The eyes are the strap of the anal sphincter, so whoever falls asleep should perform ablution.

*Sunan Abu Dawud, The book of purity*

قوله وكاء السه مبتدأ و العينان خبره السه حلقة الدبر وهو من الاست ... ومعنى الحديث أن الانسان مهما كان مستيقظاً كانت استه كالمشدودة الموكئ عليها فإذا نام إنحل وكاؤها كنى بهذا اللفظ عن الحدث وخروج الريح وهو من أحسن الكنايات وألطفها حيث جعل اليقظة للإست كالوكاء للقربة كما أن الوكاء يمنع ما في القربة أن يخرج كذلك اليقظة تمنع الإست أن تحدث إلا بإجتهاد وكنى بالعين عن اليقظة لأن النائم لا عين له تبصر
شرح سنن ابي داود للعيني باب الوضوء من النوم

His word "the strap of the anal sphincter [sah]" is the subject, and "the eyes" are its predicate. The *sah* refers to the hole of the rear end; it is part of the anus. ... The meaning of this hadith is that a person, while he is awake, his anus is essentially fastened as if it were tied up with a strap, but whenever he falls asleep, its strap is loosened. This figure of speech is used to allude to bodily occurrences [hadath] and the passing of gas, and is among the best and most pleasant allusions, in which wakefulness is ascribed to the anus like a strap to a waterskin; just as the strap prevents what is inside the waterskin from coming out, likewise wakefulness prevents the anus from having an occurrence except by exertion. And the eye is used as an allusion to wakefulness, since someone who is asleep has no eyes to perceive.

*Badr Al-deen Al-'Aini, Sharh Sunan Abi Dawud [Exposition of Sunan Abi Dawud], Chapter 70: Ablution from sleeping*

عن عبدالله بن زمعة قال سمعت النبي ﷺ يوماً يذكر الناقة والذي عقرها فقال إذ إنبعث أشقاها إنبعث لها رجل
عارم عزيز منيع في رهطه مثل ابي زمعة ثم سمعته يذكر النساء فقال إلاَم يعمد أحدكم فيجلد امرأته جلد العبد
ولعلّه أن يضاجعها من آخر يومه قال ثم وعظهم في ضحكهم من الضرطة فقال الام يضحك أحدكم مما يفعل

سنن الترمذي كتاب التفسير

From 'Abdullah ibn Zam'a who said: One day I heard the Prophet (SAW) mention the
camel and the one who had slayed her, and He said: When the most wretched of them
went forth [Al-shams 12]; a forceful and noble man went forth to her, invincible
among his troop, like Abu Zam'a. Then I heard him mention women, and He said:
None of you ought to proceed to whip his woman as a slave is whipped, for perhaps
he might go to bed with her in the latter part of his day. Then He admonished them
about laughing at farts; He said: None of you ought to laugh at what he himself does.

*Sunan Al-Tirmidhi, The book of tafsir*

عن ابي هريرة عن النبي ﷺ قال إن الشيطان إذا سمع النداء بالصلاة أحال له ضراط حتى لا يسمع صوته
فإذا سكت رجع فوسوس فإذا سمع الإقامة ذهب حتى لا يسمع صوته فإذا سكت رجع فوسوس

صحيح مسلم كتاب الصلاة

Abu Huraira related from the Prophet (SAW), who said: Indeed Satan, whenever he
hears the call to prayer, moves away and farts so as not to hear the sound, but when
it is over, he returns and whispers bad thoughts [*waswas*]; and whenever he hears the
second call immediately before prayer [*iqamah*], he goes away so as not to hear the
sound, but when it is over, he returns and whispers bad thoughts again.

*Sahih Muslim, The book of prayer*

﴾ أَئِنَّكُمْ لَتَأْتُونَ الرِّجَالَ وَتَقْطَعُونَ السَّبِيلَ وَتَأْتُونَ فِي نَادِيكُمُ الْمُنكَرَ ﴿ العنكبوت ٢٩

*{ Indeed do you all not approach men, and you cut off roadways, and you take a liking to wrongdoing in your gatherings? }* Al-'ankabut 29

عن القاسم بن محمد بن أبي بكر الصديق رضي الله عنه أنه سئل عن قول الله ﴿ وتأتون في ناديكم المنكر ﴾ ماذا كان المنكر الذي كانوا يأتون قال كانوا يتضارطون في مجالسهم يضرط بعضهم على بعض

الدر المنثور للسيوطي

Qasim ibn Muhammad ibn Abi Bakr Al-Sadiq (may Allah be pleased with him) related that he was asked about the word of Allah { and you take a liking to wrongdoing in your gatherings } – what was the wrongdoing that they took a liking to? He said: They would mutually fart in their meetings; people would fart on each other.

*Al-Suyuti, Al-durr Al-manthur*

﴿ وتأتون في ناديكم المنكر ﴾ إختلف أهل التأويل في المنكر الذي عناه الله الذي كان هؤلاء القوم يأتونه في ناديهم فقال بعضهم كان ذلك أنهم كانوا يتضارطون في مجالسهم ... عن عائشة في قوله ﴿ وتأتون في ناديكم المنكر ﴾ قال الضراط

تفسير الطبري

{ And you take a liking to wrongdoing in your gatherings } : Expositors differ regarding the "wrongdoing" that Allah has indicated, to which these people took a liking in their gatherings; some of them said that they would mutually fart on each other in their meetings. ... 'Aishah, regarding His word { and you take a liking to wrongdoing in your gatherings } , said: Farting [*durat*].

*Tafsir Al-Tabari*

ومن قائل كانوا يتضارطون ويتضاحكون قالته عائشة رضي الله عنها والقاسم ومن قائل كانوا يناطحون بين الكباش ويناقرون بين الديوك

تفسير ابن كثير

There were those who said that people would mutually fart on each other and mutually laugh at each other; 'Aishah (may Allah be pleased with her) said this, and Al-Qasim; and there were others who said that people would make rams butt each other or set up cockfights.

*Tafsir Ibn Kathir*

﴿ المنكر ﴾ كالجماع والضراط وحل الإزار وغيرها من القبائح عدم مبالاة بها

تفسير البيضاوي

{ Wrongdoing } : Such as sex, farting, undoing one's waistwrap, and other abominations that show a lack of consideration.

*Tafsir Al-Baydawi*

•  •  •

منها أنه إذا كان يقرأ فعرض له ريحٌ فينبغي أن يُمسك عن القراءة حتى يتكامل خروجها ثم يعود إلى القراءة كذا رواه إبن ابي داود وغيره عن عطاء وهو أدب حسن

التبيان في آداب حملة القران للنووي  الباب السادس في أدب القران فصل في مسائل غريبة تدعو الحاجة إليها

Among these issues is that whenever one is reciting, and the passing of gas becomes evident to him, he ought to discontinue the recitation until it has completely exited, and then he may resume recitation. Ibn Abi Dawud and others narrated this from 'Ataa; and it is a good course of conduct.

*Al-Nawawi, Al-tibyan fi Adab Hamala Al-Quran, Chapter six: On proper conduct with the Qur'an, Section: regarding certain peculiar issues that necessity calls for*

قال وليس على من ناب أو خرجت منه ريح إستنجاء

لا نعلم في هذا خلافاً قال أبو عبدالله ليس في الريح إستنجاء في كتاب الله ولا في سنة رسوله انما عليه الوضوء وقد روي عن النبي ﷺ أنه قال من استنجى من ريح فليس منا رواه الطبراني في معجمه الصغير

المغني لإبن قدامة باب الاستطابة والحدث

He [Al-Khiraqi] said: Ritual cleansing [*istinjaa*] is not required of anyone who falls asleep or passes gas.

We know of no disagreement regarding this. Abu Abdullah said: *Istinjaa* is not made obligatory in the case of gas, neither in the book of Allah nor in the *sunnah* of His Prophet, but ablution [*wudu'*] does become obligatory. It is narrated from the Prophet (SAW) that He said: Anyone who performs *istinjaa* after passing gas is not one of us. (Narrated by Al-Tabarani in *Al-mu'jam Al-saghir*].

*Ibn Qudama, Al-mughni, Chapter: Cleansing from filth [istitaba] and bodily occurrences [hadath]*

وقد نقل صالح عن أبيه في المرأة يخرج من فرجها الريح ما خرج من السبيلين ففيه الوضوء وقال القاضي خروج الريح من الذكر وقبل المرأة ينقض الوضوء

المغني لإبن قدامة باب باب ما ينقض الطهارة

Salih transmitted from his father regarding a woman who passes gas from her vagina; whatever comes out of the two passages [i.e. the front and the rear] makes ablution obligatory. Al-Qadi said: Passing gas out of the penis or from the front part of a woman invalidates ablution.

*Ibn Qudama, Al-mughni, Chapter: Things that annul a state of purity*

{ *Allah; there is no god but He, the Living, the Everlasting* } Al-baqara 255

وأخرج أبو عبيد في فضائله والدارمي والطبراني وأبو نعيم في دلائل النبوة والبيهقي عن إبن مسعود قال خرج
رجل من الإنس فلقيه رجل من الجن فقال هل لك أن تصارعني فإن صرعتني علمتك آية إذا قرأتها حين
تدخل بيتك لم يدخله شيطان فصارعه فصرعه الانسي فقال تقرأ آية الكرسي فإنه لا يقرأها أحد إذا دخل بيته
إلا خرج الشيطان له خبج تكبج الحمار

الدر المنثور للسيوطي

Abu 'Ubaid reported in his *Fada'il*, and Al-Darimi, and Al-Tabarani, and Abu Nu'im in
*Dala'il Al-nubuwa*, and Al-Bayhaqi, from Ibn Mas'ud, who said: A certain man from among
the humans set out, and a man from among the genies [*jinn*] met up with him, and said:
Do you have what it takes to wrestle with me? If you bring me down I will teach you a
verse that, whenever you recite it upon entering your house, no devil will enter. And so
he wrestled with him, and the human man brought him down. So he [the *jinn*] said: Do
you recite the throne verse [*Al-baqara* 255]? Indeed anyone who recites it when he enters
his house, Satan leaves with loud farting noises [*khabaj*] like those of a donkey.

*Al-Suyuti, Al-durr Al-manthur*

... قال تقرأ آية الكرسي ﴿ الله لا إلا هو الحي القيوم ﴾ قال نعم قال فانك لا تقرأها في بيت إلا خرج منه
الشيطان له خَبَج تكبج الحمار ثم لا يدخله حتى يصبح أخرجه أبو نعيم عن ابي عاصم الثقفي عن الشعبي

تفسير القرطبي

... He asked him: Do you recite the throne verse { Allah; there is no god but He, the
Living, the Everlasting } ?  The man replied: Yes. He said: Indeed any house in which
you recite this, Satan departs from it with loud farting noises like those of a donkey,
and then he does not enter again until morning. Abu Nu'im reported this from Abu
'Asim Al-Thaqafi who reported it from Al-Sha'bi.

*Tafsir Al-Qurtubi*

•    •    •

# الحيض والاستحاضة

*Menstruation and vaginal bleeding*

﴿ وَيَسْأَلُونَكَ عَنِ الْمَحِيضِ قُلْ هُوَ أَذًى فَاعْتَزِلُوا النِّسَاءَ فِي الْمَحِيضِ وَلَا تَقْرَبُوهُنَّ حَتَّى يَطْهُرْنَ فَإِذَا تَطَهَّرْنَ فَأْتُوهُنَّ
مِنْ حَيْثُ أَمَرَكُمُ اللَّهُ إِنَّ اللَّهَ يُحِبُّ التَّوَّابِينَ وَيُحِبُّ الْمُتَطَهِّرِينَ ﴾ البقرة ٢٢٢

*{ And they ask you about menstruation; say: It is harm; therefore keep away from women during menstruation; and do not get close to them until they have become pure; and when they have purified themselves come to them where Allah has ordered you. Indeed Allah loves those who turn in repentance, and He loves those who purify themselves }* Al-baqara 222

﴿ وَيَسْأَلُونَكَ عَنِ الْمَحِيضِ ﴾ أَيِ الْحَيْضِ أَوْ مَكَانِهِ مَاذَا يُفْعَلُ بِالنِّسَاءِ فِيهِ ﴿ قُلْ هُوَ أَذًى ﴾ قَذَرٌ أَوْ مَحَلُّهُ ﴿ فَاعْتَزِلُوا النِّسَاءَ ﴾ اتْرُكُوا وَطْأَهُنَّ ﴿ فِي الْمَحِيضِ ﴾ أَيْ وَفِيهِ أَوْ مَكَانِهِ ﴿ وَلَا تَقْرَبُوهُنَّ ﴾ بِالْجِمَاعِ ﴿ حَتَّى يَطْهُرْنَ ﴾ ... أَيْ يَغْتَسِلْنَ بَعْدَ انْقِطَاعِهِ ﴿ فَإِذَا تَطَهَّرْنَ فَأْتُوهُنَّ ﴾ بِالْجِمَاعِ ﴿ مِنْ حَيْثُ أَمَرَكُمُ اللَّهُ ﴾ وَبِتَجَنُّبِهِ فِي الْحَيْضِ وَهُوَ الْقُبُلُ وَلَا تَعْدُوهُ إِلَى غَيْرِهِ ﴿ إِنَّ اللَّهَ يُحِبُّ ﴾ يُثِيبُ وَيُكْرِمُ ﴿ التَّوَّابِينَ ﴾ مِنَ الذُّنُوبِ ﴿ وَيُحِبُّ الْمُتَطَهِّرِينَ ﴾ مِنَ الْأَقْذَارِ

تفسير الجلالين

{ And they ask you about menstruation } : that is, the blood flow or the location of it – what should be done with women about it? { Say: It is harm } : filth, or the location of it; { therefore keep away from women } : stop having intercourse with them; { during menstruation } : during it or in its location; { and do not get close to them } : for sex; { until they have become pure } ... that is, they have bathed after it has ceased; { and when they have purified themselves, come to them } : for sex; { where Allah has ordered you } : avoiding it during menstruation, this being the front part – and do not do it somewhere else; { indeed Allah loves } : rewards and honors; { those who turn in repentance } : of sins; { and He loves those who purify themselves } : of any kind of filth.

*Tafsir Al-Jalalain*

﴿ قُلْ هُوَ أَذًى ﴾ يَعْنِي تَعَالَى ذِكْرُهُ قُلْ لِمَنْ سَأَلَكَ مِنْ أَصْحَابِكَ يَا مُحَمَّدُ عَنِ الْمَحِيضِ هُوَ أَذًى وَالْأَذَى هُوَ مَا يُؤْذَى بِهِ مِنْ مَكْرُوهٍ فِيهِ وَهُوَ فِي هَذَا الْمَوْضِعِ يُسَمَّى أَذًى لِنَتْنِ رِيحِهِ وَقَذَرِهِ وَنَجَاسَتِهِ وَهُوَ جَامِعٌ لِمَعَانٍ شَتَّى مِنْ خِلَالِ الْأَذَى غَيْرِ وَاحِدَةٍ

تفسير الطبري

{ Say: It is harm } ; He (may His remembrance be exalted) means by this: Say to whoever of your Companions asks you, Oh Muhammad, about menstruation, that it is harm. "Harm" is anything disagreeable by which one may be harmed; in this instance it is called "harm" due to its strong and offensive odor, its filth, and its impurity. This is comprehensive, by saying "harm", for more than one diverse meaning.

*Tafsir Al-Tabari*

فقوله ﴿ فاعتزلوا النساء في المحيض ﴾ يعني الفرج لقوله اصنعوا كل شيء إلا النكاح ولهذا ذهب كثير من العلماء أو أكثرهم إلى أنه تجوز مباشرة الحائض فيما عدا الفرج

تفسير ابن كثير

And His word { Therefore keep away from women during menstruation } means the vagina, in reference to His (SAW) word: Do everything except relations [*nikah*]. For this reason many or most scholars have reached the conclusion that intimate contact [*mubashara*] is permissible with a menstruating women except with the vagina.

*Tafsir Ibn Kathir*


عن ابن مسعود قال الحيض ثلاث وأربع وخمس وست وسبع وثمان وتسع وعشر فإن زاد فهي استحاضة ... عن مجاهد في قوله ﴿ قل هو أذى ﴾ قال الأذى الدم ... عن ابن عباس في قوله ﴿ فاعتزلوا النساء ﴾ يقول اعتزلوا نكاح فروجهن ... عن بعض أزواج النبي ﷺ أن النبي ﷺ كان إذا أراد من الحائض شيئاً ألقى على فرجها ثوباً ثم صنع ما أراد

الدر المنثور للسيوطي

From Ibn Mas'ud, who said: Menstruation is three [days], or four, or five, or six, or seven, or eight, or nine, or ten; if it exceeds that then it is vaginal bleeding. ... Mujahid, regarding His word { Say: It is harm } , said: The blood is the harm. ... Ibn 'Abbas, regarding His word { Therefore keep away from women } , said: Keep away from marital relations with their vaginas. ... One of the Prophet's (SAW) wives related that the Prophet (SAW), whenever He wanted something from a menstruating woman, would throw a garment over her vagina, and then He would do what He wanted.

*Al-Suyuti, Al-durr Al-manthur*


وفرض على الرجل أن يجامع امرأته التي هي زوجته وأدنى ذلك مرة في كل طُهر إن قدر على ذلك وإلا فهو عاص لله تعالى برهان ذلك قول الله عز وجل ﴿ فإذا تطهرن فأتوهن من حيث أمركم الله ﴾ سورة البقرة ٢٢٢

المحلى لابن حزم كتاب النكاح

It is obligatory for a man to have sex with his woman that is his wife, and this at a minimum once every pure period [i.e. between menstruations], if he is able to do this, otherwise he transgresses against Allah Most High. Evidence for this is the word of Allah Mighty and Sublime { And when they have purified themselves come to them where Allah has ordered you } (*Al-baqara* 222).

*Ibn Hazm, Al-muhalla, The book of marital relations*


•         •         •

إذا رأت الصبية الدم ولها تسع سنين فهو حيض فأما قبل ذلك فهو دم فساد لا دم حيض وإذا رأت دماً
بعد خمسين سنة فليس بحيض

أحكام النساء لابن الجوزي الباب الخامس عشر في ذكر الحيض

Whenever a young girl sees blood at the age of nine, it is menstruation, although
before this it is abnormal bleeding, not menstrual blood. Whenever a woman sees
blood after the age of fifty, it is not menstrual blood.

*Ibn Al-Jawzi, Ahkam Al-nisaa, Chapter fifteen: mention of menstruation*

عن عائشة قالت قال النبي ﷺ إذا أقبلت الحيضة فدعي الصلاة وإذا أدبرت فاغسلي عنك الدم وصلي

صحيح البخاري كتاب الحيض

From 'Aishah, who said: The Prophet (SAW) said: Whenever you get your period,
refrain from prayer, and when it is over, wash the blood off of yourself and pray.

*Sahih Al-Bukhari, The book of menstruation*

عن ابي سعيد الخدري ... قلن وما نقصان ديننا وعقلنا يا رسول الله قال أليس شهادة المرأة مثل نصف
شهادة الرجل قلن بلى قال فذلك من نقصان عقلها أليس إذا حاضت لم تصلِّ ولم تصُم قلن بلى قال فذلك
من نقصان دينها

صحيح البخاري كتاب الحيض

Abu Sa'id Al-Khudri related ... The women asked: And what is the deficiency in our
religion and our intellect, oh Messenger of Allah? He said: Is not the testimony of a
woman like half the testimony of a man? They said: Yes indeed. He said: And that is
the deficiency in her intellect; is it not true that whenever a woman menstruates, she
has not prayed nor fasted? They said: Yes indeed. He said: And that is the deficiency
in their religion.

*Sahih Al-Bukhari, The book of menstruation*

عن إبن جريج قال قلت لعطاء هل للحائض من غسل معلوم قال لا إلا أن تستنقي تغرف على رأسها ثلاث
غرفات أو تزيد فإنّ الحيضة أشد من الجنابة

المصنف لعبد الرزاق كتاب الحيض

From Ibn Juraij who said: I said to 'Ataa: Is there a specific washing [*ghusl*] for a
menstruating woman? He said: No, except that she should seek to be pure by pouring
three scoops of water on her head, or more; indeed menstruation is more serious than
sexual impurity [*janaba*].

*'Abd Al-Razzaq, the Musannaf, The book of menstruation*

عن عائشة قالت دخلت أسماء على رسول الله ﷺ فقالت يا رسول الله كيف تغتسل إحدانا إذا طهُرت من
المحيض قال تأخذ سدرها وماءها فتوضأ ثم تغسل رأسها وتدلكه حتى يبلُغ الماء أصول شعرها ثم تُفيض على
جسدها ثم تأخذ فِرصتها فتطَّهر بها قالت يا رسول الله كيف أتطهر بها قالت عائشة فعرفت الذي يكني عنه
رسول الله ﷺ فقلت لها تَتبعين بها آثار الدم

سنن أبي داود كتاب الطهارة

From 'Aishah, who said: Asmaa went in to see the Messenger of Allah (SAW), and she
said: Oh Messenger of Allah, how should any one of us women wash once we are
purified from our menstruation? He said: She should take her *sidr* tree preparation,
and her water, and perform ablution; then she should wash and rub her head until the
water reaches the roots of her hair; then she should pour water generously over her
body; then she should take her cloth and cleanse herself with it. Asmaa said: Oh
Messenger of Allah, how do I cleanse myself with it? And 'Aishah said: I knew what
the Messenger of Allah (SAW) was getting at, so I said to her: You get out the marks
of blood with it.

*Sunan Abu Dawud, The book of purity*


عن إبن جريج قال لي عطاء تغسيل المرأة جسدها إذا تطهَّرت من الحيض بالسِدر قلت تنشر شعرها قال
لا وإن لم تجد إلا الأرض كفاها فإن لم تجد ماءً تمسَّحت بالتراب

المصنف لعبد الرزاق كتاب الحيض

From Ibn Juraij who said: 'Ataa said to me: A woman should wash her body with *sidr*
tree preparation whenever she purifies herself from menstruation. I said: Should she
undo her hair? He said: No; and if she can only find earth, it is sufficient for her; if
she can not find water she can wipe herself with the dust.

*'Abd Al-Razzaq, the Musannaf, The book of menstruation*


عن عائشة أن إمرأة من الأنصار قالت للنبي ﷺ كيف أغتسل من الحَيض قال خذي فِرصة ممسكة فتوضَّئي
ثلاثاً ثم إن النبي ﷺ استحيا فأعرض بوجهه أو قال توضئي بها فأخذتها بِجذبتها فأخبرتها بما يريد النبي ﷺ

صحيح البخاري كتاب الحيض

'Aishah related that a certain woman from the *Ansar* said to the Prophet (SAW):
How should I wash myself from my period? He said: Take a piece of cloth scented
with musk and perform ablution three times. Then indeed the Prophet (SAW) felt
embarrassed and turned his face away – or He said: perform ablution with it. So I
took her aside towards me and explained to her what the Prophet (SAW) meant
to say.

*Sahih Al-Bukhari, The book of menstruation*

عن مجاهد قال قالت عائشة ما كان لإحدانا إلا ثوب واحد تحيض فيه فإذا أصابه شيء من دم قالت بريقها فتقصعته بظُفرها

صحيح البخاري كتاب الحيض

From Mujahid who said: 'Aishah said: None of us women had more than one garment that she would menstruate in; and whenever some blood got on it, she would put her saliva on it and work it out with her fingernails.

*Sahih Al-Bukhari, The book of menstruation*

عن عائشة أن إمرأة سألت النبي ﷺ عن غسلها من الحيض فأمرها كيف تغتسل قال خذي فرصة من مسك فتطهّري بها قالت كيف أتطهر قال تطهري بها قالت كيف قال سبحان الله تطهري فإجتبذتُها إليّ فقلت تتبّعي أثر الدم

صحيح البخاري كتاب الحيض

'Aishah related that a certain woman asked the Prophet (SAW) about her washing from menstruation. He told her how she should wash herself; He said: Take a cloth of musk and purify yourself with it. She said: How should I purify myself? He said: Purify yourself with it. She said: How? He said: Allah be exalted! Purify yourself! So I ['Aishah] pulled her aside towards me and said: Work over where the stain of blood is.

*Sahih Al-Bukhari, The book of menstruation*

عن عائشة عن النبي ﷺ أنه قال لا يقبل الله صلاة حائض إلا بخمار

سنن أبي داود كتاب الصلاة

'Aishah related that the Prophet (SAW) said: Allah does not accept the prayer of a menstruating woman except if veiled.

*Sunan Abu Dawud, The book of prayer*

الوقت الذي يجب فيه الغسل من الحيض على المرأة خرج القطن ولا شيء عليه أو كان عليه بلة بيضاء

أحكام النساء لإبن الجوزي الباب الحادي عشر في ذكر ما يوجب الغسل

The time at which washing from menstruation is obligatory for women is when a piece of cotton comes out with nothing on it, or just white moisture on it.

*Ibn Al-Jawzi, Ahkam Al-nisaa, Chapter eleven: mention of what necessitates washing [ghusl]*

عن فاطمة بنت المنذر عن أسماء بنت ابي بكر وكانت تكون في حجرها أن إمرأة استفتت النبي ﷺ عن دم
الحيض يصيب الثوب فقال حُتيه ثم اقرُضيه بالماء ثم انضَحيه وصلي فيه

سنن النسائي كتاب الطهارة

Fatimah bint Al-Mundhir related from Asmaa bint Abi Bakr – she was under her
care – that a certain woman sought guidance from the Prophet (SAW) regarding
menstrual blood getting on a garment; and He said: Scrape it, then rub it with water,
then sprinkle it with water, and pray in it.

*Sunan Al-Nasa'i, The book of purification*

عن جابر إبن صبح سمعت خلاساً الهجري قال سمعت عائشة رضي الله عنها تقول كنت أنا ورسول الله ﷺ
نبيت في الشِّعار الواحد وأنا حائض طامث فإن أصابه مني شيءُ غسل مكانه ولم يعدُه ثم صلى فيه وإن أصاب
تعني ثوبه منه شيءُ غسل مكانه ولم يعده ثم صلى فيه

سنن ابي داود كتاب الطهارة

Jabir ibn Subh said: I heard from Khilas Al-Hajari, who said: I heard 'Aishah (may
Allah be pleased with her) say: It was me and the Messenger of Allah (SAW), we spent
the night in one garment while I was menstruating heavily. And if anything from me
got on him, He washed that spot, but no more than that, and then He prayed; and if
anything from me got on – she meant his garment – he washed that spot, but no
more, and then He prayed in it.

*Sunan Abu Dawud, The book of purity*

سألت إمرأة رسول الله ﷺ فقالت يا رسول الله أرأيت إحدانا إذا أصاب ثوبها الدم من الحيضة كيف تصنع
فقال رسول الله ﷺ إذا أصاب ثوب إحداكن الدم من الحيضة فلتقرصه ثم لتنضحه بماءٍ ثم لتصلي فيه

صحيح البخاري كتاب الحيض

A woman asked the Messenger of Allah (SAW) and said: Oh Messenger of Allah, what
do you find proper for one of us if menstruation blood gets on her dress – what
should she do? And the Messenger of Allah (SAW) said: When menstruation blood
gets on the dress of any of you, she should squeeze it out then sprinkle water on it
then pray in it.

*Sahih Al-Bukhari, The book of menstruation*

عن أنس أنَّ اليهود كانوا لا يجلسون مع الحائض في بيتٍ ولا يأكلون ولا يشربون قال فذُكر ذلك للنبي ﷺ
فأنزل الله ﴿ ويسألونك عن المحيض قل هو أذى فاعتزلوا النساء في المحيض ﴾ فقال رسول الله ﷺ اصنعوا
كل شيء إلا الجماع

سنن ابن ماجه كتاب الطهارة وسننها

Anas related that the Jews would not sit together at home with menstruating women, and they would not eat or drink with them. This was mentioned to the Prophet (SAW), and Allah sent down { And they ask you about menstruation; say: it is a harmful thing, so keep away from women during menstruation } [Al-baqara 222]. And the Messenger of Allah (SAW) said: Do everything except sex.

*Sunan Ibn Majah, The book of purity and its sunnah*

عن عائشة أن فاطمة بنت ابي حبيش كانت تُستحاض فقال لها رسول الله ﷺ إن دم الحيض دم أسود
يُعرف فإذا كان ذلك فامسكي عن الصلاة وإذا كان الآخر فتوضئي وصلي

سنن النسائي كتاب الطهارة

'Aishah related that Fatimah bint Abi Hubaish suffered from vaginal bleeding, and the Messenger of Allah (SAW) said to her: Indeed menstrual blood is black blood and is recognizable, so whenever it is that, discontinue prayer, and whenever it is the other, perform ablution [*wudu'*] and pray.

*Sunan Al-Nasa'i, The book of purity*

عن ميمونة بنت الحارث أن رسول الله ﷺ كان إذا أراد أن يباشر إمرأةً من نسائه وهي حائض أمرها أن
تتّزر ثم يباشرها

سنن ابي داود كتاب النكاح

Maimuna bint Al-Harith related that whenever the Messenger of Allah (SAW) desired to be intimate with one of his women and she was menstruating, He bid her to put on a waist robe [*izar*] and then he was intimate with her.

*Sunan Abu Dawud, The book of marital relations*

فقوله ﴿ فاعتزلوا النساء في المحيض ﴾ يعني الفرج لقوله اصنعوا كل شيء إلا النكاح ولهذا ذهب كثير من
العلماء أو أكثرهم إلى أنه تجوز مباشرة الحائض فيما عدا الفرج عن بعض أزواج النبي ﷺ أن النبي ﷺ كان
إذا أراد من الحائض شيئاً ألقى على فرجها ثوباً

تفسير ابن كثير

And His word { Therefore keep away from women during menstruation } means the vagina, in reference to His (SAW) word: Do everything except relations [*nikah*]. For this reason many or most scholars have reached the conclusion that intimate contact [*mubashara*] is permissible with a menstruating women except with the vagina. Some of the wives of the Prophet (SAW) related that the Prophet (SAW), whenever He desired something from a menstruating woman, would throw a garment over her vagina.

*Tafsir Ibn Kathir (Al-baqara 222)*

عن عكرمة عن بعض أزواج النبي ﷺ أن النبي ﷺ كان إذا أراد من الحائض شيئاً ألقى على فرجها ثوباً

سنن ابي داود كتاب الطهارة

'Ikrama related from one of the wives of the Prophet (SAW) that the Prophet (SAW), whenever He desired something from a menstruating woman, would throw a garment over her vagina.

*Sunan Abi Dawud, The book of purity*

عن عائشة رضي الله عنها قالت كان رسول الله ﷺ يأمرنا في فوح حيضنا أن نتّزر ثم يباشرنا وأيكم يملك اربه كما كان رسول الله ﷺ يملك إربه

سنن ابي داود كتاب الطهارة

From 'Aishah (may Allah be pleased with her) who said: The Messenger of Allah (SAW) would bid us, when we began to menstruate, to put on a waist wrap, and then He would be intimate with us; and none of you has control over his member like the Messenger of Allah (SAW) had control over His member.

*Sunan Abi Dawud, The book of purity*

جميع بن عمير قال دخلت على عائشة مع أمي وخالتي فسألتاها كيف كان رسول الله ﷺ يصنع إذا حاضت إحداكن قالت كان يأمرنا إذا حاضت إحدانا أن نتزر بإزار واسع ثم يلتزم صدرها وثديها

سنن النسائي كتاب الحيض والاستحاضة

Jumai' ibn 'Umair said: I went in to see 'Aishah with my mother and my aunt, and they asked her: What did the Messenger of Allah (SAW) do whenever one of you was menstruating? She said: He would bid us, if one of us was menstruating, to put on a loose robe, and then He would embrace her chest and her breasts.

*Sunan Al-Nasa'i, The book of menstruation and vaginal bleeding*

عن زيد بن أسلم أن رجلاً سأل رسول الله ﷺ فقال ما يحل لي من امرأتي وهي حائض فقال رسول الله ﷺ لتشُدَّ عليها إزارها ثم شأنك بأعلاها

موطأ مالك كتاب الطهارة باب ما يحل للرجل من امرأته وهي حائض

Zaid ibn Aslam related that a certain man asked the Messenger of Allah (SAW), saying: What am I allowed to do with my woman when she is menstruating? The Messenger of Allah (SAW) said: Let her tighten her waist wrap [izar] around herself, then have your way with the top part of her.

*Muwatta Malik, The book of purity, Section: what a man is permitted to do with his woman when she is menstruating*

عن حرام بن حكيم عن عمه أنه سأل رسول الله ﷺ ما يحل لي من امرأتي وهي حائض قال لك ما فوق الإزار

سنن أبي داود كتاب الطهارة

Haram ibn Hakim related from his uncle that he asked the Messenger of Allah (SAW): What am I allowed to do with my woman when she is menstruating? He said: You can have whatever is above the waist wrap.

*Sunan Abi Dawud, The book of purity*

فيجوز الاستمتاع بالسرة وما فوقها والركبة وما تحتها ولو بلا حائل وكذا بما بينهما بحائل بغير الوطء ولو تلطخ دماً

رد المحتار على الدر المختار لإبن عابدين كتاب الطهارة باب الحيض

Permitted is enjoyment of the navel and what is above it, and the knees and what is below them, if there is no covering; and accordingly, what is between the two if there is a covering – as long as there is no intercourse – even if the covering becomes smeared with blood.

*Ibn Abidin, Radd Al-muhtar 'ala Al-durr Al-mukhtar, The book of purity, Section on menstruation*

عن منصور إبن صفية أن أمه حدثته أن عائشة حدثتها أن النبي ﷺ كان يتَّكئ في حَجري وأنة حائض ثم يقرأ القرآن

صحيح البخاري كتاب الحيض

Mansur ibn Safiyya related that his mother told him that 'Aishah said to her: The Prophet (SAW) used to recline in my lap while I was menstruating, and then recite the Qur'an.

*Sahih Al-Bukhari, The book of menstruation*

قولها [عائشة] كان رسول الله ﷺ يتكئ في حجري وأنا حائض فيقرأ القران فيه جواز قراءة القران مضطجعاً
ومتكئاً على الحائض وبقرب موضع النجاسة والله أعلم

المنهاج في شرح صحيح مسلم للنووي كتاب الحيض باب جواز غسل الحائض رأس زوجها وترجيله وطهارة سؤرها والاتكاء في حجرها
وقراءة القرآن فيه

Regarding her ['Aishah's] account: "The Messenger of Allah (SAW) used to recline in
my lap while I was menstruating and recite the Qur'an." Here is the permissibility of
reciting the Qur'an while lying down and reclining on a menstruating woman, close
to the location of filth; but Allah knows better.

*Al-Nawawi, Al-minhaj fi Sharh Sahih Muslim, The book of menstruation, Section: the permissibility for a
menstruating woman to wash her husband's head, and comb him, and purify what is left over after her; and reclining
in her lap and reciting the Qur'an there.*


مباشرة الحائض أقسام احدها أن يباشرها بالجماع في الفرج فهذا حرام بإجماع المسلمين بنص القران العزيز
وألسنة الصحيحة قال أصحابنا ولو إعتقد مسلم حل جماع الحائض في فرجها صار كافراً مرتداً ولو فعله إنسان
غير معتقد حله فإن كان ناسياً أو جاهلاً بوجود الحيض أو جاهلاً بتحريمه أو مكرهاً فلا إثم عليه ولا كفارة
وإن وطئها عامداً عالماً بالحيض والتحريم مختاراً فقد إرتكب معصية كبيرة

المنهاج في شرح صحيح مسلم للنووي كتاب الحيض باب مباشرة الحائض فوق الإزار

Intimate contact with a menstruating woman falls into several categories; the first of
these is having intimacy with her by sex in the vagina, which is forbidden by univeral
consensus among Muslims, according to the texts of the Noble Qur'an and the sound
*sunnah*. Our companions have said: If a Muslim even considers the act of sex with a
menstruating woman in her vagina, he has become a disbeliever and an apostate. If a
man who does not consider this permissible does it, because he forgets, is unaware of
the menstruation, unaware of its prohibition, or is compelled, there is no sin on him
and no expiation needed. If he has intercourse wilfully, aware of the menstruation and
the prohibition, chosing to do so, he has committed a grave transgression.

*Al-Nawawi, Al-minhaj fi Sharh Sahih Muslim, The book of menstruation, Section: intimate contact with a
menstruating woman above the waist wrap*


عن ابن عباس عن النبي ﷺ في الذي يأتي امرأته وهي حائض قال يتصدق بدينار أو نصف دينار

السنن الكبرى للبيهقي كتاب الطهارة باب ما روي في كفارة من أتى امرأته حائض

Ibn 'Abbas related from the Prophet (SAW) regarding someone who has sex with
his woman while she is menstruating. He said: He is to give a charity of one dinar
or half a dinar.

*Al-Bayhaqi, Al-sunan Al-kubra, The book of purity, Section: what is related regarding atonement for someone who
comes to his woman when she is menstruating*

عن إبن عباس قال إذا أصابها في أول الدم فدينار وإذا أصابها في إنقطاع الدم فنصف دينار

سنن أبي داود كتاب الطهارة

From Ibn 'Abbas who said: If a man enjoys a woman when bleeding has begun, one dinar; and if he comes upon her when bleeding is subsiding, half a dinar.

*Sunan Abi Dawud, The book of purity*

عن إبن عباس عن النبي ﷺ قال إذا كان دماً أحمر فدينار وإذا كان دماً أصفر فنصف دينار

جامع الترمذي كتاب الطهارة

Ibn 'Abbas related that the Prophet (SAW) said: If it is red blood, then one dinar, and if it is yellow blood, then half a dinar.

*Sunan Al-Tirmidhi, The book of purity*

عن إبن عباس أن النبي ﷺ أمره يتصدق بدينار أو نصف دينار وفسر ذلك مقسم فقال إن غشيها في الدم فدينار وإن غشيها بعد إنقطاع الدم قبل أن تغتسل فنصف دينار

السنن الكبرى للبيهقي كتاب الطهارة باب ما روي في كفارة من أتى امرأته حائض

Ibn 'Abbas related that the Prophet (SAW) ordered him to give a charity of one dinar or half a dinar, and He explained this accordingly; He said: If a man has sex with a woman during bleeding, one dinar, but if he has sex with her after bleeding has stopped, before she has bathed, then half a dinar.

*Al-Bayhaqi, Al-sunan Al-kubra, The book of purity, Section: what is related regarding atonement for someone who comes to his woman when she is menstruating*

اختلفوا في وطء الحائض في طهرها وقبل الاغتسال فذهب مالك والشافعي والجمهور إلى أن ذلك لا يجوز حتى تغتسل وذهب أبو حنيفة وأصحابه إلى أن ذلك جائز إذا طهرت لأكثر أمد الحيض وهو عنده عشرة أيام وذهب الأوزاعي إلى أنها إن غسلت فرجها بالماء جاز وطؤها

بداية المجتهد ونهاية المقتصد لإبن رشد كتاب الطهارة من الحدث

There is disagreement regarding intercourse with a menstruating woman, once she has become pure [of menstruation], but before she has bathed [ghusl]. Malik, Al-Shafi'i, and the majority held that this is not permissible until she bathes, but Abu Hanifa and his companions held that this is permissible whenever she becomes pure for the maximum duration of menstruation, which for him is ten days. Al-Awza'i held that if the woman washes her vagina with water it is permissible to have intercourse with her.

*Ibn Rushd, Bidaya Al-mujtahid wa Nihaya Al-Muqtasid, The book of purification from bodily occurrences [hadath]*

عن ابراهيم قال طهُرت الحائض لم يقرَبْها زوجها حتى تغتسل ... عن عطاء وطاوس قال إذا طهرت المرأة
من الدم فأراد الرجل الشبِق أن يأتيها فليأمرها أن توضأ ثم لِيُصب منها إن شاء ... عن مجاهد في الحائض
ينقطع عنها الدم قال لا يأتيها حتى تحلّ لها الصلاة ... عن عطاء قال إذا إنقطع الدم فأصاب زوجها شُبَقٌ
يخاف فيه على نفسه فليأمرها بغسل فرجها ثم يصيب منها إن شاء ... عن الحسن أنه كرِه أن يأتي الرجل
امرأته وقد طهرت قبل أن تغتسل ... عن ابي سلمة وسليمان بن يسار قالا لا يأتيها زوجها حتى تغتسل ...
عن مكحول أنه كان يقول لا يغشى الرجل المرأة إذا طهرت من الحيضة حتى تغتسل ... عن عكرمة قال إذا
إنقطع عنها الدم فلا يأتيها حتى تطهُر فإذا طهرت فليأتها كما أمره الله

المصنف لإبن ابي شيبة كتاب الطهارة

From Ibrahim, who said: Once a menstruating woman has become pure [free of
menstruation], her husband is not to have sex with her until she bathes [*ghusl*]. ... from
'Ataa and Tawus, who said: Whenever a woman becomes purified of her blood, and an
aroused man wants to have sex with her, he should order her to perform ablution, then
he may enjoy her if he wishes. ... From Mujahid, regarding a menstruating woman whose
bleeding has ceased; he said: Let him not have sex with her until prayer is again
permissible for her. ... From 'Ataa, who said: Whenever bleeding has ceased, and arousal
comes upon her husband, who fears for himself because of it, he should order her to
wash her vagina, then he may enjoy her if he wishes. ... Al-Hasan related that he disliked
for a man to have sex with his woman, who had become pure of menstruation, before
she had bathed. ... From Abu Salama and Sulaiman ibn Yasar, who said: Her husband is
not to have sex with her until she bathes. ... Makhul related that he said: A man is not to
have intercourse with a woman, whenever she has become pure from a menstrual course,
until she bathes. ... From 'Ikrama, who said: Whenever a woman's flow of blood has ceased,
a man is not to have sex with her until she has become pure; and then when she has
become pure, let him have sex with her as Allah has ordered.

*Ibn Abi Shayba, Al-musannaf, The book of purity*


ويستحب للمرأة أن تتبع في غسلها مجاري الدم بالماء ثم بقطعة من قطن فيها مسك فإن لم تجد فبالطين فإن لم تجد
فالماء كاف وانما إستحببنا ذلك لأن للدم زفورة ويستحب للحائض إذا كانت جنباً أن تغتسل من غير وجوب

أحكام النساء لإبن الجوزي الباب الثالث عشر في صفة الغسل

It is desirable for a woman to follow up with water when bathing from places blood
has flowed out of, and then with a piece of cotton with musk on it; if she does not
have this, then with some mud; if she does not have this, then water suffices. Indeed
we recommend this since blood can take on a bad smell. And it is desirable for a
menstruating woman, whenever she is sexually impure, to bathe herself, although this
is not obligatory.

*Ibn Al-Jawzi, Ahkam Al-nisaa, Chapter thirteen: manner of performing a bath [ghusl]*

عن عطاء قال إذا طهرت الحائض فلم تجد ماءً تتيمم ويأتيها زوجها

المصنف لابن ابي شيبة كتاب الطهارة

From 'Ataa, who said: Whenever a menstruating woman becomes pure of her menstruation, but can not find any water, she is to wipe with dust [tayammum], and her husband may have sex with her.

*Ibn Abi Shayba, Al-musannaf, The book of purity*


عن معمر قال سألت الزهري عن الحائض وأ لجنب أيذكرون الله قال نعم قلت أفيقرءون القرآن قال لا قال معمر وكان الحسن وقتادة يقولان لا يقرأان شيئاً من القرآن

المصنف لعبد الرزاق كتاب الحيض

From Ma'mar who said: I asked Al-Zuhri about menstruating women and those who are sexually impure – should they make remembrance [dhikr] of Allah? He said: Yes. I said: And can they recite the Qur'an? He said: No. Ma'mar said: Al-Hasan and Qatada both said that they may not recite anything from the Qur'an.

*'Abd Al-Razzaq, the Musannaf, The book of menstruation*


عن إبن عمر عن رسول الله ﷺ قال لا يقرأ أ لجنب ولا الحائض شيئاً من القران

السنن الكبرى للبيهقي كتاب الطهارة باب ذكّ الحديث الذي ورد في نهي الحائض عن قراءة القران

Ibn 'Umar related from the Messenger of Allah (SAW), who said: Those who are sexually impure, and menstruating women, are not to recite anything from the Qur'an.

*Al-Bayhaqi, Al-sunan Al-kubra, The book of purity, Section: mention of the hadith that was reported regarding the prohibition on menstruating women reciting the Qur'an*


عن ابي هريرة قال بينما رسول الله ﷺ في المسجد فقال يا عائشة ناوليني الثوب فقالت إني حائض فقال إن حيضتَكِ ليست في يدك فناولته

صحيح مسلم كتاب الحيض

From Abu Huraira, who said: Once while the Messenger of Allah (SAW) was in the mosque, He said: Oh 'Aishah, bring me that garment. But she said: Indeed I am menstruating. And He said: Indeed your menstruation is not in your hand. So she brought it to him.

*Sahih Muslim, The book of menstruation*

عن علقمة بن أبي علقمة عن أمه مولاة عائشة أم المؤمنين أنها قالت كان النساء يبعثنَ إلى عائشة أم المؤمنين بالدِّرجة فيها الكُرْسُف فيه الصُّفرة من دم الحيضة يسألنَها عن الصلاة فتقول لهن لا تعجلنَ حتى ترينَ القَصّة البيضاء تريد بذلك الطُهر من الحيضة

موطأ مالك كتاب الطهارة باب ما يحل للرجل من امرأته وهي حائض

'Alqama ibn Abi 'Alqama related that his mother, the freed slave of 'Aishah, mother of the Believers, said: The women used to send 'Aishah, mother of the Believers, little boxes containing cotton with yellow post-menstrual discharge on it, asking her about prayer. And she would tell them: Do not be hasty until you see the cotton white; by this she meant full purity from menstruation.

*Muwatta Malik, The book of purity*

عبدالله بن سعد قال سألت النبي ﷺ عن مواكلة الحائض فقال واكلها

جامع الترمذي كتاب الطهارة

Abdullah ibn Sa'd said: I asked the Prophet (SAW) about eating with menstruating women, and He said: Eat with them.

*Sunan Al-Tirmidhi, The book of purity*

﴿ واللائي لم يحضن ﴾ يقول وكذلك عدد اللائي لم يحضن من الجواري الصغار إذا طلقهن أزواجهن بعد الدخول

تفسير الطبري

{ And those who have not yet menstruated } [*Al-talaq* 4] He is saying: And likewise the waiting periods for those young girls who have not yet menstruated, if their husbands divorce them after having entered [*dukhul*, i.e. after having sex].

*Tafsir Al-Tabari*

عن سعيد بن جبير قال تصلي المستحاضة وتطوف بالبيت
عن الحسن قال تصلي ويصيبها زوجها

المصنف لعبد الرزاق كتاب الحيض

From Sa'id ibn Jubair who said: A woman with vaginal bleeding may pray and walk around the house.

From Hasan, who said: She may pray, and her husband may come to her.

*'Abd Al-Razzaq, the Musannaf, The book of menstruation*

عن عكرمة قال المستحاضة يأتيها زوجها ... عن عطاء قال يأتيها زوجها ... عن الزهري قال يغشاها زوجها
إن شاء ... عن ابن المسيب والحسن في المستحاضة تصوم وتصلي وتقضي المناسب ويغشاها زوجها

المصنف لابن ابي شيبة كتاب النكاح من قال يأتي المستحاضة زوجها

From 'Ikrama who said: A woman with vaginal bleeding – her husband may come to
her ... from 'Ataa who said: Her husband may have sex with her ... From Al-Zuhri who
said: Her husband may get on her if he wishes ... from Ibn Al-Musayyib and Al-Hasan
regarding a woman with vaginal bleeding: She is to fast, pray, and take care of what is
appropriate, and her husband may have sex with her.

*Ibn Abi Shayba, Al-musannaf, The book of marital relations, Section: someone who asks: The husband may come to*
*a woman with vaginal bleeding [mustahadah]*


عن سالم الأفطس عن سعيد بن جبير أنه سأله عن المستحاضة أتجامَع قال الصلاة أعظم من الجماع

المصنف لعبد الرزاق كتاب الحيض

From Salim Al-Aftas, from Sa'id ibn Jubair, who asked him about women with vaginal
bleeding – can sex be had with them? He said: Prayer is greater than sex.

*'Abd Al-Razzaq, the Musannaf, The book of menstruation*


عن عكرمة عن حمنة بنت جحش أنها كانت مستحاضة وكان زوجها يجامعها

سنن ابي داود كتاب الطهارة

'Ikrama related from Hamnah bint Jahsh that she would have vaginal bleeding but her
husband would still have sex with her.

*Sunan Abi Dawud, The book of purity*


عن إسماعيل بن شروس قال سمعت عكرمة مولى إبن عباس سئل عن المستحاضة أيصيبها زوجها قال نعم وإن
سال الدم على عقبها

المصنف لعبد الرزاق كتاب الحيض

From Isma'il ibn Sharus who said: I heard 'Ikrama, the freed slave of Ibn 'Abbas, being
asked about women with vaginal bleeding – can their husbands come to them? He
said: Yes, even if blood runs down their backsides.

*'Abd Al-Razzaq, the Musannaf, The book of menstruation*

إبن جريج قال سئل عطاء عن المستحاضة فقال تصلي وتصوم وتقرأ القرآن وتستثفر بثوب ثم تطوف قال له
سليمان بن موسى أيحل لزوجها أن يصيبها قال نعم قال سليمان أرأيُ أم علم قال سمعنا أنها إذا صلت وصامت
حل لزوجها أن يصيبها

المصنف لعبد الرزاق كتاب الحيض

Ibn Juraij said: 'Ataa was asked about women with vaginal bleeding, and he said: She may pray, fast, recite the Qur'an, gather a garment between her thighs and secure it around her waist, and then walk around at home. Sulaiman ibn Musa asked him: It is permissible for her husband to enjoy her? He said: Yes. Sulaiman said: Is that an opinion or scholarly knowledge? And he said: We heard that if she prays and fasts then it is permissible for her husband to enjoy her.

'Abd Al-Razzaq, the Musannaf, The book of menstruation

عن ابراهيم قال في المستحاضة لا يقربها زوجها ... لا تصوم ولا يأتيها زوجها ولا تمس المصحف

المصنف لعبد الرزاق كتاب الحيض

From Ibrahim who said regarding women with vaginal bleeding: Her husband may not get close to her ... she may not fast, her husband may not have sex with her, and she may not touch a copy of the Qur'an.

'Abd Al-Razzaq, the Musannaf, The book of menstruation

عن ابي جعفر قال جاءت إمرأةٌ إلى النبي ﷺ فقالت إني استُحضت في غير قرئي قال فاحتشي كُرسفاً فإن
يعد فاحتشي كُرسفاً وصومي وصلي واقضي ما عليك

المصنف لعبد الرزاق كتاب الحيض

From Abu Ja'far who said: A woman came to the Prophet (SAW) and said: Indeed I have gotten vaginal bleeding outside of my period. He said: Stuff some cotton in, and if it comes back, stuff some more cotton in, and fast, and pray, and fulfill your obligations.

'Abd Al-Razzaq, the Musannaf, The book of menstruation

عن عائشة زوج النبي ﷺ أن أم حبيبة استُحيضت سبع سنين فسألت رسول الله ﷺ عن ذلك فأمرها أن
تغتسل فقال هذا عِرق فكانت تغتسل لكل صلاة

صحيح البخاري كتاب الحيض

'Aishah, wife of the Prophet (SAW), related that Umm Habibah suffered from vaginal
bleeding for seven years, so she asked the Messenger of Allah (SAW) about it, and He
told her to wash completely [*ghusl*]; He said: This is a vein. And she would wash for
every prayer.

*Sahih Al-Bukhari, The book of menstruation*

عن عائشة قالت استُحيضت أم حبيبة بنت جحش إمرأة عبد الرحمن بن عوف وهي أخت زينب بنت جحش
فاستفتت رسول الله ﷺ فقال لها رسول الله ﷺ إن هذه ليست بالحيضة ولكن هذا عرقٌ فإذا أدبرت
الحيضة فاغتسلي وصلي وإذا أقبلت فاتركي لها الصلاة قالت عائشة فكانت تغتسل لكل صلاة وتصلي وكانت
تغتسل أحياناً في مِركَنٍ في حُجرة أختها زينب وهي عند رسول الله ﷺ حتى أن حُمرة الدم لتعلو الماء وتخرج
فتصلي مع رسول الله ﷺ فما ينعها ذلك من الصلاة

سنن النسائي كتاب الطهارة

From 'Aishah, who said: Umm Habibah bint Jahsh, the woman of 'Abd Al-Rahman
ibn 'Awf and sister of Zainab bint Jahsh, suffered from vaginal bleeding, and she
sought counsel from the Messenger of Allah (SAW). And the Messenger of Allah
(SAW) said to her: Indeed this is not menstruation, but rather this is a vein. Whenever
your menstruation runs its course, perform a full washing [*ghusl*] and pray, and
whenever this appears, refrain from prayer during that time. 'Aishah said: She would
bathe for every prayer, and then pray; and sometimes she would bathe in a washbasin
in the chamber of her sister Zainab, when Zainab was with the Messenger of Allah
(SAW), to the point that the redness of blood would fill up to the top of the water.
And then she would come out and pray with the Messenger of Allah (SAW); this issue
did not keep her from prayer.

*Sunan Al-Nasa'i, The book of purity*

عمران بن طلحة عن أمه حمنة بنت جحش أنها استُحيضت على عهد رسول الله ﷺ فأتت رسول الله ﷺ فقالت
إني استُحضت حيضة مُنكَرةً شديدةً قال لها إحتشي كُرسُفاً قالت له إنه أشد من ذلك اني أثُجُّ ثَجًّا قال تلجَّمي
وتحيَّضي في كل شهر في علم الله ستة أيام أو سبعة أيام ثم اغتسلي غسلاً فصلي وصومي ثلاثة وعشرين أو أربعة
وعشرين وأخّري الظهر وقدّمي العصر واغتسلي لهما غسلاً وأخري المغرب وعجِّلي العشاء واغتسلي لهما غسلاً
وهذا أحبُّ الأمرين إليَّ

سنن إبن ماجه كتاب الطهارة وسننها

'Imran ibn Talha related from his mother Hamnah bint Jahsh that she suffered from vaginal bleeding during the time of the Messenger of Allah (SAW), so she went to the Messenger of Allah (SAW) and said: Indeed I have been suffering from very aggravating and intense bleeding. He said to her: Stuff some cotton in. She said to him: It is more intense than that; indeed it is really coming out a lot. He said: Put something around yourself to hold it in and wait out the bleeding every month, as Allah is aware, for six or seven days; then wash yourself really well and pray and fast for 23 or 24 days; postpone the *dhuhr* prayer but do the *'asr* prayer earlier, washing yourself really well for both of them; and postpone the *maghrab* prayer but hasten the *'ishaa* prayer, washing yourself really well for both of them; this is how I best prefer these issues.

*Sunan Ibn Majah, The book of purity and its sunnah*

عن علي رضي الله عنه قال المستحاضة إذا إنقضى حيضها اغتسلت كل يوم واتخذت صوفةً فيها سمن أو زيت

سنن ابي داود كتاب الطهارة

From 'Ali (may Allah be pleased with him), who said: A women with vaginal bleeding, whenever her menstruation finishes, should bathe every day, and get and use a fleece cloth with fat or oil in it.

*Sunan Abu Dawud, The book of purity*

ويستحب للمستحاضة أن تغتسل لكل صلاة ولا يجب عليها ذلك

أحكام النساء لإبن الجوزي الباب الثالث عشر في صفة الغسل

It is desirable for a woman with vaginal bleeding to bathe for every prayer, although this is not obligatory for her.

*Ibn Al-Jawzi, Ahkam Al-nisaa, Chapter thirteen: manner of performing a bath [ghusl]*

عن عائشة قالت اعتكفت مع رسول الله ﷺ إمرأة من أزواجه فكانت ترى الدم والصُفرة والطست تحتها وهي تصلي

صحيح البخاري كتاب الحيض

From 'Aishah who said: One of the wives of the Prophet (SAW) remained with Him in the mosque for devotion, and she was having bleeding and yellow discharge, so she had a basin under herself while she was praying.

*Sahih Al-Bukhari, The book of menstruation*

# الجماع

# و الجنابة

*Sex and sexual impurity*

ميمونة بنت الحارث زوج النبي ﷺ قالت كان رسول الله ﷺ إذا إغتسل من الجنابة يبدأ فيغسل يديه ثم يُفرغ بيينه على شماله فيغسل فرجه ثم يضرب بيده على الأرض ثم يمسحها ثم يغسلها ثم يتوضأ وضوء للصلاة ثم يفرغ على رأسه وعلى سائر جسده ثم يتنحّى فيغسل رجليه

سنن النسائي كتاب الغسل والتيمم

Maimuma bint Al-Harith, the Prophet's (SAW) wife, said: whenever the Messenger of Allah (SAW) washed himself from sexual impurity [janabah], He began by washing his hands, then emptied water from his right side onto his left and washed between his legs, then He struck the ground with his hand, wiped it, and washed it, then He performed ablution as if for prayer, then He emptied water on his head and on the rest of his body, then He moved back and washed his legs.

*Sunan Al-Nasa'i, The book of washing and wiping with dust [tayammum]*


عن عائشة قالت كان رسول الله ﷺ إذا إغتسل من الجنابة دعا بشيءٍ نحو الحلاب فأخذ بكفه بدأ بشق رأسه الأيمن ثم الأيسر ثم أخذ بكفيه فقال بهما على رأسه

صحيح مسلم كتاب الحيض

'Aisha said: Whenever the Messenger of Allah (SAW) washed himself from sexual impurity [janabah], He called for something like a vessel used for milking, and with his palm started on the right side of his head, then the left, then took up some with both his palms and turned them over his head.

*Sahih Muslim, The book of menstruation*


عن معاوية بن ابي سفيان أنه سأل أخته أم حبيبة زوج النبي ﷺ هل كان رسول الله ﷺ يصلي في الثوب الذي يجامعها فيه فقالت نعم إذا لم ير فيه أذى

سنن ابي داود كتاب الطهارة

Mu'awiya ibn Abi Sufyan related that he asked his sister Umm Habibah, wife of the Prophet (SAW): Did the Messenger of Allah (SAW) pray in the garment in which he had sex with her? She said: Yes, as long as he did not find anything harmful on it.

*Sunan Abi Dawud, The book of purity*

عن ابي سعيد الخدري قال قال رسول الله ﷺ إذا أتى أحدكم أهله ثم أراد أن يعود فليتوضأ

صحيح مسلم كتاب الحيض

From Abu Sa'id Al-Khudri who said: The Messenger of Allah (SAW) said: Whenever one of you comes to a woman of his household, and then wants it again, he should perform ablution.

*Sahih Muslim, The book of menstruation*

عن ابي سعيد عن النبي ﷺ قال إذا أراد أحدكم العود فليتوضأ فإنه أنشط له في العود

صحيح إبن خزيمة كتاب الوضوء

Abu Sa'id related that the Prophet (SAW) said: Whenever any of you wants to go again, he should perform ablution, for indeed it will make him more energetic upon returning.

*Sahih Ibn Khuzaima, The book of ablution*

عن عمر عن النبي ﷺ قال إذا أتى أحدكم أهله ثم أراد أن يعود فليغسل فرجه

مجمع الزوائد ومنبع الفوائد للهيثمي كتاب النكاح باب فيمن يأتي أهله ثم يريد أن يعود

From 'Umar from the Prophet (SAW) who said: Whenever any of you comes to a woman of his household and then desires to go again, he should wash his crotch.

*Al-Haythami, Majma' Al-zawa'id wa Manba' Al-fawa'id, The book of marital relations, Section: regarding who comes to a woman of his household and then desires it again*

اخبرنا أبو طاهر قال حدثنا أبو بكر قال حدثنا سعيد بن عبد الرحمان المخزومي قال حدثنا سفيان عن عاصم الأحول قال إذا أراد أحدكم أن يعود فليتوضأ وضوءه للصلاة يعني يجامع ثم يعود قبل أن يغتسل

صحيح إبن خزيمة كتاب الوضوء

Abu Tahir related to us saying: Abu Bakr told us and said: Sa'id ibn 'Abd Al-Rahman Al-Makhzumi told us and said: Sufyan told us from 'Asim Al-Ahwal, who said: If any of you wants to go again, let him perform ablution [*wudu'*] as he would for prayer; in other words, when he has sex and goes again before he washes himself fully [*ghusl*].

*Sahih Ibn Khuzaima, The book of ablution*

وإن أراد أن يجامع ثانياً بعد أخرى فليغسل فرجه أولاً وإن احتلم فلا يجامع حتى يغسل فرجه أو يبول

إحياء علوم الدين للغزالي كتاب آداب النكاح الباب الثالث في آداب المعاشرة وما يجري في دوام النكاح والنظر فيما على الزوج وفيما على الزوجة

If a man desires to have sex a second time after one time, let him wash his crotch first. And if he has a wet dream, he is not to have sex until he washes his crotch or urinates.

*Al-Ghazali, Ihyaa 'Ulum Al-din, The book of proper conduct in marital relations, Section three: concerning proper conduct in intimacy, what should be observed for the duration of marital relations, and consideration of the obligations of the husband and the obligations of the wife*

عن ابي هريرة قال قال رسول الله ﷺ إنّ تحت كل شعرةٍ جنابة فاغسلوا الشعر وانقوا البشر

سنن ابي داود كتاب الطهارة

From Abu Huraira who said: The Messenger of Allah (SAW) said: Indeed under every hair there is sexual impurity [*janabah*], so wash the hair and cleanse the skin.

*Sunan Abi Dawud, The book of purity*

عن إبن عباس أن إمرأة من أزواج النبي ﷺ اغتسلت من الجنابة فتوضأ النبي ﷺ أو إغتسل من فضلها

صحيح إبن خزيمة كتاب الوضوء

Ibn 'Abbas related that one of the Prophet's (SAW) wives washed herself from sexual impurity, and the Prophet (SAW) performed ablution – or washed – with what was left over from her.

*Sahih Ibn Khuzaima, The book of ablution*

عن عائشة أن النبي ﷺ كان إذا أراد أن يطعم وهو جنب غسل يديه ثم طعم

صحيح إبن خزيمة كتاب الوضوء

'Aishah related that the Prophet (SAW), if He wanted to eat when He was sexually impure, would wash His hands and then eat.

*Sahih Ibn Khuzaima, The book of ablution*

عن عائشة أنها قالت كنت اغتسل أنا ورسول الله ﷺ في إناءٍ واحد من الجنابة

صحيح إبن خزيمة كتاب الوضوء،

'Aishah related: I used to wash myself from sexual impurity, me and the Messenger of Allah (SAW), in a single vessel.

*Sahih Ibn Khuzaima, The book of ablution*


عن عائشة قالت كنت اغتسل أنا ورسول الله ﷺ من إناءٍ بيني وبينه واحد فيبادرني حتى أقول دع لي دع لي قالت وهما جنبان

صحيح مسلم كتاب الحيض

From 'Aishah who said: I would bathe, me and the Messenger of Allah (SAW), from a single vessel between us; and He would become so engaged before me that I had to say "leave some for me, leave some for me". She said that they had become impure from sex.

*Sahih Muslim, The book of menstruation*


عن عائشة رضي الله عنها قالت كنت اغتسل أنا ورسول الله ﷺ من إناءٍ واحد يبادرني وأبادره حتى يقول دعي لي وأقول أنا دع لي

سنن النسائي كتاب الطهارة

From 'Aishah (may Allah be pleased with her) who said: I used to bathe, me and the Messenger of Allah (SAW), from one vessel; He would make a move on me and I would make a move on him, until He would say "Leave some for me" and I would say "Leave some for me".

*Sunan Al-Nasa'i, The book of purity*


عن أنس أن رسول الله ﷺ كان يطوف على نسائه في غسلٍ واحد

سنن النسائي كتاب الطهارة

Anas related that the Messenger of Allah (SAW) would go around to His women with one bath [*ghusl*].

*Sunan Al-Nasa'i, The book of purification*

وكان رسول الله ﷺ ربما جامع نساءه كلهن بغسل واحد وربما إغتسل عند كل واحدة منهن

الطب النبوي لإبن قيّم

The Messenger of Allah (SAW) would perhaps have sex with all of His women from one bath, or perhaps He would wash after each one of them.

*Ibn Qayyim, Al-tibb Al-nabawi*

عن صفوان بن سليم وقالت سلمى مولاته طاف النبي ﷺ ليلة على نسائه التسع وتطهر من كل واحدة قبل أن يأتي الاخرى وقال هذا أطيب واطهر

الشفا للقاضي عياض اليحصبي القسم الأول الباب الثاني في تكميل الله تعالى له المحاسن خَلْقاً خُلُقاً وقرانه جميع الفضائل الدينية والدنيوية فيه نسقاً

Safwan ibn Sulaim related, and Salma his mistress said: The Prophet (SAW) went around in one night to His nine wives, and He purified Himself after each one of them before going to the next one. He said: This is better and purer.

*Al-qadi 'Iyad Al-Yahsubi, Al-shifa, Part one, Section two: concerning how Allah most high perfected in Him the good features of creation and character and brought together all religious and worldly virtues in Him*

من غسل) روي مشدداً ومخففاً قيل أي جماع امرأته قبل الخروج الى الصلاة لأنه أغض للبصر في الطريق من غسل امرأته بالتشديد والتخفيف إذا جامعها وقيل أراد غسل غيره لأنه إذا جامعها احوجها إلى الغسل

سنن النسائي بشرح السيوطي كتاب الجمعة

"Whoever washes" : narrated as "completely bathes" or "washes"; in other words, as it is said, sex with his wife before heading out to prayer, since this is best for keeping the gaze low along the way; whoever washes his woman ("completely bathes" or "washes") when he has sex with her. It is said that He desired washing someone other than oneself, since whenever a man has sex with a woman he makes it obligatory for her to wash.

*Al-Suyuti, Commentary on Sunan Al-Nasa'i, The book of Friday assembly*

عن وهب بن منبّه أن رجلاً قال لرسول الله ﷺ يا رسول الله إذا تبطّن الرجل إمرأته إغتسل فقال وأنا إذا تبطنتها اغتسلت

أدب النساء لعبد الملك بن حبيب باب ما جاء في ثواب الجماع وحب الاستكثار منه

Wahb ibn Munabbih related that a certain man said to the Messenger of Allah (SAW): Oh Messenger of Allah, when a man gets into his woman, should he wash? And He said: As for me, whenever I get into a woman I wash.

*'Abd Al-Malik ibn Habib, Adab Al-nisaa, Section: what is said regarding the reward of blessing in sex and the desirability of having a great deal of it*

ذكر عمر بن الخطاب لرسول الله ﷺ أنه تصيبه جنابة من الليل فقال له رسول الله ﷺ توضأ وإغسل ذكرك
ثم نم

صحيح مسلم كتاب الحيض

'Umar ibn Al-Khatab mentioned to the Messenger of Allah (SAW) that sexual impurity [*janabah*] had come upon him during the night, and the Messenger of Allah (SAW) said to him: Perform ablution [*wudu'*] and wash your penis then sleep.

*Sahih Muslim, The book of menstruation*

عن الزهري في الرجل يرى أنه احتلم ولم يجد بللاً قال ليس عليه غسل

المصنف لعبد الرزاق كتاب الطهارة

From Al-Zuhri regarding a man who thinks that he has had a wet dream but does not find any wetness; he said: He is not obliged to wash.

*'Abd Al-Razzaq, the Musannaf, The book of purity*

عن علي قال سألت النبي ﷺ عن المذي فقال من المذي الوضوء ومن المني الغسل

جامع الترمذي كتاب الطهارة

From 'Ali who said: I asked the Prophet (SAW) about pre-ejaculate [*madhy*] and He said: For pre-ejaculate, ablution [*wudu'*]; and for semen [*maniy*], a full washing [*ghusl*].

*Sunan Al-Tirmidhi, The book of purity*

عن إبن عباس قال في المذي والودي والمني من المني الغسل ومن المذي والودي الوضوء يغسل حشفته
ويتوضأ

المصنف لعبد الرزاق كتاب الطهارة

From Ibn 'Abbas, who said regarding pre-ejaculate, prostatic secretion [*wady*], and semen: for semen, a full washing, and for pre-ejaculate and prostatic secretion, ablution – he should wash the head of the penis and then perform ablution.

*'Abd Al-Razzaq, the Musannaf, The book of purity*

والمذي ماء رقيق يخرج بعد الشهوة متسبباً لا يحس بخروجه فلا غسل فيه ويجب منه الوضوء لما روى سهل
بن حنيف رضي الله عنه قال كنت ألقي من المذي شدة وعناء فكنت أكثر منه الاغتسال فذكرت ذلك
لرسول الله ﷺ وسألته عنه فقال يجزيك من ذلك الوضوء حديث صحيح وهل يوجب غسل الذكر والانثيين
على روايتين إحداهما لا يوجب لحديث سهل والثانية يوجب لما روى علي رضي الله عنه قال كنت رجلاً
مذاءً فاستحييت أن أسأل رسول الله ﷺ لمكان ابنته فأمرت المقداد فسأله فقال يغسل ذكره وأنثييه ويتوضأ
رواه أبو داود

الكافي لإبن قدامة كتاب الطهارة باب ما يوجب الغسل

The pre-ejaculate [*madhy*] is delicate fluid that comes out as a result of desire; its emission is not felt. There is no washing [*ghusl*] regarding it, but ablution [*wudu'*] from it is required, based on what Sahl ibn Hunaif (may Allah be pleased with him) related. He said: I used to release pre-ejaculate strongly and uncomfortably, and I washed myself more because of it; I mentioned this to the Messenger of Allah (SAW) and asked him about it. He said: For that, ablution is sufficient for you. A sound [*sahih*] hadith. But does this necessitate washing the penis and testicles? There are two applicable accounts; one of them is that this is not necessitated, from a hadith of Sahl. The second is that it is necessitated, based on what 'Ali (may Allah be pleased with him) related. He said: I was a man who pre-ejaculated a lot, and I was ashamed to ask the Messenger of Allah (SAW) in the presence of his daughter. So I sent Miqdad and he asked Him for me. He said: He must wash his penis and testicles and perform ablution. Abu Dawud narrated this.

*Ibn Qudama, Al-kafi fi Fiqh Al-imam Ibn Hanbal, The book of purification, Section: that which necessitates washing*

عن حرام بن حكيم عن عمه عبدالله بن سعد الأنصاري قال سألت رسول الله ﷺ عما يوجب الغسل وعن الماء
يكون بعد الماء فقال ذلك المذي وكل فحل يُمذي فتغسل من ذلك فرجك وانثييك وتوضأ وضوءك للصلاة

سنن ابي داود كتاب الطهارة

Haram ibn Hakim related from his uncle Abdullah ibn Sa'd Al-Ansari, who said: I asked the Messenger of Allah (SAW) about what makes full washing obligatory, and about the fluid that shows up after the wash water. And He said: That is pre-ejaculate [*madhy*]; every virile male makes pre-ejaculate. You should wash your crotch and your testicles and perform ablution like your ablution for prayer.

*Sunan Abi Dawud, The book of purity*

عمر بن الخطاب قال إني لأجده يخذر مني مثل الخريزة فإذا وجد ذلك فليغسل أحدكم ذكره وليتوضأ وضوءه
للصلاة يعني المذي

موطأ مالك كتاب الطهارة باب الوضوء من المذي

'Umar ibn Al-Khattab said: Indeed I find it flowing from me like little beads; and whenever any of you finds it, he should wash his penis and perform his ablution as for prayer. This is regarding pre-ejaculate [*madhy*].

*Muwatta Malik, The book of purity, Section: ablution for pre-ejaculate*

فإن شكّ هل الخارج مني أو مذي تخيّر إن شاء جعله منياً واغتسل فقط وإن شاء جعله مذياً وغسل ما
أصاب بدنه وثوبه منه وتوضأ ولا يغتسل والأفضل أن يفعل جميع ذلك

عمدة السالك وعدة الناسك لإبن النقيب المصري كتاب الطهارة باب الغسل

If one doubts as to whether what has come out is semen or pre-ejaculate, he may, if he wishes, prefer to consider it semen and simply wash himself fully, or if he wishes, to consider it pre-ejaculate, wash the part of his body and garment that it touched, perform ablution, and not wash himself fully. But the best is for him do all of that.

*Ibn Al-Naqib Al-Misri, 'Umda Al-salik wa 'Udda Al-nasik, The book of purity, Section: washing [ghusl]*

والودي ماء أبيض يخرج عقيب البول فليس فيه إلا الوضوء لأن الشرع لم يرد فيه بزيادة عليه فإن خرج منه
شيء ولم يدر أمني هو أو غيره في يقظة فلا غسل فيه لأن المني الموجب للغسل يخرج دفقاً بشهوة فلا يشتبه
بغيره وإن كان في نوم وكان نومه عقيب شهوة بملاعبة أهله أو تذكر فهو مذي لأن ذلك سبب المذي والظاهر
أنه مذي وإن لم يكن كذلك إغتسل لحديث عائشة في الذي يجد البلل ولأن خروج المني في النوم معتاد وغيره
نادر فحمل الأمر على المعتاد

الكافي في فقه الإمام أحمد بن حنبل لإبن قدامة كتاب الطهارة باب ما يوجب الغسل

The prostatic secretion [*wady*]: white fluid that comes out after urine; only ablution [*wudu'*] is required regarding it, since the Law does not bear on anything beyond this regarding it. And what if something comes out from a man and he does not know whether it is semen or something else? Attentiveness is in order but no washing necessary, because the semen that necessitates washing comes out forcefully from desire and can not be suspected to be anything else. And if it happens during sleep, and his sleep followed arousal as a result of playing with a woman of his household or a thought of something, then it is pre-ejaculate [*madhy*], since this is the cause of pre-ejaculate, and it is clear that it is pre-ejaculate. And if it is not such, then he must wash himself, based on the hadith of 'Aishah regarding one who finds wetness, and because the emission of semen during sleep is familiar, and other things are rare, and the issue is borne on what is familiar.

*Ibn Qudama, Al-kafi fi Fiqh Al-imam Ahmad ibn Hanbal, The book of purity, Section: that which necessitates washing*

ويُعرف المني بتدفق أو تلذذ أو ريح طلع أو عجين إذا كان رطباً أو بياض بيض إذا كان جافاً فتى وُجد واحد منها كان منياً موجباً للغسل

عمدة السالك وعدة الناسك لإبن النقيب المصري كتاب الطهارة باب الغسل

Semen is recognized by gushing, or delight, or the emanating smell either like dough when it is moist or egg white when it is dry. And when one of these is noted, it was semen, making washing necessary.

*Ibn Al-Naqib Al-Misri, 'Umda Al-salik wa 'Udda Al-nasik, The book of purity, Section: washing [ghusl]*

عن المقداد بن الأسود أنه سأل النبي ﷺ عن الرجل يدنو من امرأته فلا ينزل قال إذا وجد أحدكم ذلك فلينضح فرجه - يعني ليغسله - ويتوضأ

سنن إبن ماجه كتاب الطهارة

Miqdad ibn Al-Aswad related that he asked the Prophet (SAW) about if a man gets close with his woman but does not ejaculate. He said: Whenever any of you see that this is the case with him, let him sprinkle his crotch – in other words, wash it – and perform ablution.

*Sunan Ibn Majah, The book of purity*

عن عمرو بن ميمون قال سألت سليمان بن يسار عن الثوب يصيبه المنيّ أيغسله أم يغسل الثوب كله قال سليمان قالت عائشة كان النبي ﷺ يصيب ثوبه فيغسله من ثوبه ثم يخرج في ثوبه إلى الصلاة وأنا أرى أثر الغسل فيه

سنن إبن ماجه كتاب الطهارة وسننها

'Amr ibn Maimun said: I asked Sulaiman ibn Yasar about a garment that semen gets on – should he wash it or wash the whole garment – and Sulaiman said that 'Aisha said: It used to get on the Messenger of Allah's (SAW) garment, and He washed it from his garment and then went to prayer in his garment; and I saw the wash spot on it.

*Sunan Ibn Majah, The book of purity and its sunnah*

عن عائشة في المني قالت كنت أفركه من ثوب رسول الله ﷺ

صحيح مسلم كتاب الطهارة

From 'Aishah who said regarding semen: I used to scrape it off the Messenger of Allah's (SAW) garment.

*Sahih Muslim, The book of purification*

عن همام بن الحارث قال نزل بعائشة ضيفٌ فأمرت له بملحفة لها صفراء فإحتلم فيها فإستحيى أن يرسل بها وفيها أثر الإحتلام فغمسها في الماء ثم أرسل بها فقالت عائشة لِمَ أفسدت علينا ثوبنا إنما كان يكفيك أن تفركه بإصبعك ربما فركته من ثوب رسول الله ﷺ بإصبعي

سنن إبن ماجه كتاب الطهارة وسننها

From Hammam ibn Al-Harith who said: A guest came to 'Aishah, and she ordered that he be given a yellow blanket of hers. He had a wet dream on it and was embarrassed to send it back with the stain of the wet dream on it, so he dipped it in water and then sent it back. And 'Aishah said: Why have you ruined our garment for us?! It would have been enough for you to scrape it with your finger; sometimes I would scrape it off the Messenger of Allah's (SAW) garment with my finger.

*Sunan Ibn Majah, The book of purity and its sunnah*

عن أُبيّ بن كعب عن رسول الله ﷺ أنه قال في الرجل يأتي أهله ثم لا يُنْزل قال يغسل ذكره ويتوضأ

صحيح مسلم كتاب الحيض

From Ubayy ibn Ka'b who related that the Messenger of Allah (SAW) said regarding a man who comes to a woman of his household but then does not ejaculate; He said: He should wash his penis and perform ablution.

*Sahih Muslim, The book of menstruation*

أُبَي بن كعب قال يا رسول الله إذا جامع الرجل المرأة فلم يُنْزل قال يغسل ما مسّ المرأة منه ثم يتوضأ ويصلي

صحيح البخاري كتاب الغسل

Ubayy ibn Ka'b said: Oh Messenger of Allah, what if a man has sex with a women and does not ejaculate? He said: He should wash whatever of him touched the woman, then perform ablution, and pray.

*Sahih Al-Bukhari, The book of washing [ghusl]*

عن أُبَيّ بن كعب قال سألت رسول الله ﷺ عن الرجل يصيب من المرأة ثم يُكسل فقال يغسل ما اصابه
من المرأة ثم يتوضأ ويصلي

صحيح مسلم كتاب الحيض

From Ubayy ibn Ka'b who said: I asked the Messenger of Allah (SAW) about a man
who comes to a woman but then dwindles and does not finish, and He said: He should
wash whatever got on him from the woman, then perform ablution, and pray.

*Sahih Muslim, The book of menstruation*


عن ابي سلمة أن عطاء بن يسار أخبره أن زيد بن خالد أخبره أنه سأل عثمان بن عفان رضي الله عنه قلت
أرأيت إذا جامع فلم يُمنِ قال عثمان يتوضأ للصلاة ويغسل ذكره

صحيح البخاري كتاب الوضوء

Abu Salama related that 'Ataa ibn Yasar told him that Zayd ibn Khalid had told him
that he asked 'Uthman ibn 'Affan (may Allah be pleased with him): Do you have an
opinion about a man who has sex but does not release semen? 'Uthman said: He
should perform ablution as for prayer and wash his penis.

*Sahih Al-Bukhari, The book of ablution*


عن عائشة زوج النبي ﷺ قالت إن رجلاً سأل رسول الله ﷺ عن الرجل يجامع أهله ثم يُكسل هل عليهما
الغسل وعائشة جالسة فقال رسول الله ﷺ اني لافعل ذلك أنا وهذه ثم نغتسل

صحيح مسلم كتاب الحيض

From 'Aishah, the wife of the Prophet (SAW), who said: A certain man asked the
Messenger of Allah (SAW) about someone who has sex with a woman of his household
but then dwindles and does not finish; is it obligatory for them to wash? And 'Aishah
was sitting there. The Messenger of Allah (SAW) said: Indeed I do that, me and her,
and then we wash.

*Sahih Muslim, The book of menstruation*


عن عمرو بن شعيب عن أبيه عن جده قال قال رسول الله ﷺ إذا إلتقى الختانان وتوارت الحشفة فقد
وجب الغسل

سنن إبن ماجه كتاب الطهارة وسننها

'Amr ibn Shu'ib related from his father, from his grandfather, who said: The
Messenger of Allah (SAW) said: Whenever the two circumcised parts meet, and the
tip of the penis vanishes, washing [ghusl] is obligatory.

*Ibn Majah, Sunan ibn Majah, The book of purity and its sunnah*

عن عائشة قالت قال النبي ﷺ إذا جاوز الختان الختان وجب الغسل

جامع الترمذي كتاب الطهارة

From 'Aishah who said: The Prophet (SAW) said: Whenever the circumcised part goes
past the circumcised part, washing is obligatory.

*Sunan Al-Tirmidhi, The book of purity*


عن أبي موسى قال إختلف في ذلك رهط من المهاجرين والأنصار فقال الأنصاريون لا يجب الغسل إلا من
الدفق أو من الماء وقال المهاجرون بل إذا خالط فقد وجب الغسل قال أبو موسى فأنا أشفيكم من ذلك فقمت
فإستأذنت على عائشة فأذن لي فقلت لها يا أُمّاه - أو يا أم المؤمنين - اني أريد أن أسألك عن شيءٍ واني أستحييك
فقالت لا تستحيي أن تسأليني عما كنت سائلاً عنه أمك التي ولدتكَ فإنما أنا أمك قلت فما يوجب الغسل قالت
على الخبير سقطت قال رسول الله ﷺ إذا جلس بين شُعبها الأربع ومسّ الختان الختان فقد وجب الغسل

صحيح مسلم كتاب الحيض

From Abu Musa who said: There arose a dispute regarding this between a group of
the emigrants [*Muhajirun*] and the helpers [*Ansar*]. The Ansaris said: Full washing
[*ghusl*] is not necessary except upon gushing, that is, from semen. And the Muhajirun
said: Rather, if there is any sexual activity at all, full washing becomes necessary. Abu
Musa said: I will remedy this for you. And so I went and asked permission of 'Aishah,
and it was granted to me, and I said to her: Oh Mother – or Oh Mother of the
Believers – Indeed I wish to ask you something, but I feel bashful with you. And she
said: Do not be bashful about asking me what you used to ask your mother, the one
who gave birth to you, for indeed I am your mother. I said: What makes washing
obligatory? She said: You have come across the expert; the Messenger of Allah (SAW)
said: Whenever a man sits between the four limbs [*shu'ab*] of a woman, and the
circumcised part touches the circumcised part, then washing is obligatory.

*Sahih Muslim, The book of menstruation*


عن أُمّ سلمة قالت قلت يا رسول الله اني إمرأةٌ أشد ضفر رأسي فأنقضه لغسل الجنابة قال لا انما يكفيك أن
تحثي على رأسك ثلاث حثيات ثم تفيضين عليك الماء فتطهرين

صحيح مسلم كتاب الحيض

From Umm Salamah who said: Oh Messenger of Allah, I am a woman with a lot of
braids on my head; should I undo them to wash from sexual impurity [*janabah*]? He
said: No, rather it is enough for you to pour three handfuls over your head and then
generously pour the water on yourself, and you will be purified.

*Sahih Muslim, The book of menstruation*

عن اُمّ سلمة قالت جاءت أم سليم إلى النبي ﷺ فقالت يا رسول الله إنّ الله لا يستحيي من الحق فهل على
المرأة من غسل إذا احتلمت فقال رسول الله ﷺ نعم إذا رأت الماء فقالت أم سلمة يا رسول الله وتحتلم المرأة
فقال تَرِبت يداكِ فبِمَ يُشبهها ولدها

صحيح مسلم كتاب الحيض

From Umm Salamah who said: Umm Sulaim came to the Prophet (SAW) and said:
Oh Messenger of Allah, indeed Allah is not shy of the truth; is it obligatory for a
woman to wash if she has a wet dream [*ihtalamat*]? The Messenger of Allah (SAW)
said: Yes, if she sees the fluid. And Umm Salamah said: Oh Messenger of Allah, do
women really have wet dreams? And He said: May your hand be covered in dust [i.e.
Come on, of course!]; otherwise how does her child resemble her?

*Sahih Muslim, The book of menstruation*

عن اُمّ سلمة قالت جاءت أم سليم إلى النبي ﷺ فسألته عن المرأة ترى في المنام ما يرى الرجل قال إذا رأت
الماء فلتغتسل قالت قلتُ فضحتِ النساء وهل تحتلم المرأة فقال النبي ﷺ تربت يمينك وفيما يشبهها ولدها إذاً

صحيح إبن خزيمة كتاب الوضوء

From Umm Salama who said: Umm Sulaim came to the Prophet (SAW) and asked
Him about women when they find in their sleep what a man finds; He said: Whenever
she sees fluid let her wash herself. I said [to her]: You've disgraced women; do women
really have wet dreams?! And the Prophet (SAW) said: May your right hand be covered
in dust; how then does her child resemble her?

*Sahih Ibn Khuzaima, The book of ablution*

عن شقيق عن عبدالله قال كا نصلي مع النبي ﷺ فلا نتوضأ من موطئ

صحيح إبن خزيمة كتاب الوضوء باب ذكر الدليل على أن وطء الأنجاس لا يوجب الوضوء

Shaqiq related from Abdullah who said: We used to pray with the Prophet (SAW) and
we did not perform ablution from having intercourse.

*Sahih Ibn Khuzaima, The book of ablution, Section: citing the evidence that intercourse with the unclean does not*
*necessitate ablution*

ويجب الغسل بالإيلاج في كل فرج قبل أو دبر من آدمي أو بهيمة حي أو ميت لأنه أشبه قبل المرأة
فإن أولج في قبل الخنثى المشكل فلا غسل عليهما لأنه لا يتيقن كونه فرجاً فلا يجب الغسل بالشك

الكافي في فقه الإمام أحمد بن حنبل لإبن قدامة كتاب الطهارة باب ما يوجب الغسل

And full washing [*ghusl*] is made obligatory by penetration of any opening, front or
rear, human or animal, alive or dead, because it is an opening that resembles the front

part of a woman. And if a man penetrates the front part of an ambiguous hermaphrodite, they are not obliged to wash, since its constitution can not be ascertained as a vagina; washing is not made obligatory based on uncertainty.

*Ibn Qudama, Al-kafi fi Fiqh Al-imam Ahmad ibn Hanbal, The book of purity, Section: that which necessitates washing*

ولو لفّ على ذكره خرقة وأولجه في فرج إمرأة ففيه ثلاثة أوجه لأصحابنا الصحيح منها والمشهور أنه يجب عليهما الغسل والثاني لا يجب لأنه أولج في خرقة والثالث إن كانت الخرقة غليظة تمنع وصول اللذة والرطوبة لم يجب الغسل وإلا وجب والله أعلم

المنهاج في شرح صحيح مسلم للنووي كتاب الحيض باب بيان أن الجماع كان في أول الاسلام لا يوجب الغسل إلا أن ينزل المني وبيان نسخه وأن الغسل يجب بالجماع

If a man wraps a cloth around his penis and inserts it into a woman's vagina, there are three points of view among our companions. The correct and well-known of these is that washing is obligatory for both of them; the second is that it is not obligatory, since he has penetrated in a cloth; and the third, if the cloth is thick and prevents the attainment of pleasure or moisture, that washing is not obligatory – otherwise it is. But Allah knows better.

*Al-Nawawi, Al-minhaj fi Sharh Sahih Muslim, The book of menstruation, Section: substantiating that in sex at the beginning of Islam, washing [ghusl] was not obligatory unless semen was discharged, and substantiating that this was abrogated and that washing is always obligatory upon sex*

ولو استدخلت المرأة ذكر بهيمة وجب عليها الغسل ولو استدخلت ذكراً مقطوعاً فوجهان أصحهما يجب عليها الغسل

المنهاج في شرح صحيح مسلم للنووي كتاب الحيض باب بيان أن الجماع كان في أول الاسلام لا يوجب الغسل إلا أن ينزل المني وبيان نسخه وأن الغسل يجب بالجماع

If a woman inserts an animal's penis into herself, she is obliged to wash, and if she inserts a severed penis there are two points of view; the more correct of the two is that she is obliged to wash.

*Al-Nawawi, Al-minhaj fi Sharh Sahih Muslim, The book of menstruation, Section: substantiating that in sex at the beginning of Islam, washing [ghusl] was not obligatory unless semen was discharged, and substantiating that this was abrogated and that washing is always obligatory upon sex*

عن عائشة رضي الله عنها قالت لتعدّ إحداكن الخرقة لزوجها إذا أتاها

كنز العمال للهندي كتاب النكاح المباشرة وآدابها

From 'Aishah (may Allah be pleased with her) who said: Any of you women should prepare a cloth for her husband whenever he comes to her.

*Al-Hindi, Kanz Al-'Ummal, The book of marital relations, Intimate contact and its conduct*

عن عائشة قالت إن المرأة لتتخذ الخرقة لزوجها فإذا قضى الرجل حاجته إمتسحت بها ثم ناولته فمسح عنها

كنز العمال لابن حسام الدين الهندي كتاب النكاح المباشرة وآدابها

From 'Aishah who said: Indeed a woman ought to grab a cloth for her husband, for when a man fulfills his need she can use it to wipe, then pass it to him to wipe from her.

*Al-Hindi, Kanz Al-'Ummal, The book of marital relations, Intimate contact and its conduct*

عن عائشة عن النبي ﷺ قال إذا أراد الرجل أن يجامع امرأته اتخذت خرقة فإذا فرغ ناولته اياها فمسح عنه الأذى ومسحت عنها

علل الحديث لابن ابي حاتم علل أخبار في النكاح

'Aishah related from the Prophet (SAW) that He said: Whenever a man wants to have sex with his woman, she should grab a cloth, then when he finishes she can pass it to him so he can wipe off the harm from himself, and she can wipe herself off.

*Ibn Abi Hatim, 'Ilal Al-hadith, Occasions for the accounts regarding marital relations*

عن سالم بن عبدالله عن أبيه عبدالله ابن عمر أنه كان يقول قبلة الرجل إمرأته وجسّها بيده من الملامسة فن قبّل امرأته أو جسها بيده فعليه الوضوء

موطأ الإمام مالك كتاب الطهارة باب الوضوء من قبلة الرجل امرأته

Salim ibn Abdullah related that his father Abdullah ibn 'Umar used to say: A man kissing his wife or fondling her with his hand is part of intimate contact; so whoever kisses his woman or fondles her with his hand must perform ablution.

*Muwatta Malik, The book of purity, Section: ablution from a man kissing his woman*

عن قتادة في الرجل يغشى امرأته في السفر وليس معه ماء قال لا بأس بذلك

المصنف لعبد الرزاق كتاب الطهارة

From Qatada regarding a man who has sex with his woman while on a journey, and does not have any water; he said: There is no issue with that.

*'Abd Al-Razzaq, the Musannaf, The book of purity*

سئل شيخ الاسلام عن قوله تعالى ﴿ قل للمؤمنين يغضوا من أبصارهم ويحفظوا فروجهم ذلك أزكى لهم إن الله
خبير بما يصنعون ﴾ والحديث عن النبي ﷺ في ذكر زنا الأعضاء كلها وماذا على الرجل إذا مس يد الصبي
الأمرد فهل هو من جنس النساء ينقض الوضوء أم لا وما على الرجل إذا جاء إلى عبده المردان ومد يده إلى
هذا وهذا ويتلذذ بذلك وما جاء في التحريم من النظر إلى وجه الأمرد الحسن وهل هذا الحديث المروي أن
النظر إلى الوجه المليح عبادة صحيح أم لا وإذا قال أحد أنا ما أنظر إلى المليح الأمرد لأجل شيء ولكني إذا
رأيته قلت سبحان الله تبارك الله أحسن الخالقين فهل هذا القول صواب أم لا أفتونا مأجورين فأجاب قدس
الله روحه ونور ضريحه ورحمه ورضي عنه ونفع بعلومه وحشرنا في زمرته الحمد لله إذا مس الأمرد لشهوة ففيه
قولان في مذهب أحمد وغيره احدهما أنه كمس النساء لشهوة ينقض الوضوء وهو المشهور في مذهب مالك وذكره
القاضي أبو يعلى من شرح المذهب وهو أحد الوجهين في مذهب الشافعي والثاني أنه لا ينقض وهو المشهور من
مذهب الشافعي والقول الأول أظهر فإن الوطء في الدبر يفسد العبادات التي تفسد بالوطء في القبل كالصوم
والاحرام والاعتكاف ويوجب الغسل كما يوجبه هذا

التفسير الكبير لإبن تيمية سورة النور

The Sheikh of Islam [Ibn Taymiyya] was asked regarding the word of the Most High { Tell the believers to lower their looking and to guard their private parts, for that is purer for them; truly Allah is well aware of what they do } , and regarding the hadith of the Prophet (SAW) in mentioning adultery of the all the members, and what a man must do if he touches the hand of a smooth and beardless boy [amrad]; is this in the same category as women, invalidating ablution, or not? And what must a man do if he comes to a smooth, beardless servant of his, and puts his hand on this and that, and takes pleasure from it? And what has been said regarding the prohibition of looking at the pleasing face of a smooth, beardless boy? And is the hadith that has been related – that looking at a nice face is worship – sound or not? And if someone says: I do not look at a nice smooth, beardless boy for any reason, but if I see one I say "Exalted is Allah, blessed is Allah, the best of creators" – is it correct to say this or not? Grant us the reward of your judgment. And he (may Allah consecrate his spirit and illuminate his grave and have mercy on him and be pleased with him and make profitable his knowledge and bring us close together in his party) answered: Praise be to Allah, if a man "touches" a smooth, beardless boy out of desire, there are two opinions in the school of Ahmad and others. The first of these is that, like touching women out of desire, ablution is invalidated; this is widespread in the school of Malik, mentioned by Qadi Abu Ya'la in commentary on this school. This is one of two views in the school of Al-Shafi'i. The second opinion is that it is not invalidated; this is widespread in the school of Al-Shafi'i. The first opinion is the purest, for indeed intercourse in the rear annuls the acts of worship that are annulled by intercourse in the front, such as fasting, ritual purity for pilgrimage [ihram], and remaining in the mosque for devotion [i'tikaf], and necessitates washing just as that necessitates it.

*Ibn Taymiyya, Al-tafsir Al-kabir, Surah Al-nur*

وسئل مالك عن رجل له نسوة وجواري هل يطؤهن جميعاً قبل أن يغتسل فقال لا بأس بأن يصيب الرجل
جاريتيه قبل أن يغتسل فأما النساء الحرائر فيُكره أن يصيب الرجل المرأة الحرة في يوم الاخرى فأما أن يصيب
الجارية ثم يصيب الاخرى وهو جنب فلا بأس بذلك

موطأ الإمام مالك كتاب الطهارة

Malik was asked about a man who had women and servant girls – may he have sex
with all of them before he washes himself? And he said: There is no problem with a
man coming to two of his servant girls before he washes himself, but as to free women,
it is disapproved for a man to come to one free woman on another one's day; however
as regards his coming to one maid and then to another, being in a state of impurity
[*junub*], there is no issue with that.

*Muwatta Malik, The book of purity*

وإن أحس بإنتقال المني من ظهره فأمسك ذكره فلم يخرج ففيه روايتان إحداهما لا غسل عليه لقول النبي ﷺ
إذا رأت الماء والثانية يجب لأنه خرج عن مقره أشبه ما لو ظهر

الكافي في فقه الإمام أحمد بن حنبل لإبن قدامة كتاب الطهارة باب ما يوجب الغسل

If a man feels the movement of semen down his back but takes hold of his penis and
nothing comes out, then regarding this there are two accounts. One of them says that
he is not obliged to wash, based on what the Prophet (SAW) said: "If she sees fluid …"
The second is that it is necessary, since it has come out of its resting place, similar to
if it had actually appeared.

*Ibn Qudama, Al-kafi fi Fiqh Al-imam Ahmad ibn Hanbal, The book of purity, Section: that which necessitates
washing*

يجب على الرجل من خروج المنيّ ومن إيلاج الحشفة في أي فرج كان قبلاً ذكراً أو دبراً ذكراً أو أنثى ولو بهيمة أو
صغيراً في صغيرة ويجب على المرأة من خروج منيّها ومن أي ذكر دخل في قبلها أو دبرها ولو أشلّ أو من صبي
أو بهيمة ومن الحيض والنفاس وخروج الولد جافاً وإنما يتعلق بتغييب جميع الحشفة ولو رأى منياً في ثوب أو
فراش ينام فيه مع من يمكن كونه منه نُدب لهما الغسل

عمدة السالك وعدة الناسك لإبن النقيب المصري كتاب الطهارة باب الغسل

It [washing] is obligatory for a man upon discharge of semen [*maniy*] and upon
penetration of the head of the penis into any opening, whether in the front or the
rear, male or female, even an animal, or a little boy into a little girl. And it is obligatory
for a woman upon discharge of her semen [*maniy*] and from any penis that enters her
front part or her rear, even if it is crippled or it is of a young boy or animal, and in
menstruation and the postpartum period, or in the dry birth of a child; this is

84

contingent upon the entire head of the penis becoming concealed. And if a man sees semen on a garment or a bed that he sleeps in with someone from whom he is able to produce progeny, both of them are obliged to wash.

*Ibn Al-Naqib Al-Misri, 'Umda Al-salik wa 'Udda Al-nasik, The book of purity, Section: washing [ghusl]*

ولو جُومِعت في قبلها فاغتسلت ثم خرج منيّه منها لزمها غسل آخر بشرطين احدهما أن تكون ذات شهوة لا صغيرة الثاني أن تكون قضت شهوتها لا نائمة ومكرهة

عمدة السالك وعدة الناسك لإبن النقيب المصري كتاب الطهارة باب الغسل

If a woman has had sex done to her in the front, and has washed herself, and then the man's semen comes out of her, another washing is necessary upon two conditions: the first of them is that she is capable of desire, not like a little girl; the second is that she was fulfilling her desire and was not sleeping or coerced.

*Ibn Al-Naqib Al-Misri, 'Umda Al-salik wa 'Udda Al-nasik, The book of purity, Section: washing [ghusl]*

إيجاب الغسل لا يتوقف على نزول المني بل متى غابت الحشفة في الفرج وجب الغسل على الرجل والمرأة وهذا لا خلاف فيه اليوم وقد كان فيه خلاف لبعض الصحابة ومن بعدهم ثم إنعقد الاجماع على ما ذكرناه وقد تقدم بيان هذا قال أصحابنا ولو غيب الحشفة في دبر إمرأة أو دبر رجل أو فرج بهيمة أو دبرها وجب الغسل سواء كان المولج فيه حياً أو ميتاً صغيراً أو كبيراً وسواء كان ذلك عن قصد أم عن نسيان وسواء كان مختاراً أو مكرهاً أو استدخلت المرأة ذكره وهو نائم وسواء إنتشر الذكر أم لا وسواء كان مختوناً أم أغلف فيجب الغسل في كل هذه الصور على الفاعل والمفعول به إلا إذا كان الفاعل أو المفعول به صبياً أو صبية فإنه لا يقال وجب عليه لأنه ليس مكلفاً ولكن يقال صار جنباً فإن كان مميزاً وجب على الولي أن يأمره بالغسل كما يأمره بالوضوء

المنهاج في شرح صحيح مسلم للنووي كتاب الحيض باب بيان أن الجماع كان في أول الاسلام لا يوجب الغسل إلا أن ينزل المني وبيان نسخه وأن الغسل يجب بالجماع

The necessity for washing [ghusl] does not depend on the emission of semen; rather when the head of the penis disappears inside the vagina, washing is obligatory for the man and the woman. There is no disagreement on this today, although there was disagreement among some of the Companions and those after them, but then all convened on what we have mentioned and evidence of this has been presented. Our companions have said that if the head of the penis goes into the rear of a woman or the rear of a man, or the vagina of an animal or its rear, washing is obligatory whether the one penetrated is alive or dead, small or grown, whether it was intentional or absentminded, and whether it was by choice or compulsion; or if a woman inserts a man's penis into herself while he is sleeping, whether the penis is erect or not, and whether it is circumcised or uncircumcised.

Washing is obligatory in all of these instances, for the one doing it and the one getting it done to them, except if the one doing it or the one getting it done to them is a young boy or young girl, in which case it is not said to be obligatory, since the young boy is not yet responsible for his actions, although it can be said that he has become sexually impure, and if he is of the age of discernment it is obligatory for his guardian to ask him to wash, just as he asks him to perform ablution.

*Al-Nawawi, Al-minhaj fi Sharh Sahih Muslim, The book of menstruation, Section: substantiating that in sex at the beginning of Islam, washing [ghusl] was not obligatory unless semen was discharged, and substantiating that this was abrogated and that washing is always obligatory upon sex*

لو نزل المني إلى أصل الذكر ثم لم يخرج فلا غسل وكذا لو صار المني في وسط الذكر وهو في صلاة فأمسك بيده على ذكره فوق حائل فلم يخرج المني حتى سلم من صلاته صحت صلاته فإنه مازال مطهراً حتى خرج والمرأة كالرجل في هذا إلا أنها إذا كانت ثيباً فنزل المني إلى فرجها ووصل الموضع الذي يجب عليها غسله في الجنابة والإستنجاء وهو الذي يظهر حال قعودها لقضاء الحاجة وجب عليها الغسل بوصول المني إلى ذلك الموضع

المنهاج في شرح صحيح مسلم للنووي كتاب الحيض باب وجوب الغسل على المرأة بخروج المني منها

If semen [maniy] comes down to the opening of the penis, but then does not come out, there is no washing required. Likewise if the semen reaches the middle of the penis, and a man is in prayer but takes hold of his penis with his hand above a covering, and the semen does not come out until he concludes his prayer, then his prayer is valid, since he remains pure until it comes out. And the woman is like the man in this regard, except in the case that she is a formerly married woman, and the semen [maniy] comes down to her vagina and reaches the place which requires washing from sexual impurity and cleaning in general, that is, the parts that are visible when she is sitting down to fulfill her need; then it is required for her to wash, since the semen reached this location.

*Al-Nawawi, Al-minhaj fi Sharh Sahih Muslim, The book of menstruation, Section: obligation for a woman to wash [ghusl] if semen comes out of her.*

قوله وتواري حشفة في قبل أو دبر عليهما التواري في فرج البهيمة لا يوجب الغسل إلا بالإزال ... التواري في الميتة والصغيرة لا يوجب الغسل إلا بالإزال

البحر الرائق شرح كنز الدقائق لزيد الدين إبن نجيم كتاب الطهارة

Regarding his [Al-Nasafi's] words "and the concealment of the head of a penis in the front part or the rear; both require". Concealment in an animal's vagina does not necessitate washing except in the case of ejaculation ... concealment in a dead woman or in a little girl does not necessitate washing except in the case of ejaculation.

*Ibn Nujaim, Al-bahr Al-ra'iq, The book of purity*

عن ابي هريرة أن النبي ﷺ لقيه في بعض طريق المدينة وهو جنب فانخنست منه فذهب فإغتسل ثم جاء فقال أين كنت يا أبا هريرة قال كنت جنباً فكرهت أن أجالسك وأنا على غير طهارة فقال سبحان الله إن المؤمن لا ينجُس

صحيح البخاري كتاب الغسل

Abu Huraira related that the Prophet (SAW) met up with him in one of the streets of Medina while he was sexually impure. "So I withdrew from Him."; and he went and washed himself. Then He came and said: Where were you oh Abu Huraira? He said: I was sexually impure and did not want to keep you company while I was impure. But He said: Praise be to Allah! Truly a believer does not become filthy.

*Sahih Al-Bukhari, The book of washing*

عن عبدالله بن مالك الغافقي أنه سمع رسول الله ﷺ يقول لعمر بن الخطاب إذا توضأت وأنا جنب أكلت وشربت ولا أصلي ولا اقرأ حتى اغتسل

السنن الكبرى للبيهقي كتاب الطهارة باب نهي الجنب عن قراءة القرآن

Abdullah ibn Malik Al-Ghafiqi related that he heard the Messenger of Allah (SAW) say to 'Umar ibn Al-Khattab: Whenever I perform ablution and I am sexually impure, I eat and drink but I do not pray or recite until I have fully washed.

*Al-Bayhaqi, Al-sunan Al-kubra, The book of purity, Section*: the prohibition for those sexually impure to recite the Qur'an

عن إبن عباس قال إغتسل بعض أزواج النبي ﷺ في جفنة لجاء رسول الله ﷺ ليغتسل منها أو ليتوضأ فقالت يا رسول الله إني كنت جنباً فقال النبي ﷺ إن الماء لا يُجنِب

المصنف لإبن ابي شيبة كتاب الطهارة

From Ibn 'Abbas, who said: One of the Prophet's (SAW) wives bathed herself in a basin, and the Messenger of Allah (SAW) came to bathe after her or to perform ablution. And she said: Oh Messenger of Allah, indeed I was sexually impure. But the Prophet (SAW) said: Indeed water does not make anyone sexually impure.

*Ibn Abi Shayba, Al-musannaf, The book of purity*

﴾ يا أيها الذين آمنوا لا تقربوا الصلواة وأنتم سكارى حتى تعلموا ما تقولون ولا جنباً إلا عابري سبيل حتى تغتسلوا وإن كنتم مرضى أو على سفر أو جاء أحد منكم من الغائط أو لامستم النساء فلم تجدوا ماء فتيمموا صعيداً طيباً فامسحوا بوجوهكم وأيديكم إن الله كان عفواً غفوراً ﴿ النساء ٤٣

{ *Oh you who have believed! Do not come for prayer when you are drunk, until you are aware of what you are saying, nor being sexually impure, unless you are on your way along a road, until you have bathed; and if you are sick or on a journey, or any of you has come from defecating, or you have touched women, and you can not find any water, then dry wipe with clean earth, and wipe your faces and your hands. Indeed Allah is forbearing, forgiving.* } Al-nisaa 43


﴾ يا أيها الذين آمنوا إذا قمتم إلى الصلوة فاغسلوا وجوهكم وأيديكم إلى المرافق وامسحوا برؤوسكم وأرجلكم إلى الكعبين وإن كنتم جنباً فاطهروا وإن كنتم مرضى أو على سفر أو جاء أحد منكم من الغائط أو لامستم النساء فلم تجدوا ماء فتيمموا صعيداً طيباً فامسحوا بوجوهكم وأيديكم منه ما يريد الله ليجعل عليكم من حرج ولكن يريد ليطهركم وليتم نعمته عليكم لعلكم تشكرون ﴿ المائدة ٦

{ *Oh you who have believed! Whenever you all get up to go to prayer, wash your faces and your hands up to the elbows, and wipe your heads and your feet up to the ankles; if you are sexually impure, then purify yourselves, and if you are ill, or on a journey, or any of you have come back from defecating, or you have touched women, and you can not find any water, then dry wipe with clean earth, and wipe your faces and your hands with it; Allah does not wish to make things awkward for you, but wishes to purify you and to perfect his grace upon you so that perhaps you might give thanks.* } Al-ma'ida 6

﴿ أو لامستم النساء ﴾ وفي قراءة ﴿ لمستم ﴾ بلا ألف وكلاهما بمعنى اللمس وهو الجس باليد قاله اب
عمر وعليه الشافعي وألحق به الجس بباقي البشرة وعن ابن عباس هو الجماع ﴿ فلم تجدوا ماء ﴾ تطهرون
به للصلاة بعد الطلب والتفتيش وهو راجع إلى ما عدا المرضى ﴿ فتيمموا ﴾ اقصدوا بعد دخول الوقت
﴿ صعيداً طيباً ﴾ تراباً طاهراً فاضربوا به ضربتين ﴿ فامسحوا بوجوهكم وأيديكم ﴾ مع المرفقين منه

تفسير الجلالين

{ Or you have touched women } ; there is another recitation without the letter *alef*;
both mean to touch, that is, exploring with the hand; Ibn 'Umar said this, and Al-
Shafi'i affirmed it; included in this is exploring with the rest of the skin. According to
Ibn 'Abbas this means sex. { And you can not find any water } : to cleanse yourselves
with for prayer, after having looked around for it and sought out for it – and this
goes back to what exempts those who are sick; { then dry wipe } : then settle for,
when the time comes, { clean earth } : pure dirt, and strike it twice; { and wipe your
faces and your hands } : up to the elbows with it.

*Tafsir Al-Jalalain* (Al-nisaa 43)

فالتيمم في اللغة هو القصد يقول العرب تيممك الله بحفظه أي قصدك ومنه قول امرىء القيس شعراً ...
﴿ فامسحوا بوجوهكم وأيديكم ﴾ التيمم بدل عن الوضوء في التطهر به لا أنه بدل منه في جميع أعضائه بل
يكفي مسح الوجه واليدين فقط بالإجماع ولكن إختلف الأئمة في كيفية التيمم على أقوال ... عن إبن
عبد الرحمن بن أبزى أن رجلاً أتى عمر فقال اني أجنبت فلم أجد ماء فقال عمر لا تصل فقال عمار أما
تذكر يا أمير أمؤمنين إذ أنا وأنت في سرية فأجنبنا فلم نجد ماء فأما أنت فلم تصل وأما أنا فتمعكت في
التراب فصليت فلما أتينا النبي ﷺ ذكرت ذلك له فقال اما كان يكفيك وضرب النبي ﷺ بيده الأرض
ثم نفخ فيها ومسح بها وجهه وكفيه ... وقوله ﴿ ما يريد الله ليجعل عليكم من حرج ﴾ أي في الدين الذي
شرعه لكم ﴿ ولكن يريد ليطهركم ﴾ فلهذا أباح لكم إذا لم تجدوا الماء أن تعدلوا إلى التيمم بالصعيد
﴿ وليتمّ نعمته عليكم لعلكم تشكرون ﴾ ولهذا كانت هذه الامة مخصوصة بمشروعية التيمم دون سائر الأمم

تفسير إبن كثير

*Tayammum* [dry wiping], linguistically, derives from "to intend towards"; the Arabs
say "May Allah betake Himself towards you in His safeguarding", that is, may He
intend towards you; Imru' Al-Qais used this poetically. ... { Wipe your faces and your
hands } : *tayammum* can substitute for ablution [*wudu'*] as regards purification, not
that it substitutes for it regarding all the body parts, but it is sufficient to wipe just
the face and hands according to universal consensus; the Imams did, however, differ
regarding how to perform *tayammum*. ... Ibn 'Abd Al-Rahman ibn Abza related that a
certain man came to 'Umar and said: Indeed I became sexually impure but did not

find any water. 'Umar said: Do not pray. But 'Ammar said: Do you not recall, oh Leader of the Believers, when you and me were out as part of a detachment, and we became sexually impure, and did not find any water, and you did not pray, but I rolled around in the dirt and then prayed. And when we came back to the Prophet (SAW), you mentioned this to him, and He said: Indeed this would have been good enough for you – and the Prophet (SAW) struck his hand on the ground, then blew into it, and wiped his face and hands with it. … His word { Allah does not wish to make things awkward for you } [Al-ma'ida 6]; that is, in the religion He has ordained for you all; { but wishes to purify you } : this is why He made it permissible for you all, whenever you can not find any water, to instead perform *tayammum* with earth; { to perfect his grace upon you so that perhaps you might give thanks } : this is why this people [*ummah*] is privileged by the lawfulness of *tayammum*, as opposed to all other people.

*Tafsir Ibn Kathir (Al-nisaa 43)*

ثم إختلف أهل التأويل في اللمس الذي عناه الله بقوله ﴿ أو لامستم النساء ﴾ فقال بعضهم عنى بذلك الجماع ... عن سعيد بن جبير قال ذكروا اللمس فقال ناس من الموالي ليس بالجماع وقال ناس من العرب اللمس الجماع قال فأتيت إبن عباس فقلت إن ناساً من الموالي والعرب اختلفوا في اللمس فقالت الموالي ليس بالجماع فقالت العرب الجماع قال من أي الفريقين كنت قلت كنت من الموالي قال غلب فريق الموالي إن المس واللمس والمباشرة الجماع ولكن الله يكني ما شاء بما شاء

تفسير الطبري

The expositors then differed regarding the "touching" that Allah indicated by His word { Or you have touched women } ; some of them said that by this He meant sex … From Sa'id ibn Jubair, who said: They mentioned "touching", and some of the leaders said that it is not sex, while some of the Arabs said that "touching" is sex. He said: So I went to Ibn 'Abbas and said: Indeed some of the leaders disagree with the Arabs regarding "touching"; the leaders say that it is not sex, while the Arabs say that it is sex. He said: Which of the two groups are you with? I said: I'm with the leaders. He said: The group of the leaders is defeated; indeed "touch" and "touching" and "intimate contact" are sex – Allah can allude to whatever He wants with whatever He wants.

*Tafsir Al-Tabari*

قوله ﴿ أو لامستم النساء ﴾ عن ابي عثمان قال اللمس باليد ... عن إبن عباس قال هو الجماع ... عن عبدالله قال اللمس ما دون الجماع ... عن علي ﴿ أو لامستم النساء ﴾ قال هو الجماع ... عن إبن سيرين قال سألت عبيدة عن قوله تعالى ﴿ أو لامستم النساء ﴾ فقال بيده فظننت ما عنى فلم أسأله ... عن ابي عبيدة قال ما

دون الجماع ... عن الحسن قال الملامسة الجماع ... عن الشعبي قال الملامسة ما دون الجماع ..... عن سعيد بن
جبير قال اختلفت أنا وأُناس من العرب في اللمس فقلت أنا وأناس من الموالي اللمس ما دون الجماع وقالت
العرب هو الجماع فأتينا إبن عباس فقال غلبت العرب هو الجماع
المصنف لإبن أبي شيبة كتاب الطهارة

His word { Or you have touched women } . Abu 'Uthman said: Touching with the hand.
... Ibn 'Abbas said: This means sex. ... Abdullah said: Touching other than sex. ... 'Ali
said about { Or you have touched women } : this means sex. ... Ibn Sirin said: I asked
'Ubaida about the word of the Most High { Or you have touched women } , and he said:
With one's hand. And I grasped what he meant, and didn't ask him. ... Abu 'Ubaida said:
Anything other than sex. ... Al-Hasan said: Touching [*mulamasa*] is sex. ... Al-Sha'bi
said: Touching is anything besides sex. ... Sa'id ibn Jubair said: Some people among the
Arabs and I disagreed about "touching"; Some of the leaders and I said that touching
means anything besides sex, but the Arabs said that it is sex. So we went to Ibn 'Abbas,
and he said: The Arabs win; it is sex.

*Ibn Abi Shayba, Al-musannaf, The book of purity*

واختلفوا في معنى اللمس والملامسة فقال قوم المجامعة وهو قول إبن عباس والحسن ومجاهد وقتادة وكنّي
باللمس عن الجماع لأن الجماع لا يحصل إلا باللمس وقال قوم هما إلتقاء البشرتين سواء كان بجماع أو غير جماع
وهو قول إبن مسعود وإبن عمر والشعبي والنخعي وإختلف الفقهاء في حكم الآية فذهب جماعة إلى أنه إذا
أفضى الرجل بشيء من بدنه إلى شيء من بدن المرأة ولا حائل بينهما ينتقض وضوؤهما وهو قول إبن مسعود
وإبن عمر رضي الله عنهما وبه قال الزهري والأوزاعي والشافعي رضي الله عنهم وقال مالك والليث بن سعد
وأحمد وإسحاق إن كان اللمس بشهوة نقض الطهر وإن لم يكن بشهوة فلا ينتقض
تفسير البغوي

There is disagreement regarding the meaning of "touching" and "intimate contact".
Some people say that it is sex; this is what Ibn 'Abbas, Al-Hasan, Mujahid, and Qatada
say. Sex is alluded to as "touching" since sex can only occur with touching. Some
people say that both of these refer to the coming together of two skins, whether with
or without sex; this is what Ibn Mas'ud, Ibn 'Umar, Al-Sha'bi, and Al-Nakh'i say. The
jurists disagree regarding the ruling of this verse. One group holds that whenever a
man brings any part of his body to any part of a woman's body, there being no barrier
between the two of them, then both of their ablutions are invalidated; this is what Ibn
Mas'ud and Ibn 'Umar (may Allah be pleased with both of them) say, and Al-Zuhri,
Al-Awza'i, and Al-Shafi'i (may Allah be pleased with them) said this as well. Malik,
Al-Laith ibn Sa'd, Ahmad, and Ishaq said that if the touching is out of desire, purity
is invalidated, while if it is not out of desire, it does not become invalidated.

*Tafsir Al-Baghawi*

عن عائشة أنها استعارت من أسماء قلادة فهلكت فأرسل رسول الله ﷺ ناساً من أصحابه في طلبها فأدركتهم
الصلاة فصلوا بغير وضوء فلما أتوا النبي ﷺ شكوا ذلك إليه فنزلت آية التيمم فقال أسيد بن حضير جزاك الله
خيراً فوالله ما نزل بك أمرٌ قط إلا جعل الله لك منه مخرجاً وجعل للمسلمين فيه بركة
صحيح مسلم كتاب الحيض

'Aishah related that she borrowed a necklace from Asmaa but it got lost. So the
Messenger of Allah (SAW) sent some men from among his Companions to go look
for it. And the time for prayer came upon them, so they prayed without having
performed ablution. When they came back to the Prophet (SAW) they complained
about this to him, and so the verse about wiping with dust [tayammum] came down.
And Usaid ibn Hudair said [to 'Aishah]: May Allah reward you richly! I swear by
Allah, any issue that has ever come down because of you, Allah has made from it a
way out for you, and made from it a blessing for the Muslims.

*Sahih Muslim, The book of menstruation*


عن عائشة رضي الله عنها سقطتْ قلادة لي بالبيداء ونحن داخلون المدينة فأناخ النبي ﷺ ونزل فثنى رأسه في
حجري راقداً أقبل أبو بكر فلكزني لكزةً شديدة وقال حبستِ الناس في قلادة في الموت لمكان رسول الله ﷺ
وقد أوجعني ثم إن النبي ﷺ إستيقظ وحضرت الصبح فالتُمس الماء فلم يوجد فنزلت ﴿ يا أيها الذين آمنوا إذا
قمتم إلى الصلاة ﴾ الآية
صحيح البخاري كتاب التفسير

'Aishah (may Allah be pleased with her) related: A necklace of mine fell off at Al-
baidaa when we were on our way to Medina. The Prophet (SAW) made his camel
kneel, got down, and laid his head on my lap to sleep. Abu Bakr came at me and
punched me hard and said: You have held people back because of a necklace. And
I played dead because of where the Messenger of Allah (SAW) was, although it
hurt me. Then the Prophet (SAW) awoke at the time of the morning [subh] prayer,
and water was sought, but none was found, so this verse came down { Oh you who
have believed, whenever you all get up to go to prayer } [Al-ma'ida 6] [i.e.
permitting tayammum].

*Sahih Al-Bukhari, The book of tafsir*

•　　　•　　　•

فقال أبو موسى ألم تسمع قول عمار لعمر بعثني رسول الله ﷺ في حاجة فأجنبتُ فلم أجد الماء فتمرّغت في الصعيد كما تمرّغ الدابة فذكرت ذلك للنبي ﷺ فقال إنما كان يكفيك أن تصنع هكذا فضرب بكفّه ضربة على الأرض ثم نفضها ثم مسح بها ظهر كفه بشماله أو ظهر شماله بكفه ثم مسح بهما وجهه

صحيح البخاري كتاب التيمم

Abu Musa said: Did you not hear what 'Ammar said to 'Umar: The Messenger of Allah (SAW) sent me out on an errand, and I became sexually impure but could not find any water. So I rolled around on the ground like an animal. Then I mentioned this to the Prophet (SAW), and He said: Indeed it would have been enough for you to do like this. And He slapped the ground with his hand, shook it off, and then wiped off the back of his right hand with his left – or the back of his left with his hand – then wiped his face with both hands.

*Sahih Al-Bukhari, The book of dry wiping [tayammum]*

إختلف العلماء في إيجاب الوضوء من لمس النساء باليد أو بغير ذلك من الأعضاء الحساسة فذهب قوم إلى أن من لمس امرأة بيده مفضياً إليها ليس بينها وبين حجاب ولا ستر فعليه الوضوء وكذلك من قبلها لأن القبلة عندهم لمس سواء ما سواء التذ أم لم يلتذ وبهذا القول قال الشافعي وأصحابه إلا أنه مرة فرق بين اللامس والملموس فأوجب الوضوء على اللامس دون الملموس ومرة سوّى بينهما ومرة أيضاً فرق بين ذوات المحارم والزوجة فأوجب الوضوء من لمس الزوجة دون ذوات المحارم ومرة سوى بينهما وذهب آخرون إلى إيجاب الوضوء من اللمس إذا قارنته اللذة أو قصد اللذة في تفصيل لهم في ذلك وقع بحائل أو بغير حائل بأي عضو اتفق ما عدا القبلة فإنهم لم يشترطوا لذة في ذلك وهو مذهب مالك وجمهور أصحابه ونفى قوم إيجاب الوضوء لمن لمس النساء وهو مذهب ابي حنيفة ولكلٍّ سلف من الصحابة إلا إشترط اللذة فإني لا أذكر أحداً من الصحابة اشترطها وسبب اختلافهم في هذه المسألة إشتراك إسم اللمس في كلام العرب فإن العرب تطلقه مرة على اللمس الذي هو باليد ومرة تكني به على الجماع فذهب قوم إلى أن اللمس الموجب للطهارة في آية الوضوء هو الجماع في قوله تعالى ﴿ أو لامستم النساء ﴾ وذهب آخرون إلى أنه اللمس باليد ومن رآه من هؤلاء من باب العام أريد به الخاص فإشترط فيه اللذة ومنهم من رآه من باب العام أريد به العام فلم يشترط اللذة فيه ومن إشترط اللذة فإنما دعاه إلى ذلك ما عارض عموم الآية من أن النبي ﷺ كان يلمس عائشة عند سجوده بيده وربما قبلها لمسته وخرج أهل الحديث حديث حبيب بن ابي ثابت عن عروة عن عائشة عن النبي ﷺ أنه قبل بعض نسائه ثم خرج إلى الصلاة ولم يتوضأ فقلت من هي إلا أنت فضحكت قال أبو عمر هذا الحديث وهنه الحجازيون وصححه الكوفيون وإلى تصحيحه مال أبو عمر بن عبد البر قال وروي هذا الحديث أيضاً من طريق معبد بن نباتة وقال الشافعي إن ثبت حديث معبد بن نباتة في القبلة لم ار فيها ولا في اللمس وضوءاً وقد إحتج من أوجب الوضوء من اللمس باليد بأن اللمس ينطلق حقيقة على اللمس باليد وينطلق مجازاً على الجماع وأنه إذا تردد اللفظ بين الحقيقة والمجاز فالأولى أن يحمل على الحقيقة حتى يدل الدليل على المجاز وأولئك أن يقولوا

إن المجاز إذا كثر إستعماله كان أدل منه على الحقيقة كالحال في إسم الغائط الذي هو أدل على الحدث الذي هو فيه مجاز منه على المطمئن من الأرض الذي هو فيه حقيقة والذي أعتقده أن اللمس وإن كانت دلالته على المعنيين بالسواء أو قريباً من السواء أنه أظهر عندي في الجماع وإن كان مجازاً لأن الله تبارك وتعالى قد كنى بالمباشرة والمس في معنى الجماع وهما في معنى اللمس وعلى هذا التأويل في الآية يحتج بها في إجازة التيمم للجنب دون تقدير تقديم فيها ولا تأخير على ما سيأتي بعد وترتفع المعارضة التي بين الآثار والآية على التأويل الآخر وأما من فهم من الآية اللمسين معاً فضعيف فإن العرب إذا خاطبت بالاسم المشترك إنما تقصد به معنى واحداً من المعاني التي يدل عليها الاسم لا جميع المعاني التي يدل عليها وهذا بين بنفسه في كلامهم

بداية المجتهد ونهاية المقتصد لإبن رشد كتاب الطهارة من الحدث

Scholars differ as to the obligation to perform ablution [*wudu'*] for anyone who touches women with the hand or with any of the tactile limbs other than the hand. One group held that whoever touches a woman with his hand, getting close to her, there being no veil or curtain between him and her, he is obliged to perform *wudu'* ; similarly for whoever kisses a woman, since kissing is touching, whether he takes pleasure in it or not. Al-Shafi'i and his companions expressed this view, except that on one occasion he made the distinction between the one touching and the one being touched, and made *wudu'* obligatory for the one touching but not the one being touched, but on another occasion he considered them both equal. On yet another occasion he made the distinction between non-marriageable relatives and wives, making *wudu'* obligatory for someone who touches his wife but not for touching a non-marriageable relative, but on another occasion he considered them both equal. Another group held that touching makes *wudu'* obligatory if it is accompanied by pleasure or the intention of pleasure; in their elaboration of the details on this is the participation of any limb that is involved, with a screen or with something other than a screen, except kissing, for indeed they did not impose the condition of pleasure in this case; this is the doctrine of Malik and most of his companions. A group of people dismissed the obligation of *wudu'* for someone who touches women; this is the doctrine of Abu Hanifa. Each of them has predecessors from among the Companions that did not impose the condition of pleasure; indeed I can not recall any of the Companions that imposed this condition. The reason for their disagreement regarding this issue is the possibility of more than one meaning for the term "touch" in the way the Arabs spoke, since the Arabs would at times apply it to touching that is done with the hand, and other times would use it as an allusion to sex. Some people hold that the kind of touching that necessiates purification, as stated in the verse of *wudu'* , is sex, as referred to in the word of the Most High { Or you have touched women } [*Al-nisaa* 43]. Others hold that this refers to touching with the hand, and among these are some who see it from a customary aspect – by this I mean characteristic – and impose the condition of pleasure; among them as well are some who see it from the customary aspect – by this I mean commonplace – and do not impose the condition of pleasure in it. What gets the attention of those who impose the condition of pleasure is indeed what is at odds with the full verse, in that the Prophet (SAW) would touch 'Aishah with his hand during his prostrations, and perhaps she would touch him as well. The scholars of hadith report a hadith from Habib ibn Abi Thabit, from 'Urwa, from 'Aishah, from the Prophet (SAW), that He kissed one of his women, and then went out to prayer without having performed *wudu'* ; 'Urwa said: Who could it be but you? And she laughed. Abu 'Umar said: This hadith was considered weak by those from Hejaz but considered authentic by those from Kufa, and Abu 'Umar ibn 'Abd Al-Barr was inclined to take it as authentic. He said: This hadith was also narrated by way of Ma'bad ibn Nubata, and Al-Shafi'i said: Indeed the hadith of Ma'bad ibn Nubata is affirmed regarding kissing; I see no obligation for *wudu'* from either kissing or touching. Those who held that *wudu'* is obligatory from touching with the hand made objections to this, in that "touching" comes across in actuality as touching with the hand but comes across only figuratively as sex, and since whenever an expression goes back and forth between actuality and figurative, it must be taken foremost as what is in actuality until there is evidence for the figurative. Those people say that whenever usage of the figurative increases, this makes the figurative more indicative over the actual, as is the case for the term defecation, for which the figurative term is more indicative of the bodily occurrence, which is referred to figuratively, rather than the "calm, safe area of land" that is the actual literal meaning. What I find concerning "touching", even if its connotation for these two meanings is equal or close to equal, is that it is clearer in my opinion in reference to sex, even if this is figurative, since Allah Blessed and Exalted alluded to sex as intimate contact [*mubashara*] and contact [*mass*], and both of these mean to touch. On the basis of this interpretation for the verse, objection may be made to making dry wiping [*tayammum*] permissible for someone who is sexually impure, without evaluating what is presented regarding it, and without waiting for what was to follow. Discord between the hadiths and the verse is raised on the latter interpretation. However, whoever promotes the understanding that the verse refers to both kinds of touching together, this is weak, since the Arabs, whenever they discoursed using a term with a possibility of meanings, indeed they intended only one of the meanings which the term could refer to, not all of the meanings that it could refer to; and this by itself is evidence regarding the way they spoke.

*Ibn Rushd, Bidaya Al-mujtahid wa Nihaya Al-Muqtasid, The book of purification from bodily occurrences [hadath]*

عن عبد الرحمن بن حرملة أن رجلاً سأل سعيد بن المسيب عن الرجل الجنُب يتيمَّم ثم يدرك الماء فقال
سعيد إذا أدرك الماء فعليه الغسل لما يُستقبل قال مالك فيمن احتلم وهو في سفر ولا يقدر من الماء إلا على
قدر الوضوء وهو لا يعطَش حتى يأتي الماء قال يغسل بذلك فرجه وما أصابه من ذلك الأذى ثم يتيمم صعيداً
طيباً كما أمره الله وسئل مالك عن رجل جنب أراد أن يتيمم فلم يجد تراباً إلا تراب سَبَخة هل يتيمم
بالسباخ وهل تُكره الصلاة في السباخ قال مالك لا بأس بالصلاة في السباخ والتيمم منها لأن الله تبارك وتعالى
قال ﴿ فتيمموا صعيداً طيباً ﴾ فكل ما كان صعيداً فهو يُتيمم به سباخاً كان أو غيره
موطأ مالك كتاب الطهارة

'Abd Al-Rahman ibn Harmala related that a certain man asked Sa'id ibn Al-Musayyab about if someone, who is sexually impure, wipes with dust [tayammum], and then comes across some water. And Sa'id said: If he comes across water then he is to fully wash [ghusl] for what is faced. Malik said regarding someone who has a wet dream while travelling, and has no water except what is sufficient for ablution [wudu'], and who is not thirsty so as to need the water; he said: He is to wash his crotch with it, and whatever of the harm has gotten on them, then wipe with good, clean earth as Allah has ordered him. And Malik was asked about if a man, sexually impure, wishes to wipe with earth but only finds salty earth – can he wipe with salty earth? And is prayer on salty earth disapproved? Malik said: There is no issue with prayer on salty earth, or wiping with it, because Allah Blessed and Exalted has said: { So wipe with good, clean earth } [Al-nisaa 43]. Any surface material [sa'id] can be used to wipe with, salty or otherwise.

*Muwatta' Malik, The book of purity*

عن ابي ظبيان قال سئل عباس أي الصعيد أطيب قال الحرث
المصنف لعبد الرزاق كتاب الطهارة

From Abu Dhabyan, who said: 'Abbas was asked what kind of clean earth/surface material [sa'id] is best; he said: Arable land.

*'Abd Al-Razzaq, the Musannaf, The book of purity*

عن علي قال كان رسول الله ﷺ يقرأ بنا القران على كل حال إلا الجنابة
المصنف لإبن ابي شيبة كتاب الطهارة

From 'Ali, who said: The Messenger of Allah (SAW) would recite the Qur'an with us on any occasion, except sexual impurity.

*Ibn Abi Shayba, Al-musannaf, The book of purity*

عن علي قال كان رسول الله ﷺ يقرئنا القران على كل حال مالم يكن جنباً

المصنف لإبن ابي شيبة كتاب الطهارة

From 'Ali, who said: The Messenger of Allah (SAW) would have us recite the Qur'an on any occasion, as long as we were not sexually impure.

*Ibn Abi Shayba, Al-musannaf, The book of purity*

عن عكرمة أنه كان لا يرى بأساً أن يقرأ ألجنب الآية والآيتين

المصنف لإبن ابي شيبة كتاب الطهارة

'Ikrama related that he had no problem with someone who is sexually impure reciting one or two verses.

*Ibn Abi Shayba, Al-musannaf, The book of purity*

عن الزهري في المرأة والرجل يخرج منهما الشيء بعدما يغتسلان قال يغسلان فرجهما ويتوضئان

المصنف لإبن ابي شيبة كتاب الطهارة

Al-Zuhri said regarding a woman and a man, if anything comes out of them after they have washed; he said: They should wash their crotches and perform ablution.

*Ibn Abi Shayba, Al-musannaf, The book of purity*

عن ابي مجلز قال قال إبن عمر إذا إغتسل أحدكم من الجنابة فبال قبل أن يفرُغ من غسله فليُفرغ على رأسه الماء

المصنف لإبن ابي شيبة كتاب الطهارة

From Abu Mijlaz, who said: Ibn 'Umar said: Whenever any of you washes himself from sexual impurity, but urinates before he finishes washing, let him pour out the water over his head.

*Ibn Abi Shayba, Al-musannaf, The book of purity*

عن الحسن في ألجنب يعرق في الثوب حتى ينعصر قال يصلي فيه

المصنف لإبن ابي شيبة كتاب الطهارة

Al-Hasan related regarding someone who is sexually impure who sweats in his garment to the point of having to wring it out; he said: He should pray in it.

*Ibn Abi Shayba, Al-musannaf, The book of purity*

هل يحل أكل المني الطاهر فيه وجهان الصحيح المشهور أنه لا يحل لأنه مستخبث قال تعالى ﴿ ويحرم عليهم

الخبائث ﴾ والثاني يجوز وهو قول الشيخ أبي زيد المروزي لأنه طاهر لا ضرر فيه

كتاب المجموع للنووي كتاب الحيض باب إزالة النجاسة

Is it permissible to eat semen in a state of purity? There are two views on this; the correct and widespread one is that it is not permissible, since it is taken to be repulsive; the Most High said { Prohibited to them are repulsive things } [Al-A'raf 157]. And the second is that it is permissible, this being what Sheikh Abu Zaid Al-Maruzi says, since it is in a state of purity and there is no harm in it.

*Al-Nawawi, Kitab al-Majmu', The book of menstruation, Section: removing filth*


قال النبي ﷺ سبعة لا ينظر الله اليهم يوم القيامة ولا يزكيهم ويدخلهم النار مع الداخلين الناكح يده ...

وقد رخص بعض العلماء لمن إضطر إلى ذلك في سفر فلبس متاعه حتى سال منه ما كان يؤذيه فقال لا بأس به

وحكي عن أحد صاحبي أبي حنيفة أبي يوسف أو محمد لا بأس أن يأخذ المضطر حريرة فيمسحه بها حتى ينزل

محاضرات الأدباء ومحاورات الشعراء والبلغاء للراغب الاصفهاني الحد السادس عشر في المجون والسخف النبي عن ذلك والرخصة فيه

The Prophet (SAW) said: There are seven that Allah does not regard on resurrection day, will not vindicate them, and will send them to hellfire with the other ones entering: 1) someone who has relations [nikah] with his hand ... But one of the scholars gave licence for this to someone under duress on a journey who touches his goods until what was harming him flows out; he said: There is nothing wrong with this. And it was narrated from one of the companions of Abu Hanifa, Abu Yusuf or Muhammad: There is nothing wrong for someone under duress to take hold of a piece of silk and rub on it until he discharges.

*Al-Raghib Al-Asfahani, Muhadarat Al-udabaa wa Muhawarat Al-shu'raa wa Al-bulaghaa, The sixteenth outline: regarding jest and absurdity, Subsection: prohibition against rubbing, and its concession*


(الإستناء حرام) أي بالكف إذا كان لإستجلاب الشهوة أما إذا غلبته الشهوة وليس له زوجة ولا أمة ففعل

ذلك لتسكينها فالرجاء أنه لا وبال عليه كما قاله أبو الليث ويجب لو خاف الزنا (كره) الظاهر أنها كراهة تنزيه

لأن ذلك بمنزلة ما لو أنزل بتفخيذ أو تبطين وقدمنا عن المعراج في باب مفسدات الصوم يجوز أن يستمني بيد

زوجته أو خادمته وأنظر ما كتبناه هناك (ولا شيء عليه) أي من حد وتعزير وكذا من إثم على ما قلناه

رد المحتار على الدر المختار لإبن عابدين كتاب الحدود باب الوطء الذي يوجب الحد والذي لا يوجبه

"Masturbation is forbidden" : that is, with the hand, whenever desire is sought. However, if desire overpowers a man, and he does not have a wife or a servant girl, and he does it to calm the desire, then it is expected that there is no harm to him, as

Abu Al-Laith said, it being necessary if he fears adultery. "Disapproved" : the meaning is that it is slightly disliked, since this is similar to if he had caused discharge by rubbing on someone's thighs or belly. And we have expounded regarding the night ascent in the section of things that annul the fast: it is permissible for a man to masturbate with the hand of his wife or female servant; refer to what we have written there. "And there is nothing on him" : that is, of any legal punishment or reprimand, and as such, of wrongdoing, according to what we have said.

*Ibn 'Abidin, Radd Al-muhtar 'ala Al-durr Al-mukhtar, The book of legal punishments [hudud], Section: intercourse that necessitates punishment and that which does not necessitate it*

وإن قوّر بطيخةً أو عجيناً أو أديماً أو نخشاً في صنم فأولج فيه فعلى ما قدّمنا من التفصيل قلتُ وهو أسهل من إستمنائه بيده وقد قال أحمد فيمن به شهوة الجماع غالباً لا يملك نفسه ويخاف أن تنشقّ أنثياه أطعم هذا لفظ ما حكاه عنه في المغني ثم قال أباح له الفطر ، لأنه يخاف على نفسه فهو كالمريض ومن يخاف على نفسه الهلاك لعطش ونحوه وأوجب الإطعام بدلاً من الصيام وهذا محمول على من لا يرجو إمكان القضاء فإن رجا ذلك فلا فدية عليه والواجب إنتظار القضاء وفعله إذا قدر عليه لقوله ﴿ فمن كان منكم مريضاً ﴾ البقرة ١٨٤
بدائع الفوائد لإبن قيّم

If a man makes a hole in a melon, or some dough, or leather, or the worn-out part of the base of a statue, and penetrates into it, this is already related to the detailed description we have presented. I have said: This is easier than him masturbating with his hand. And Ahmad said regarding whoever has an overbearing desire such that he cannot dominate himself, and fears that his testicles might burst: "Feed it" ["*At'im*"], this being an expression related in the *Mughni*. Then he said: Breaking the fast is lawful for him, since he fears for himself, and is like a sick person, and whoever fears harm for himself due to thirst or similar issues, nourishment is necessitated rather than fasting, and this carries over to whoever has no hope for the opportunity of fulfillment, for if he hopes for this then there is no redemption and it is necessary to wait for fulfillment and act on it if he is in a position to do so, this in reference to His word: { And whoever among you is sick ... } [Al-baqara 184].

*Ibn Qayyim, Bada'ia Al-fawa'id*

روي عن أحمد في رجل خاف أن تنشقّ مثانته من الشبق أو تنشق أنثياه لحبس الماء في زمن رمضان يستخرج
الماء ولم يذكر بأي شيء يستخرجه  قال وعندي أنه يستخرجه بما لا يفسد صوم غيره  كاستمنائه بيده أو بدن
زوجته أو أمته غير الصائمة فإن كان له أمة طفلة أو صغيرة إستمنى بيدها  وكذلك الكافرة ويجوز وطؤها فيما
دون الفرج  فإن أراد الوطء في الفرج مع إمكان إخراج الماء بغيره  فعندي أنه لا يجوز  لأن الضرورة إذا
رُفعت حرم ما وراءها  كالشبع من الميتة  بل ههنا آكدُ  لأن باب الفروج آكدُ في الحظر من الأكل

بدائع الفوائد لإبن قيّم

It was narrated from Ahmad concerning a man who feared that his bladder might burst
from sex drive, or that his testicles might burst from retaining the fluid, during the time
of Ramadan: should he elicit the fluid to come out? And he made no mention of anything
by which to make the fluid come out. He said: According to me he should make it come
out in a way that does not annul the fast of anyone else, such as masturbating using his
own hand or using the body of a non-fasting wife or servant girl of his; but if he has a
small or child servant girl, he may masturbate using her hand, and the same for an
unbelieving woman, and intercourse with her is lawful provided it is not in the vagina.
And if he desires intercourse in the vagina, there being the possibility of releasing the
fluid by means other than in the vagina, then according to me it is not lawful, because
whenever necessity is elevated, what comes after is forbidden, like taking satisfaction
from dead women, but indeed this is more certain, for the entrance of vaginas is more
certain in prohibition [i.e. less of a necessity] than eating.

*Ibn Qayyim, Bada'ia Al-fawa'id*


وأما الجماع والباه فكان هديه فيه أكل هدي تُحفظ به الصحة ويتم به اللذة وسرور النفس ويحصل به مقاصده
التي وُضع لأجلها . فإن الجماع وضع في الأصل لثلاثة أمور هي مقاصده الأصلية أحدها حفظ النسل ودوام
النوع الانساني إلى أن تتكامل العدة التي قدّر الله بروزها إلى هذا العالم  الثاني  إخراج الماء الذي يضر احتباسه
واحتقانه بجملة البدن  الثالث  قضاء الوطر ونيل اللذة والتمتع بالنعمة وهذه - وحدها - هي الفائدة التي في الجنة
إذ لا تناسل هناك ولا إحتقان يستفرغه الانزال

الطب النبوي لإبن قيّم

As for sex and coitus, His ways regarding it are the most complete ways: by it health is
preserved, pleasure and the delight of the soul are attained, and the objectives for which
it was established are reached. Indeed sex was established in the beginning towards three
things, its original goals; one of them was to ensure posterity and the continuation of
humankind until the consummation of the period fixed by Allah for this world. The
second: the expulsion of fluid, the confinement and congestion of which is harmful for
the whole body. The third: fulfillment of desire and attainment of pleasure and
enjoyment in abundance. And this one – this alone – is the goal in *Jannah*, where there
is no procreation and no congestion from which relief is sought by discharge.

*Ibn Qayyim, Al-tibb Al-nabawi*

وأردأ اشكاله أن تعلوه ويجامعها على ظهره وهو خلاف الشكل الطبيعي الذي طبع الله عليه الرجل والمرأة بل
نوع الذكر والانثى وفيه من المفاسد أن ألمني تيعسر خروجه كله فربما بقى في العضو منه بقيةٌ فيتعفن ويفسد
فيضر وأيضاً فربما سال إلى الذكر رطوبات من الفرج وأيضاً فإن الرحم لا يتكن من الإشتمال على الماء
واجتماعه فيه وانضمامه عليه لتخليق الولد

الطب النبوي لإبن قيّم

The worst of positions is the woman on top of the man and he having sex with her
on his back. This is contrary to the natural position that Allah fixed for a man and a
woman even as He fashioned them male and female. And this is damaging in that it
becomes difficult for all the semen to come out, perchance some of it remaining in
the member, to become spoiled and decay, causing harm. Also perchance some fluids
from the vagina may run onto the penis. And also indeed the womb is not well seated
from being turned over the semen, to meet it there, and to unite with it, for the
creation of the child.

*Ibn Qayyim, Al-tibb Al-nabawi*


إذا قضى وطره فليتمهل على أهله حتى تقضى هي أيضاً نهمتها فإن انزالها ربما يتأخر فيهيج شهوتها ثم القعود
عنها إيذاء لها والاختلاف في طبع الانزال يوجب التنافر مهما كان الزوج سابقاً إلى الانزال والتوافق في وقت
الانزال ألذ عندها لا يشتغل الرجل بنفسه عنها فانها ربما تستحي

إحياء علوم الدين للغزالي كتاب آداب النكاح الباب الثالث في آداب المعاشرة وما يجري في دوام النكاح والنظر فيما على الزوج وفيما
على الزوجة

When a man has fulfilled his desire, let him take his time with his wife until she also
fulfills her craving, for indeed her ejaculation may perhaps be delayed; if he arouses
her desire, and then neglects her, it will cause harm to her. A difference in the nature
of the ejaculation necessarily leads to discord whenever the husband reaches it first.
But harmony at the time of ejaculation is more pleasing for her, since the man is not
occupied with himself at her expense, for indeed perhaps she may be shy.

*Al-Ghazali, Ihyaa 'Ulum Al-din, The book of proper conduct in marital relations, Section three: concerning proper*
*conduct in intimacy, what should be observed for the duration of marital relations, and consideration of the*
*obligations of the husband and the obligations of the wife*

المغني لإبن قدامة كتاب الايلاء

Four months is the length of time at which a woman suffers harm from deferring intercourse from her.

*Ibn Qudama, Al-mughni, The book of the oath*

(ولا تكون اللواطة في الجنة) قال السيوطي قال إبن عقيل الحنبلي جرت مسألة بين أبي علي بن الوليد المعتزلي وبين أبي يوسف القزويني في ذلك فقال أبن الوليد لا يمنع أن يجعل ذلك من جملة اللذات في الجنة لزوال المفسدة لأنه إنما منع في الدنيا لما فيه من قطع النسل وكونه محلاً للأذى وليس في الجنة ذلك ولهذا أبيح شرب الخمر لما ليس فيه من السكر وغاية العربدة وزوال العقل فلذلك لم يمنع من الالتذاذ بها فقال أبو يوسف الميل إلى الذكور عاهة وهو قبيح في نفسه لأنه محل لم يخلق للوطء ولهذا لم يبح في شريعة بخلاف الخمر وهو مخرج الحدث والجنة نزهت عن العاهات فقال أبن الوليد العاهة هي التلويث بالأذى فإذن لم يبق إلا مجرد الالتذاذ

رد المحتار على الدر المختار لإبن عابدين كتاب الحدود باب الوطء الذي يوجب الحد والذي لا يوجبه

"And there is no homosexuality in Jannah" : Al-Suyuti said: Ibn 'Aqil Al-Hanbali said that an issue arose between Abu 'Ali ibn Al-Walid Al-Ma'tazili and Abu Yusuf Al-Qazwini concerning this. Ibn Al-Walid said: It is not prohibited for this to be part of all the delights of *Jannah*, as there is no longer any source of corruption. Indeed it is prohibited in this world since posterity is cut off by it and by it giving occasion to harm, and this does not exist in *Jannah*. This is why fermented drink is allowed, since there is no drunkenness in it, or excessive revelry, or loss of good sense. For this reason it is not prohibited to find delight in this [homosexuality]. However Abu Yusuf said: The tendency towards males is a physical defect and is repugnant in and of itself, since it is a location that was not created for intercourse. For this reason it is not lawfully permitted, as opposed to fermented drink, since it is where feces come out; and *Jannah* is far above physical infirmities. But Ibn Walid said: Physical infirmity is defilment by harmful things; nothing remains, then, but to simply find delight.

*Ibn 'Abidin, Radd Al-muhtar 'ala Al-durr Al-mukhtar, The book of legal punishments [hudud], Section: intercourse that necessitates punishment and that which does not necessitate it*

الفم والأنف

*Nose and mouth*

عن المقدام بن شريح عن أبيه قال سألتُ عائشة قلت بأي شيء كان يبدأ النبي ﷺ إذا دخل بيته قالت بالسواك

صحيح مسلم كتاب الطهارة

Al-Miqdam ibn Shuraih related that his father said: I asked 'Aishah and said: What did the Prophet (SAW) begin with first when He entered his house? She said: The teeth-cleaning twig [siwak].

*Sahih Muslim, The book of purity*

حذيفة قال كان النبي ﷺ إذا قام من الليل يشوص فاه بالسواك

صحيح البخاري كتاب الوضوء

Hudhaifa said: The Prophet (SAW), whenever He arose after the night was over, scrubbed his mouth with a *siwak*.

*Sahih Al-Bukhari, The book of ablution*

عن ابي بردة عن أبيه قال أتيت النبي ﷺ فوجدته يستنّ بسواك بيده يقول " أُع أُع " والسواك في فيه كأنه يتهوع

صحيح البخاري كتاب الوضوء

Abu Burda related that his father said: I came to the Prophet (SAW) and I found him cleaning his teeth with a *siwak* He had in his hand, saying "U'ah u'ah" when the *siwak* was in his mouth, as if He were retching.

*Sahih Al-Bukhari, The book of ablution*

عن حذيفة قال كان رسول الله ﷺ إذا قام ليتهجد يشوص فاه بالسواك

صحيح مسلم كتاب الطهارة

From Hudhaifa who said: The Messenger of Allah (SAW), whenever He arose for night prayer [tahajjud], would clean his mouth with the *siwak*.

*Sahih Muslim, The book of purity*

عن علي بن ابي طالب قال إن قال أفواهكم طرق للقرآن فطيّبوها بالسواك

سنن إبن ماجه كتاب الطهارة وسننها

From 'Ali ibn Abi Talib, who said: Indeed your mouths are paths for the Qur'an, so freshen them with the *siwak*.

*Sunan Ibn Majah, The book of purity and its sunnah*

حدثنا أنس قال قال رسول الله ﷺ أكثرت عليكم في السواك

صحيح البخاري كتاب الجمعة

Anas told us: The Messenger of Allah (SAW) said: I have told you all over and over about the *siwak*.

*Sahih Al-Bukhari, The book of Friday assembly*

عن ابي هريرة قال كان رسول الله ﷺ إذا عطس غطى وجهه بثوبه ووضع كفيه على حاجبيه

كتاب المعجم لابن الأعرابي رقم ٤٤٢

From Abu Huraira who said: The Messenger of Allah (SAW), whenever He sneezed, covered his face with his garment and put his palms over his eyelids.

*Ibn Al-A'rabi, Kitab Al-mu'jam, number 442*

عن ابي هريرة قال كان رسول الله ﷺ إذا عطس وضع يده أو ثوبه على فيه وخفض أو غضَّ بها صوته

سنن ابي داود كتاب الأدب

From Abu Huraira, who said: Whenever the Messenger of Allah (SAW) would sneeze, He put his hand or his garment over his mouth, to lessen or lower the sound.

*Sunan Abu Dawud, The book of manners*

عن عبدالله بن ابي بكر عن أبيه أن رسول الله ﷺ قال إن عطس فشمّته ثم إن عطس فشمته ثم إن عطس فشمته ثم إن عطس فقل إنك مضنوك

موطأ مالك كتاب الاستئذان

Abdullah ibn Abi Bakr related from his father that the Messenger of Allah (SAW) said: If someone sneezes, invoke a blessing over him [by saying "May Allah have mercy on you" ("*Yarhamuka Allah*")]; if he then sneezes again, invoke a blessing on him; if he then sneezes again, invoke a blessing on him; if he then sneezes yet again, say to him: Indeed you are ill.

*Muwatta Malik, The book of seeking permission*

عن ابي هريرة أن النبي ﷺ قال إذا إستيقظ أحدكم من منامه فليستنثر ثلاث مرات فإنّ الشيطان يبيت على خياشيمه

صحيح مسلم كتاب الطهارة

Abu Huraira related that the Prophet (SAW) said: When any of you awakens from sleep let him draw water through his nose three times to clean it, for indeed Satan spends the night in his nasal cavities.

*Sahih Muslim, The book of purity*

عن أنس رضي الله عنه عن النبي ﷺ قال إذا كان في الصلاة فإنه يناجي ربه فلا يبزقنّ بين يديه ولا عن يمينه ولكن عن شماله تحت قدمه اليسرى

صحيح البخاري كتاب العمل في الصلاة

Anas (may Allah be pleased with him) related from the Prophet (SAW) that He said: When one is in prayer indeed he is in intimate discourse with his Lord, so he must by no means spit between his hands or to his right, but rather on his left under his left foot.

*Sahih Al-Bukhari, The book of actions in prayer*

أنس بن مالك قال قال النبي ﷺ البزاق في المسجد خطيئة وكفارتها دفنها

صحيح البخاري كتاب الصلاة

Anas ibn Malik said: The Prophet (SAW) said: Spitting in the mosque is a sin; expiation is made by burying it.

*Sahih Al-Bukhari, The book of prayer*

عن يزيد بن عبدالله بن الشخّير عن أبيه قال صليت مع رسول الله ﷺ فرأيته تنخّع فدلكها بنعله

صحيح مسلم كتاب المساجد ومواضع الصلاة

Yazid ibn 'Abdullah ibn Al-Shikhir related from his father, who said: I was praying with the Messenger of Allah (SAW), and I saw Him cough and spit out, and rub it off with His sandal.

*Sahih Muslim, The book of mosques and places of prayer*

عن أبي سعيد الخدري أن النبي ﷺ رأى نخامة في قبلة المسجد فحكّها بحصاة ثم نهى أن يبزق الرجل عن
يمينه أو أمامة ولكن يبزق عن يساره أو تحت قدمه اليسرى

صحيح مسلم كتاب المساجد ومواضع الصلاة

Abu Sa'id Al-Khudri related that the Prophet (SAW) saw some phlegm on the *qiblah*
of the mosque, and scratched at it with a small stone. Then He forbade anyone to
spit on his right side or in front of him, but rather to spit on his left side or under
his left foot.

*Sahih Muslim, The book of mosques and places of prayer*


عن أبي هريرة أن رسول الله ﷺ رأى نخامة في قبلة المسجد فأقبل على الناس فقال ما بال أحدكم يقوم
مستقبل ربه فيتنخّع أمامه أيحب أحدكم أن يُستقبل فيُتنخع في وجهه فإذا تنخّع أحدكم فليتنخع عن يساره تحت
قدمه فإن لم يجد فليقل هكذا ووصف القاسم فتفل في ثوبه ثم مسح بعضه على بعض

صحيح مسلم كتاب المساجد ومواضع الصلاة

Abu Huraira related that the Messenger of Allah (SAW) saw some phlegm on the
*qiblah* of the mosque, and He approached the people and said: What crosses the mind
of any of you to stand facing his Lord and then cough and spit before Him? Would
any of you like it if someone faced you and coughed and spit in his face? So whenever
any of you cough and spit, let him spit on his left side under his foot; and if he can
not find the space then let him do like this. And Qasim demonstrated by spitting into
his garment and then rubbing part of it over the other.

*Sahih Muslim, The book of mosques and places of prayer*


عن أنس أن النبي ﷺ رأى نخامة في القبلة فشقّ ذلك عليه حتى رُئِيَ في وجهه فقام فحكّه بيده فقال إن
أحدكم إذا قام في صلاته فإنه يناجي ربه أو إن ربه بينه وبين القبلة فلا يبزُقنّ أحدكم قِبَلَ قبلته ولكن عن
يساره أو تحت قدميه ثم أخذ طرف ردائه فبصق فيه ثم ردّ بعضه على بعض فقال أو يفعل هكذا

صحيح البخاري كتاب الصلاة

Anas related that the Prophet (SAW) saw some phlegm on the *qiblah*, and it troubled
him to the point that you could see it on his face. So He got up and scratched at it
with his hand, and said: Truly whenever any of you goes for his prayer, he is indeed
in intimate discourse with his Lord – or his Lord is between him and the *qiblah* – so
let none of you spit facing the *qiblah*, but rather to his left or under his feet. Then He
took the edge of his garment and spat it in, folded part of it over the other, and said:
Or he can do like this.

*Sahih Al-Bukhari, The book of prayer*

عن أبي العلاء بن الشخير عن أبيه قال رأيت رسول الله ﷺ تنخّع فدلكه برجله اليسرى

سنن النسائي كتاب المساجد

Abu Al-'Alaa Al-Shikhir related that his father said: I saw the Messenger of Allah (SAW) cough up and spit out, and then rub it with his left foot.

*Sunan Al-Nasa'i, The book of mosques*

عن أنس بن مالك قال رأى رسول الله ﷺ نخامةً في قبلة المسجد فغضب حتى إحمرّ وجهه فقامت إمرأة من الأنصار فحكّتها وجعلت مكانها خلوقاً فقال رسول الله ﷺ ما أحسن هذا

سنن النسائي كتاب المساجد

From Anas ibn Malik who said: The Messenger of Allah (SAW) saw some phlegm on the *qiblah* of the mosque, and He became enraged until his face turned red. And a woman from the Ansar got up and scratched at it and put a kind of perfume in its place. And the Messenger of Allah (SAW) said: How nice that is.

*Sunan Al-Nasa'i, The book of mosques*

عن أبي هريرة أن رسول الله ﷺ قال العطاس من الله والتثاؤب من الشيطان فإذا تثاءب أحدكم فليضع يده على فيه وإذا قال آه آه فإن الشيطان يضحك من جوفه

جامع الترمذي كتاب الأدب

Abu Huraira related that the Messenger of Allah (SAW) said: Sneezing is from Allah and yawning is from Satan, so whenever any of you yawns he should put his hand over his mouth, and whenever he says "Aah aah" indeed Satan laughs from within him.

*Sunan Al-Tirmidhi, The book of manners*

عن عدي بن ثابت عن أبيه عن جده رفعه قال العُطاس والنعاس والتثاؤب في الصلاة والحيض والقيء والرُّعاف من الشيطان

جامع الترمذي كتاب الأدب

'Adi ibn Thabit related from his father, from his grandfather, who attributed it to Muhammad (SAW); he said: Sneezing, snoozing, and yawning during prayer, and menstruation, vomiting, and nosebleeds, are of Satan.

*Sunan Al-Tirmidhi, The book of manners*

عن ابي هريرة عن النبي ﷺ قال إن الله يحب العطاس ويكره التثاؤب فإذا عطس أحدكُم وحمد الله كان حقاً
على كل مسلم سمعه أن يقول له يرحمك الله وأما التثاؤب فإنما هو من الشيطان فإذا تثاءب أحدكُم فليردده ما
إستطاع فإن أحدكُم إذا تثاءب ضحك منه الشيطان

صحيح البخاري كتاب الأدب

Abu Huraira related from the Prophet (SAW) that He said: Indeed Allah loves
sneezing, and hates yawning; so whenever any of you sneezes, and praises Allah [i.e.
says "Alhamdulillah"], indeed every Muslim who hears him must say back to him: May
Allah have mercy on you ["Yarhamuka Allah"]. And indeed yawning is of Satan, so
whenever any of you yawns, he should hold it back as much as he can, for indeed
whenever any of you yawns, Satan laughs at him.

*Sahih Al-Bukhari, The book of manners*

عن ابي هريرة عن النبي ﷺ قال إذا تثاءب أحدكُم فليكظِم ما إستطاع

الأدب المفرد للبخاري كتاب العُطاس والتثاؤب

Abu Huraira related that the Prophet (SAW) said: Whenever any of you yawns, he
should suppress it as much as he can.

*Al-Bukhari, Al-adab Al-mufrad, The book of sneezing and yawning*

عن ابي سعيد عن النبي ﷺ قال إذا تثاءب أحدكُم فليضع يده بفيه فإن الشيطان يدخل فيه

الأدب المفرد للبخاري كتاب العُطاس والتثاؤب

Abu Sa'id related that the Prophet (SAW) said: Whenever any of you yawns, he should
put his hand over his mouth, for indeed Satan might enter it.

*Al-Bukhari, Al-adab Al-mufrad, The book of sneezing and yawning*

عن إبن مسعود عن النبي ﷺ قال أربع للمسلم على المسلم يعوده إذا مرض ويشهده إذا مات ويُجيبه إذا دعاه
ويشمّته إذا عطس

الأدب المفرد للبخاري كتاب العُطاس والتثاؤب

Ibn Mas'ud related that the Prophet (SAW) said: Four things are a Muslim's obligation
to another Muslim: to visit him when he is sick, to be present with him when he dies,
to respond to him when he calls on him, and to invoke a blessing over him when he
sneezes [by saying "May Allah have mercy on you" ("Yarhamuka Allah")].

*Al-Bukhari, Al-adab Al-mufrad, The book of sneezing and yawning*

عن ابي هريرة أن رسول الله ﷺ قال إذا توضأ أحدكم فليجعل في أنفه ماءً ثم لينثر

سنن ابي داود كتاب الطهارة

Abu Huraira related that the Messenger of Allah (SAW) said: Whenever any of you performs ablution [*wudu'*], he should take up water in his nose and then shake it out.

*Sunan Abu Dawud, The book of purity*

عن ابي هريرة أن رسول الله ﷺ قال من توضأ فليستنثر ومن استجمر فليوتر

صحيح مسلم كتاب الطهارة

Abu Huraira related that the Messenger of Allah (SAW) said: Whoever performs ablution, let him rinse out his nose [*istinthar*]; and whoever wipes with stones, let him use an odd number.

*Sahih Muslim, The book of purity*

عن إبن جريج عن عطاء قال يُتوضأ من الرُعاف إذا ظهر فسال مما قلّ منه أو كثُر

المصنف لعبد الرزاق كتاب الطهارة

Ibn Juraij related from 'Ataa, who said: Ablution is to be performed from nosebleeds, whenever it appears and flows out, a little or a lot of it.

*'Abd Al-Razzaq, the Musannaf, The book of purity*

عن قتادة قال إذا رعف الانسان فلم يُقلِع فإنه يسُدّ منخَره ويصلي وإن خاف أن يدخل جوفه فليصل وإن سال فإنّ عمر قد صلى وجُرحه يثعب دماً

المصنف لعبد الرزاق كتاب الطهارة

From Qatada, who said: Whenever a man has a nosebleed that does not subside, even damming up his nostril, and he is in prayer, even if he fears that it might go inside him, let him pray, and even if it flows out; indeed 'Umar prayed while his wounds were oozing blood.

*'Abd Al-Razzaq, the Musannaf, The book of purity*

عن عبد الرحمان بن حرملة الاسلمي أنه قال رأيت سعيد بن المسيب يرعُف فيخرج منه الدم حتى تختضب
أصابعه من الدم ألذي يخرج من أنفه ثم يصلي ولا يتوضأ

موطأ مالك كتاب الطهارة

From 'Abd Al-Rahman ibn Harmala Al-Aslami, who said: I saw Sa'id ibn Al-Musayyib
having a nosebleed, and blood came out of him until his fingers became smeared with
the blood coming out of his nose; then he prayed, but did not perform ablution.

*Muwatta' Malik, The book of purity*

وقال عروة بن مسعود حين وجّهته قريش عام القضية إلى رسول الله ﷺ ورأى من تعظيم أصحابه له ما رأى
وأنه لا يتوضأ إلا ابتدروا وضوءَه وكادوا يقتتلون عليه ولا يبصُق بُصاقاً ولا يتنخّم نخامةً إلا تلقّوها بأكُفّهم
فدلكوا بها وجوههم وأجسادهم ولا تَسقط منه شعرة إلا ابتدروها وإذا أمرهم بأمر ابتدروا أمره وإذا تكلّم
خفضوا اصواتَهم عنده وما يُحدّدون إليه النظر تعظيماً له

الشفا للقاضي عياض اليحصبي القسم الثاني فيما يجب على الأنام من حقوقه ﷺ فصل في عادة الصحابة في تعظيمه ﷺ وتوقيره وإجلاله

'Urwa ibn Mas'ud said, when the Quraish directed him to the Messenger of Allah
(SAW) in the year of the issue, and he saw what he saw of how the Companions
exalted Him, that hardly did He perform ablution but that they would rush to get his
ablution water, and they almost killed each other over it. And hardly did He spit out
something, or clear his throat of phlegm, but that they would catch it in the palms
of their hands, and rub it over their faces and their bodies. And hardly did a hair fall
from him, but that they would rush to get it. Whenever He ordered them to do
something, they rushed to his order; and whenever He talked, they lowered their
voices in his presence; and they did not fix their gaze on him out of exaltation
towards him.

*Al-qadi 'Iyad Al-Yahsubi, Al-shifa, Part Two: Regarding the rights of His (SAW) that are due on all of creation,*
*Section: regarding the custom of the Companions in exalting him (SAW), venerating him, and revering him*

عن ابي ذر عن النبي ﷺ قال عُرضت عليَّ أعمال أمتي حَسَنُها وسيِّئُها فوجدت في محَاسن اعمالها الأذى يُماط
عن الطريق ووجدت في مساوئ اعمالها النخاعة تكون في المسجد لا تُدفن

صحيح مسلم كتاب المساجد ومواضع الصلاة

Abu Dharr related from the Prophet (SAW), who said: The deeds of my *ummah* were laid out before me – the best of them and the worst of them; and I saw the removal of harm from the road as among their good deeds, and phlegm on the mosque that had not been buried as among their worst deeds.

*Sahih Muslim, The book of mosques and places of prayer*


عن عائشة قالت قال رسول الله ﷺ من أصابه قيء أو رُعاف أو قلس أو مذي فلينصرف فليتوضأ ثم ليبنِ على
صلاته وهو في ذلك لا يتكلم

سنن إبن ماجه كتاب إقامة الصلاة وألسنة فيها

From 'Aishah, who said: The Messenger of Allah (SAW) said: Whoever is overtaken by vomiting, nosebleed, regurgitation, or pre-ejaculate, let him depart [from prayer] and perform ablution, then resume his prayer, all the while not talking.

*Sunan Ibn Majah, The book of calling to prayer and the sunnah regarding it*


عن ابي هريرة عن رسول الله ﷺ قال إذا صلى أحدكم نخلع نعليه فلا يؤذِ بهما أحداً ليجعلهما بين رجليه أو
ليصلِّ فيهما

سنن ابي داود كتاب الصلاة

Abu Huraira related that the Messenger of Allah (SAW) said: Whenever any of you prays, and takes off his sandals, let him not harm anyone with them; he should put them between his legs or pray with them on.

*Sunan Abu Dawud, The book of prayer*


عن مجاهد قال قال عمر من نقى أنفه أو مس إبطه توضأ

المصنف لإبن ابي شيبة كتاب الطهارة

From Mujahid, who said: 'Umar said: Whoever blows his nose or touches his armpit is to perform ablution.

*Ibn Abi Shayba, Al-musannaf, The book of purity*

# الأكل والشرب

# Eating and drinking

حارثة بن وهب الخزاعي قال حدثتني حفصة زوج النبي ﷺ أن النبي ﷺ كان يجعل يمينه لطعامه وشرابه وثيابه ويجعل شماله لما سوى ذلك

سنن ابي داود كتاب الطهارة

Haritha ibn Wahb Al-Khuza'i said: Hafsa, the Prophet's (SAW) wife, related to me that the Prophet (SAW) used his right hand for his food, his drink, and his clothing, and used his left otherwise.

*Sunan Abu Dawud, The book of purity*

عن جابر عن رسول الله ﷺ قال لا تأكلوا بالشمال فإنّ الشيطان يأكل بالشمال

صحيح مسلم كتاب الأشربة

Jabir related from the Messenger of Allah (SAW) who said: Do not eat with the left, for Satan eats with the left.

*Sahih Muslim, The book of drinks*

عبدالله بن كعب أخبره عن أبيه كعب عن أنه حدثهم أن رسول الله ﷺ كان يأكل بثلاث أصابع فإذا فرغ لعقها

صحيح مسلم كتاب الأشربة

Abdullah ibn Ka'b related from his father Ka'b that he told them that the Prophet (SAW) ate with three fingers, and when He was done He licked them.

*Sahih Muslim, The book of drinks*

عن جبر أن النبي ﷺ أمر بلعق الأصابع والصحفة وقال إنكم لا تدرون في أية البركة

صحيح مسلم كتاب الأشربة

Jabir related that the Prophet (SAW) ordered people to lick their fingers and the plate; He said: Indeed you all do not know in which part the blessing is.

*Sahih Muslim, The book of drinks*

عن أنس أن النبي ﷺ كان إذا ما أكل طعاماً لعق أصابعه الثلاث وقال إذا ما وقعت لقمة أحدكم فليُمط عنها الأذى وليأكلها ولا يدعها للشيطان

جامع الترمذي كتاب الأطعمة

Anas related that the Prophet (SAW), whenever he ate food, would lick His three fingers; and He said: Whenever a bite of food falls from any of you, he should remove what is harmful from it and then eat it and not leave it to Satan.

*Sunan Al-Tirmidhi, The book of foods*

عن إبن عباس أن النبي ﷺ قال إذا أكل أحدكم فلا يمسح يده حتى يلعَقها أو يُلعِقها

صحيح البخاري كتاب الأطعمة

Ibn 'Abbas related that the Prophet (SAW) said: Whenever any of you has eaten, he should not wipe his hand until he has licked it or gotten it licked.

*Sahih Bukhari, The book of food*

عن إبن عباس أن النبي ﷺ شرب لبناً ثم مضمض

صحيح إبن خزيمة كتاب الوضوء

Ibn 'Abbas related that the Prophet (SAW) drank milk and then rinsed his mouth.

*Sahih Ibn Khuzaimah, The book of ablution [wudu']*

عن عائشة بنت سعد بن ابي وقاص عن أبيها أن النبي ﷺ كان يشرب قائماً

الشمائل المحمدية للترمذي باب ما جاء في شرب رسول الله ﷺ

'Aishah bint Sa'd ibn Abi Waqqas related from her father that the Prophet (SAW) drank standing up.

*Al-Tirmidhi, Al-shama'il al-Muhammadiya, The section concerning how the Messenger of Allah (SAW) drank*

عن ابي سعيد الخدري قال سمعتُ رسول الله ﷺ وهو يقال له إنه يُستقى لك من بئر بُضاعة وهي بئر يُلقى فيها لحوم الكلاب والمحايض وعذِر الناس. فقال رسول الله ﷺ إنّ الماء طهور لا ينجسه شيءٌ

سنن ابي داود كتاب الطهارة

Abu Sa'id Al-Khudri said: I heard the Messenger of Allah (SAW) being told: You have been given to drink from the well of *Buda'a*, a well into which the flesh of dogs, menstrual items, and people's waste are thrown. The Messenger of Allah (SAW) said: Indeed water is pure and nothing makes it dirty.

*Sunan Abu Dawud, The book of purity*

عن أبي هريرة رضي الله عنه قال قام رسول الله ﷺ يخطب فقال إن الله عز وجل أمرني أن أعلمكم ما علمني
وأن أؤدبكم ... وإذا رفعتم المائدة فإكنسوا ما تحتها فإن الشياطين يلتقطون ما تحتها فلا تجعلوا لهم نصيباً في طعامكم

نوادر الاصول في معرفة أحاديث الرسول لحكيم الترمذي الأصل السادس والسبعون

From Abu Huraira (may Allah be pleased with him) who said: The Messenger of
Allah (SAW) got up to give a speech, and said: Truly Allah Mighty and Sublime has
ordered me to teach you all what He has taught me, and to discipline you all ...
Whenever you get up from the table, brush away what is under it, for indeed the
devils collect what is under it; do not let them have a share in your food.

*Al-Hakim Al-Tirmidhi, Nawadir Al-usul, Foundation seventy-six*


عن عبدالله بن ابي قتادة عن أبيه قال قال رسول الله ﷺ إذا شرب أحدكم فلا يتنفس في الإناء

صحيح البخاري كتاب الأشربة

'Abdullah ibn Abi Qatada related from his father, who said: The Messenger of Allah
(SAW) said: When any of you drinks, he should not not breathe in and out of the vessel.

*Sahih Al-Bukhari, The book of drinks*


أبو غطفان المُرّي أنه سمع أبا هريرة يقول قال رسول الله ﷺ لا يشربنَّ أحد منكم قائماً فمن نسي فليستقئ

صحيح مسلم كتاب الأشربة

Abu Ghatafan Al-Murri heard Abu Huraira say: The Messenger of Allah (SAW) said:
Let no one among you drink while standing up; anyone who forgets should vomit.

*Sahih Muslim, The book of drinks*


عن حذيفة قال ... فقال رسول الله ﷺ إنّ الشيطان يستحلّ الطعام إن لا يُذكَر إسم الله عليه

صحيح مسلم كتاب الأشربة

From Hudhaifa who said: ... The Messenger of Allah (SAW) said: Satan considers
permissible any food upon which the name of Allah has not been mentioned.

*Sahih Muslim, The book of drinks*


عن جابر قال: نهى رسول الله ﷺ عن أكل البصل والكراث

صحيح مسلم كتاب المساجد ومواضع الصلاة

Jabir said: The Messenger of Allah (SAW) forbade the eating of onions and leeks.

*Sahih Muslim, The book of mosques and places of prayer*

عن جابر بن عبدالله عن النبي ﷺ قال من أكل من هذه البَقلة الثوم وقال مرة من أكل البصل والثوم
والكُرّات فلا يقربنَّ مسجدنا فإن الملائكة تتأذّى مما يتأذى منه بن آدم

صحيح مسلم كتاب المساجد ومواضع الصلاة

Jabir ibn Abdullah related from the Prophet (SAW), who said: Whoever eats this garlic
plant – or at one point He may have said whoever eats onion and garlic and leeks –
let him not ever come close to our mosque, for indeed the angels are harmed by what
the children of Adam are harmed by.

*Sahih Muslim, The book of mosques and places of prayer*

عن ابي عثمان النهدي قال قال رسول الله ﷺ إذا أُعطيَ أحدكُم الريحان فلا يردّه فإنه خرج من الجنة

جامع الترمذي كتاب الأدب

From Abu 'Uthman Al-Nahdi who said: The Messenger of Allah (SAW) said:
Whenever any of you is given basil, he should not refuse it, for indeed it has come
from *Jannah*.

*Sunan Al-Tirmidhi, The book of manners*

عن ابن عباس أن النبي ﷺ قال البركة تنزل وسط الطعام فكلوا من حافتيه ولا تأكلوا من وسطه

جامع الترمذي كتاب الأطعمة

Ibn 'Abbas related that the Prophet (SAW) said: Indeed the blessing comes down in
the middle of the food, so eat from the edges and do not eat from the middle.

*Sunan Al-Tirmidhi, The book of foods*

عن ابي هريرة عن النبي ﷺ قال ... من أكل فما تخلل فليلفظ وما لاك بلسانه فليبتلع من فعل فقد أحسن
ومن لا فلا حرج

سنن أبي داود كتاب الطهارة

Abu Huraira related from the Prophet (SAW) who said: ... Whoever eats any food
should throw out what he has picked from between his teeth, and swallow what he
has worked with his tongue. Whoever does this has done well, although whoever
does not, there is no blame.

*Sunan Abu Dawud, The book of purity*

عن جابر بن عبدالله أنه قال أقبل رسول الله ﷺ من شعب من الجبل وقد قضى حاجته وبين أيدينا تمر على ترس أو جحفة فدعوناه فأكل معنا وما مس ماءً

سنن أبي داود كتاب الأطعمة

From Jabir ibn 'Abdullah who said: The Messenger of Allah (SAW) came down a side trail on the mountain, having fulfilled His need. And we had among us some dates on a shield or leather shield, so we called Him, and He ate with us, not having used any water [to wash].

*Sunan Abu Dawud, The book of foods*

قال يحيى وسئل مالك هل في القيء وضوء قال لا ولكن ليتمضمض من ذلك وليغسل فاه وليس عليه وضوء

موطأ مالك كتاب الطهارة

Yahya said: Malik was asked: Is ablution [*wudu'*] necessary from vomit? He said: No, but one should rinse his mouth out from it and wash his mouth, but there is no *wudu'* necessary.

*Muwatta Malik, The book of purity*

عن عبدالله بن عباس أن رسول الله ﷺ أكل كتف شاة ثم صلى ولم يتوضأ

موطأ مالك كتاب الطهارة

'Abdullah ibn 'Abbas related that the Messenger of Allah (SAW) ate a shoulder of lamb, then prayed, withouth having performed *wudu'*.

*Muwatta Malik, The book of purity*

عن ابي هريرة أن رسول الله ﷺ أكل كتف شاة فمضمض وغسل يديه وصلى

سنن إبن ماجه كتاب الطهارة وسننها

Abu Huraira related that the Messenger of Allah (SAW) ate a shoulder of lamb, then rinsed out his mouth, washed his hands, and prayed.

*Sunan Ibn Majah, The book of purity and its sunnah*

عن إبن عمر قال تجشّأ رجل عند النبي ﷺ فقال كُفّ جشاءك عنا فإن أطولكم جوعاً يوم القيامة أكثركم شبعاً في دار الدنيا

سنن إبن ماجه كتاب الأطعمة

From Ibn 'Umar, who said: A man belched in front of the Prophet (SAW), and He said: Stop belching around us, for truly those of you who will feel the most hunger on the day of resurrection are those of you who satisfy themselves most in the abode of this world.

*Sunan Ibn Majah, The book of foods*


عن عطاء قال إن قاء إنسان أو استقاء فقد وجب عليه الوضوء وإن قلس فقد وجب عليه الوضوء

المصنف لعبد الرزاق كتاب الطهارة

From 'Ataa who said: If a man vomits or throws up, it becomes obligatory for him to perform ablution [*wudu'*]; even if he regurgitates, it becomes obligatory for him to perform ablution.

*'Abd Al-Razzaq, the Musannaf, The book of purity*


عن ابي الدرداء أن رسول الله ﷺ قاء فأفطر فتوضأ

جامع الترمذي كتاب الطهارة

Abu Al-Dardaa related that the Messenger of Allah (SAW) vomited, thereby breaking the fast, and so He performed ablution.

*Sunan Al-Tirmidhi, The book of purity*


عن مقدام بن معديكرب قال سمعت رسول الله ﷺ يقول ما ملأ آدمي وعاءً شراً من بطنٍ بِحَسْب إبن آدم أُكلاتٌ يُقِمْنَ صُلبه فإن كان لا محالة فثُلُث لطعامه وثلث لشَرابه وثلث لنَفَسه

جامع الترمذي كتاب الزهد

From Miqdam ibn Ma'dikarib, who said: I heard the Messenger of Allah (SAW) say: No one fills a vessel worse than a belly; it is sufficient for a person to eat what will hold up his backbone; but if there is no way around it, then a third for his food, a third for his drink, and a third for him to breathe.

*Sunan Al-Tirmidhi, The book of abstaining*

عن ابن جريج قال قلت لعطاء أرأيت إن قلس رجلٌ فبلغ صدره أو حلقه ولم يبلغ الفم قال فلا وضوء عليه قلت أرأيت إن بلغ الحلق فلم يمجّها وأعادها في جوفه قال فقد وجب الوضوء إذا بلغت الفم فظهرت قلت أتكره أن يعيدها المرء في جوفه بعدما يظهر بفيه قال نعم ولا أكرهه لمأثم ولكن أقذره

المصنف لعبد الرزاق كتاب الطهارة

From Ibn Juraij, who said: I asked 'Ataa: What do you think if someone regurgitates and it reaches his chest or his throat but doesn't reach his mouth? He said: He does not need to perform ablution. I asked: What do you think if it reaches the throat and he doesn't spit it out but sends it back inside himself? He said: He is obligated to perform ablution if it reaches the mouth, since it has appeared. I asked: Do you dislike for someone to send it back inside himself after it has appeared in his mouth? He said: Yes; I don't dislike it to the point of a wrongdoing, but I see it as filthy.

*'Abd Al-Razzaq, the Musannaf, The book of purity*

عن طاوس ومجاهد قالا ليس في القلس وضوء

المصنف لعبد الرزاق كتاب الطهارة

From Tawus and Mujahid, who both said: There is no ablution for regurgitating.

*'Abd Al-Razzaq, the Musannaf, The book of purity*

عبد الرزاق قال قلت لعطاء أرأيت إن تجشأت نخرج شيءٌ من الطعام من حلقي وكان نشب في حلقي وليس من معدتي أتوضأ منه قال لا قلت أرأيت لو تجشأت لجاء من الأوداج والطعام شيء يسيرٌ قال لعَمري إني لأتنخم شيئاً كثيراً ثم يأتي الشيء من حلقي ومن الرأس فليس في ذلك وضوء إلا ما خرج من جوفك من معدتك

المصنف لعبد الرزاق كتاب الطهارة

['Abd Al-Razzaq] said: I asked 'Ataa: What do you think if I belch and some food comes out of my throat that was stuck in my throat, but it didn't come from my stomach – should I perform ablution from it? He said: No. I said: What do you think if I belch and it comes from the bottom of my neck and just a little bit of food? He said: I swear by my life, indeed I clear a lot of stuff from my throat, then it comes up from my throat and from the top part, but there is no ablution for that, only what comes out from inside you, from your stomach.

*'Abd Al-Razzaq, the Musannaf, The book of purity*

عن علي بن الأقمر قال سمعت أبا جحيفة قال قال رسول الله ﷺ لا آكل مُتَّكِئًا

سنن أبي داود كتاب الطهارة

From 'Ali ibn Al-Aqmar who said: I heard Abu Juhaifa say: The Messenger of Allah (SAW) said: I do not eat reclining.

*Sunan Abu Dawud, The book of purity*

عن إبن عباس قال نهى رسول الله ﷺ أن يُتَنَفَّس في الإناء أو يُنفخ فيه

سنن أبي داود كتاب الأشربة

From Ibn 'Abbas who said: The Messenger of Allah (SAW) forbade people to breathe in and out of a [drinking] vessel, or to blow in it.

*Sunan Abu Dawud, The book of beverages*

عزرة بن ثابت قال أخبرني ثمامة بن عبدالله قال كان أنس يتنفس في الإناء مرتين أو ثلاثاً وزعم أن النبي ﷺ كان يَتنفس ثلاثاً

صحيح البخاري كتاب الأشربة

'Azra ibn Thabit said: Thumama ibn Abdullah related to me, saying that Anas would breathe in and out of a vessel twice or three times; and he alleged that the Prophet (SAW) would breathe in and out three times.

*Sahih Al-Bukhari, The book of drinks*

عن ابي هريرة رضي الله عنه عن النبي ﷺ قال كل عمل إبن آدم له إلا الصوم فإنه لي وأنا أجزي به ولخلوف فم الصائم أطيب عند الله من ريح المسك

صحيح البخاري كتاب اللباس

Abu Huraira (may Allah be pleased with him) related from the Prophet (SAW), who said: All of the deeds of a son of Adam are for him, except fasting; for indeed that is for me, and I give the reward for it; and the altered smell of the mouth of a fasting person is more fragrant to Allah then the scent of musk.

*Sahih Al-Bukhari, The book of dress*

وهو أن يُمسك عن الأكل قبل السبع ويلعق أصابعه ثم يمسحها بالمنديل ثم يغسلها ويلتقط فتات الطعام قال رسول الله ﷺ من أكل ما يسقط من المائدة عاش في سعة

إحياء علوم الدين للغزالي كتاب آداب الأكل القسم الثالث ما يستحب بعد الطعام

And this [what is desirable after food] is that a person cease from eating before becoming satiated, and that he lick his fingers and then wipe them with a napkin, then wash them and gather the food crumbs. The Messenger of Allah (SAW) said: Whoever eats what falls from the tablespread will live in abundance.

*Al-Ghazali, Ihyaa 'Ulum Al-din, The book of conduct in eating, Section three: what is desirable after food*

أبو اليمان المعلى بن راشد قال حدثتني جدتي أم عاصم وكانت أم ولد لسنان بن سلمة قالت دخل علينا نبيشة الخير ونحن نأكل في قَصعة فحدثنا أن رسول الله ﷺ قال من أكل في قصعة ثم لحسها استغفرت له القصعة

جامع الترمذي كتاب الأطعمة

Abu Al-Yaman Al-Mu'alla ibn Rashid said: My grandmother Umm 'Asim – she was a servant-mother [*umm walad*, "mother of children"] to Sinan ibn Salama – she said: Nubaisha Al-Khair came in to see us while we were eating from a large bowl. He related to us that the Messenger of Allah (SAW) said: Whoever eats from a bowl and then licks it up – the bowl will seek forgiveness for him on his behalf.

*Sunan Al-Tirmidhi, The book of foods*

روى الطبراني من حديث العرباض بن سارية قال قال رسول الله ﷺ من لعق الصحفة ولعق أصابعه أشبعه الله في الدنيا والآخرة

عمدة القاري لبدر الدين العيني كتاب الأطعمة باب لعق الأصابع ومصها قبل أن تُمسح بالمنديل

Al-Tabarani relates from a hadith of Al-'Irbad ibn Sariya, who said: The Messenger of Allah (SAW) said: Whoever licks the dish and licks his fingers – Allah will satisfy him in this world and the next.

*Badr Al-deen Al-'aini, 'Umdat Al-qari, The book of foods; Section: licking and sucking the fingers before wiping them with a napkin*

عن إبن عباس قال كان رسول الله ﷺ يُنبَذ له الزبيب في السِّقاء فيشربه يومه والغد وبعد الغد فإذا كان مساء الثالثة شربه وسقاه فإن فضل شيء أهراقه

صحيح مسلم كتاب الأشربة

From Ibn 'Abbas, who said: Raisins would be soaked and fermented [*yunbadh*] for the Messenger of Allah (SAW) in waterskins, and He would drink it on the day it was made, the day after, and the day after that. And on the evening of the third day, He would drink it and give it to people to drink, and then if anything was left over He would spill it out.

*Sahih Muslim, The book of drinks*

عن عطاء بن يسار أن رسول الله ﷺ نهى أن ينبذ البُسر والرطب جميعاً والتمر والزبيب جميعاً

موطأ مالك كتاب الأشربة

'Ataa ibn Yasar related that the Messenger of Allah (SAW) forbade for unripe and ripe dates to be soaked and fermented together, or dates and raisins together.

*Muwatta Malik, The book of drinks*

وثبت في صحيح مسلم أنه ﷺ كان يُنتبذ له أول الليل ويشربه إذا أصبح يومه ذلك والليلة التي تجيء والغد والليلة الأخرى والغد إلى العصر فإن بقى منه شيء سقاه الخادم أو أمر به فصب

وهذا النبيذ هو ماء يطرح فيه تمرُ يحلِّيه وهو يدخل في الغذاء والشراب وله نفع عظيم في زيادة القوة وحفظ الصحة ولم يكن يشربه بعد ثلاث خوفاً من تغيّره إلى الاسكار

الطب النبوي لإبن قيّم

It is affirmed in *Sahih Muslim* that wine [*nabidh*] would be prepared for Him (SAW) at the beginning of the night, and He would drink it – whenever He arose – on its day, and on the following night, and the next day and night, and the day after that up until the afternoon. If anything remained, He would give it to the servants to drink, or order it to be poured out.

This *nabidh* is water into which dates are added to sweeten it, and is included as part of food and drink, and is of great benefit in increasing strength and staying healthy; however He did not drink it after three days, out of fear that it might have become intoxicating.

*Ibn Qayyim, Al-tibb Al-nabawi*

عن جابر قال سمعت النبيّ ﷺ يقول إن أهل الجنة يأكلون فيها ويشربون ولا يتفُلون ولا يبولون ولا يتغوّطون ولا يمتخطون قالوا فما بال الطعام قال جشاءٌ ورشح كرشح المسك يلهَمون التسبيح والتحميد كما يلهمون النفس

صحيح مسلم كتاب الجنة وصفة نعيمها وأهلها

From Jabir who said: I heard the Prophet (SAW) say: Indeed the people of *Jannah* eat and drink there, but they do not spit, urinate, defecate, or clear themselves of mucus. The people said: So what happens to food? He said: Belching and sweat like sweat of musk; and *tasbih* ["Subhana Allah"] and *tahmid* ["Alhamdu lillah"] will come to them naturally just like breathing comes to them naturally.

*Sahih Muslim, The book of Jannah and the description of its bliss and its people*

# النظافة

## Cleanliness

عن ابي مالك الأشعري قال قال رسول الله ﷺ الطُّهور شَطر الايمان

صحيح مسلم كتاب الطهارة

From Abu Malik Al-Ash'ari, who said: The Messenger of Allah (SAW) said: Purity is half of belief.

*Sahih Muslim, The book of purity*

﴿ إِذْ يُغَشِّيكُمُ النُّعَاسَ أَمَنَةً مِّنْهُ وَيُنَزِّلُ عَلَيْكُم مِّنَ السَّمَاءِ مَاءً لِّيُطَهِّرَكُم بِهِ وَيُذْهِبَ عَنكُمْ رِجْزَ الشَّيْطَانِ وَلِيَرْبِطَ عَلَى قُلُوبِكُمْ وَيُثَبِّتَ بِهِ الْأَقْدَامَ ﴾ الأنفال ١١

*{ Behold He covered you with slumber as a means of safety from Him, and sent down water from heaven on you to purify you with it, to remove the filth of Satan from you, to strengthen your hearts, and to affirm your feet by it. }* Al-anfal 11

وقوله ﴿ لِيُطَهِّرَكُم بِهِ ﴾ أي من حدث أصغر أو أكبر وهو تطهير الظاهر ﴿ وَيُذْهِبَ عَنكُمْ رِجْزَ الشَّيْطَانِ ﴾ أي من وسوسة أو خاطر سيئ وهو تطهير الباطن

تفسير ابن كثير

His word: { To purify you with it } : that is, from any bodily occurrence, large or small; this is outer purification. { To remove the filth of Satan from you } : that is, whisperings and evil notions; this is inner purification.

*Tafsir Ibn Kathir*

•     •     •

فنقول إنه إتفق المسلمون على أن الطهارة الشرعية طهارتان طهارة من الحدث وطهارة من الخبث واتفقوا على
أن الطهارة من الحدث ثلاثة اصناف وضوء وغسل وبدل منهما وهو التيمم

بداية المجتهد ونهاية المقتصد لإبن رشد كتاب الطهارة من الحدث

We can say that Muslims are in agreement that legitimate purification [tahara] consists of two kinds of purification: purification from hadath [bodily occurrences that make one ritually impure] and purification from khabath [harmful external impurities]. And they are in agreement that there are three manners of purity from hadath: ablution [wudu'], full washing/bathing [ghusl], and a substitute for these two, this being dry wiping with dust [tayammum].

*Ibn Rushd, Bidaya Al-mujtahid wa Nihaya Al-Muqtasid, The book of purification from bodily occurrences [hadath]*

عن إبن عباس قال من ألسنة أن لا يصلي الرجل بالتيمم إلا صلاة واحدة ثم يتيمم للصلاة الاخرى

المصنف لعبد الرزاق كتاب الطهارة

From Ibn 'Abbas, who said: It is *sunnah* that after *tayammum* a man may only pray one prayer; then he must perform *tayammum* for the next prayer.

*'Abd Al-Razzaq, the Musannaf, The book of purity*

فأما الدليل على وجوبها فالكتاب وألسنة والاجماع أما الكتاب فقوله تعالى ﴿ يا أيها الذين آمنوا إذا قمتم إلى
الصلاة فاغسلوا وجوهكم وأيديكم إلى المرافق ﴾ الآية فإنه إتفق المسلمون على أن إمتثال هذا الخطاب واجب
على كل من لزمته الصلاة إذا دخل وقتها وأما ألسنة فقوله ﷺ لا يقبل الله صلاة بغير طهور ولا صدقة من
غلول وقوله ﷺ لا يقبل الله صلاة من أحدث حتى يتوضأ وهذان الحديثان ثابتان عند أئمة النقل وأما الاجماع
فإنه لم ينقل عن أحد من المسلمين في ذلك خلاف ولو كان هناك خلاف لنقل إذ العادات تقتضي ذلك
وأما من تجب عليه فهو البالغ العاقل وذلك أيضاً ثابت بالسنة والاجماع أما ألسنة فقوله ﷺ رُفع القلم عن
ثلاث فذكر الصبي حتى يحتلم والمجنون حتى يُفيق

بداية المجتهد ونهاية المقتصد لإبن رشد كتاب الطهارة من الحدث

Proof that it [ablution, *wudu'*] is obligatory is in the Book, the *sunnah*, and universal consensus. From the Book: the word of the Most High { Oh you who have believed, whenever you get up to go to prayer, wash your faces and your arms up to the elbows } and the rest of the verse [Al-ma'ida 6]. Indeed Muslims agree that complying with this message is obligatory for all who are to observe prayer, whenever they come upon its appointed time. Regarding *sunnah*, He (SAW) has said: Allah does not accept prayer without purification, nor charity from ill-gotten wealth [*ghulul*, i.e. taken from the booty before it is duly divided] [Sahih Muslim]. And He (SAW) said: Allah does not accept the prayer of anyone who has had a bodily occurrence [hadath] until he performs wudu' [Sahih Al-Bukhari]. These two hadiths are firm among the authorities in the transmitting of tradition. As for universal consensus: indeed no disagreement has been reported from any Muslim regarding this; and if there were a disagreement, it would have been reported; customary practice calls for this. As regards those for whom this is obligatory: those who have come of age and are of sound mind. This is also affirmed by the sunnah and by universal consensus; in the sunnah by what He (SAW) said: The pen is lifted from three [i.e. they are not held accountable] – and He mentioned young boys before they have a wet dream as well as someone who is insane before he comes to his senses. [Abu Dawud and others]

*Ibn Rushd, Bidaya Al-mujtahid wa Nihaya Al-Muqtasid, The book of purification from bodily occurrences [hadath]*

أنّ رجلاً أتى النبي ﷺ فقال يا رسول الله كيف الطهور فدعا بماءٍ في إناءٍ فغسل كفيه ثلاثاً ثم غسل وجهه ثلاثاً ثم غسل ذراعيه ثلاثاً ثم مسح برأسه فأدخل إصبعيه السباحتين في أذنيه ومسح بإبهاميه على ظاهر أذنيه وبالسباحتين باطن أذنيه ثم غسل رجليه ثلاثاً ثم قال هكذا الوضوء فمن زاد على هذا أو نقص فقد أساء وظلم

سنن أبي داود كتاب الطهارة

A certain man came to the Prophet (SAW) and said: Oh Messenger of Allah, how is purification performed? So He called for some water in a vessel and washed his palms three times, then He washed his face three times, then He washed his arms three times, then He wiped his head, then He inserted his two index fingers into his ears and wiped the outside of his ears with his thumbs and with the index fingers the front inside of his ears, then He washed his feet three times, then He said: This is how ablution is, and whoever adds to this or takes away from it has acted wrongly and unjustly.

*Sunan Abu Dawud, The book of purity*

عروة قالت ذكر رسول الله ﷺ ما يتوضَّأ منه فقال من مسّ الذكر

سنن النسائي كتاب الغسل والتيمم

'Urwah said: The Messenger of Allah (SAW) mentioned why you have to do ablution [wudu']; He said: From touching your penis.

*Sunan Al-Nasa'i, The book of washing and dry wiping with dust [tayammum]*

والأصل في وجوب الطهارة بالمياه قوله تعالى ﴿ ويُنزِّل عليكم من السماء ماءً ليُطهركم به ﴾ وقوله ﴿ فلم تجدوا ماءً فتيمموا صعيداً طيباً ﴾ وأجمع العلماء على أن جميع أنواع المياه طاهرة في نفسها مطهرة لغيرها إلا ماء البحر

بداية المجتهد ونهاية المقتصد لإبن رشد كتاب الطهارة من الحدث

The basis for the obligation to perform purification with water is the word of the Most High { And He sent down water from heaven on you, to purify you with it } [Al-anfal 11], and His word { ... and can not find any water, then dry wipe with clean earth } [Al-ma'ida 6]. Scholars have come together unanimously that all types of water are pure in themselves, and can serve to purify other things, except sea water.

*Ibn Rushd, Bidaya Al-mujtahid wa Nihaya Al-Muqtasid, The book of purification from bodily occurrences [hadath]*

كيفية الغسل وهو أن يضع الاناء عن يمينه ثم يسمي الله تعالى ويغسل يديه ثلاثاً ثم يستنجي ويزيل ما على بدنه من نجاسة إن كانت ثم يتوضأ وضوءه للصلاة كما سبق إلا غسل قدميه فإنه يؤخرهما فإن غسلهما ثم وضعهما على الأرض كالاضاعة للماء ثم يصب الماء على شقّه الأيمن ثلاثاً ثم على شقه الأيسر ثلاثاً ثم على رأسه ثلاثاً ثم يدلك ما أقبل من بدنه وما أدبر ويخلل شعر الرأس واللحية ويوصل الماء إلى منابتها ما كثف منه أو حفّ وليس على المرأة نقض الضفائر إلا إذا علمت أن الماء لا يصل إلى خلل الشعر ويتعهد معاطف البدن وليتقِ أن يمس ذكره في أثناء ذلك فإن فعل ذلك فليعد الوضوء وإن توضأ قبل الغسل فلا يعيده بعد الغسل

إحياء علوم الدين للغزالي كتاب أسرار الطهارة ومهماتها

[Manner of performing *ghusl*, full washing] is that one place the vessel on his right side, then invoke the name of Allah Most High [i.e. by saying "*Bismillah...*"], wash his hands three times, then perform a general cleansing as we have described, removing the filth from his body if there is any. Then he is to perform ablution [*wudu'*] as is done for prayer, as stated earlier, but without washing his feet; these he is to delay, for indeed if he washes them, and then places them on the ground, it is a waste of water. Then he is to pour water over his right side three times, then over his left side three times, then over his head three times, then he is to rub down his front and back sides, then run through his head and beard hair, then return the water to where it came from, whether much or little. (A woman is not required to undo her hairlocks unless she knows that the water will not reach down to the roots.) And he is to pay attention to the crooks of his body, and take care not to touch his penis during all of this; if he does, he is to repeat ablution. And if he performs *wudu'* before *ghusl*, he does not need to repeat it following *ghusl*.

*Al-Ghazali, Ihyaa 'Ulum Al-din, The book of the foundations of purity [tahara] and its requirements*

إختلف علماء الأمصار في انتقاض الوضوء مما يخرج من الجسد من النجس على ثلاثة مذاهب فإعتبر قوم في ذلك الخارج وحده من أي موضع خرج وعلى أي جهة خرج وهو أبو حنيفة وأصحابه والثوري وأحمد وجماعة ولهم من الصحابة السلف فقالوا كل نجاسة تسيل من الجسد وتخرج منه يجب منها الوضوء كالدم والرعاف الكثير والفصد والحجامة والقيء إلا البلغم عند ابي حنيفة وقال أبو يوسف من أصحاب ابي حنيفة إنه إذا ملأ الفم ففيه الوضوء ولم يعتبر أحد من هؤلاء اليسير من الدم إلا مجاهد وإعتبر قوم آخرون المخرجين الذكر والدبر فقالوا كل ما خرج من هذين السبيلين فهو ناقض الوضوء من أي شيء خرج من دم أو حصا أو بلغم وعلى أي وجه كان خروجه على سبيل الصحة أو على سبيل المرض وممن قال بهذا القول الشافعي وأصحابه ومحمد بن عبد الحكم من أصحاب مالك وإعتبر قوم آخرون الخارج والمخرج وصفة الخروج فقالوا كل ما خرج من السبيلين مما هو معتاد خروجه وهو البول والغائط والمذي والودي والريح إذا كان خروجه على وجه الصحة فهو ينقض الوضوء فلم يروا في الدم والحصاة والدود وضوءاً ولا في السلس وممن قال بهذا القول مالك وجل أصحابه والسبب في اختلافهم أنه لما أجمع المسلمون على انتقاض الوضوء مما يخرج من السبيلين من غائط وبول وريح ومذي لظاهر الكتاب ولتظاهر الآثار بذلك تطرق إلى ذلك ثلاثة إحتمالات أحدها أن يكون الحكم انما علق بأعيان هذه الأشياء فقط المتفق عليها على ما رآه مالك رحمه الله الاحتمال الثاني أن يكون الحكم انما علق بهذه من جهة أنها أنجاس خارجة من البدن لكون الوضوء طهارة والطهارة إنما يؤثر فيها النجس والاحتمال الثالث أن يكون الحكم أيضاً انما علق بها من جهة أنها خارجة من هذين السبيلين

بداية المجتهد ونهاية المقتصد لإبن رشد كتاب الطهارة من الحدث

Scholars of the major cities disagree regarding the invalidation of *wudu'* by impurity [*najas*] that comes out of the body, into three schools of doctrine. In this regard, one group considers that what comes out is all the same, from whatever location it comes out of, on any side it comes out of; in this group are Abu Hanifa and his companions, Al-Thawri, Ahmad, and another group, and among them are some of the Companions the forefathers; they said: All impurity that flows from the body and comes out makes *wudu'* obligatory, such as blood, severe nosebleeds, bleeding, cupping, vomiting, except mucus in Abu Hanifa's opinion. Abu Yusuf, from Abu Hanifa's companions, said: Indeed if it fills the mouth, *wudu'* is to be performed. And none of them considered a minor amount of blood except Mujahid. A second group considered the two outlets to be the penis and the anus; they said: Everything that comes out of these two passages invalidates *wudu'*, whatever blood, stones, or mucus comes out, and from whichever side it comes out, whether it comes out in a normal healthy state or in illness. Those who said this are Al-Shafi'i and his companions, Muhammad ibn 'Abd Al-Hakam from Malik's companions. Yet another group considered that what comes out as well as the place it comes out from both describe the event; they said: Everything that comes out of the two passages that normally comes out, this being urine, defecation, pre-ejaculate, prostatic fluid, and gas, whenever it comes out in a normal healthy state, invalidates *wudu'*. They did not consider *wudu'* necessary for blood, stones, or worms, nor for urinary incontinence. Among those who said this are

Malik and the majority of his companions. The reason for the disagreement is that when the Muslims unanimously agreed on the invalidation of *wudu'* by the defecation, urine, gas, and pre-ejaculate that come out of the two passages, based on the clear meaning of the Book and what the hadith make apparent, they examined three possible considerations on this. The first of these is that the ruling should rest on the substance of these things only, those that are agreed on, according to the view of Malik (may Allah have mercy on him). The second possible consideration is that the ruling rests on these because they are impure things that come out of the body, *wudu'* being purification, and indeed purification is affected by impurity. The third possible consideration is that the ruling also rests on these considering that they come out from the two passages.

*Ibn Rushd, Bidaya Al-mujtahid wa Nihaya Al-Muqtasid, The book of purification from bodily occurrences [hadath]*

فقد قال النبي ﷺ بني الدين على النظافة وقال ﷺ مفتاح الصلاة الطهور وقال الله تعالى ﴿ فيه رجال يحبون أن يتطهروا والله يحب المطهرين ﴾ وقال النبي ﷺ الطهور نصف الايمان وقال الله تعالى ﴿ ما يريد الله ليجعل عليكم من حرج ولكن يريد ليطهّركم ﴾ فتفطنَ ذوو البصائر بهذه الظواهر أن أهم الأمور تطهير السرائر إذ يبعد أن يكون المراد بقوله ﷺ الطهور نصف الايمان عمارة الظاهر بالتنظيف بإفاضة الماء والقائه وتخريب الباطن وابقاءه مشحوناً بالأخباث والأقذار هيهات هيهات والطهارة لها أربع مراتب الاولى تطهير الظاهر عن الأحداث وعن الأخباث والفضلات والثانية تطهير الجوارح عن الجرائم والآثام والثالثة تطهير القلب عن الاخلاق المذمومة والرذائل الممقوتة والرابعة تطهير السر عما سوى الله تعالى وهي طهارة الأنبياء والصديقين إحياء علوم الدين للغزالي كتاب أسرار الطهارة ومهماتها

The Prophet (SAW) has said: The religion [*deen*] is built upon cleanliness; and He said: The key to prayer is purity; and Allah Most High said: { In it there are men who love to purify themselves; and Allah loves those who purify themselves } [*Al-tawba* 108]; and the Prophet (SAW) said: Purity is half of belief; and Allah Most High said: { Allah does not wish to make things awkward for you, but wishes to purify you } [*Al-ma'ida* 6]. And so those with understanding realize from these clear indications that the most important of issues is the purification of the innermost; it is unlikely that his (SAW) words "Purity is half of belief" mean improving the outward appearance through cleansing by pouring out and tossing aside copious amounts of water, while undermining what is inside, leaving it fraught with harmful and filthy things; oh how impossible! how impossible!

Purity consists of four degrees; the first: Purification of the outward aspect from bodily occurrences [*hadath*], harmful things [*khabith*], and secretions. Second, purification of the limbs from offenses and wrongdoings. Third, purification of the heart from loathsome character and abhorrent depravities. Fourth, purification of the innermost being from that which might be elevated as equal to Allah Most High; this is the purity of the prophets and the righteous.

*Al-Ghazali, Ihyaa 'Ulum Al-din, The book of the foundations of purity [tahara] and its requirements*

عن جابر بن عبدالله رضي الله عنهما قال قال رسول الله ﷺ مفتاح الجنة الصلاة ومفتاح الصلاة الوضوء

جامع الترمذي كتاب الطهارة

From Jabir ibn Abdullah (may Allah be pleased with both of them), who said: The Messenger of Allah (SAW) said: The key to *Jannah* is prayer, and the key to prayer is performing ablution [*wudu'*].

*Sunan Al-Tirmidhi, The book of purity*

عن عمرو بن عبسة قال قال رسول الله ﷺ إن العبد إذا توضأ فغسل يديه خَرَّت خطاياه من يديه فإذا غسل وجهه خرت خطاياه من وجهه فإذا غسل ذراعيه ومسح برأسه خرت خطاياه من ذراعيه ورأسه فإذا غسل رجليه خرت خطاياه من رجليه

سنن إبن ماجه كتاب الطهارة وسننها

From 'Amr ibn 'Abasa, who said: The Messenger of Allah (SAW) said: Indeed someone, whenever he performs ablution and washes his hands, his sins fall out from his hands; whenever he washes his face, his since fall out from his face; whenever he washes his arms and wipes his head, his sins fall out from his arms and his head; whenever he washes his feet, his sins fall out from his feet.

*Sunan Ibn Majah, The book of purity and its sunnah*

قال أبو القاسم والذي ينقُض الطهارة ما خرج من قُبُل أو دبر

وجملة ذلك أن الخارج من السبيلين على ضربين معتاد كالبول والغائط والمني والمذي والودي والريح فهذا ينقض الوضوء إجماعاً قال إبن المنذر أجمع أهل العلم على أن خروج الغائط من الدبر وخروج البول من ذكر الرجل وقبل المرأة وخروج المذي وخروج الريح من الدبر أحداثُ ينقض كل واحد منها الطهارة ويوجب الوضوء ودم الاستحاضة ينقض الطهارة في قول عامة أهل العلم إلا في قول ربيعة الضرب الثاني نادرٌ كالدم والدود والحصا والشعر فينقض الوضوء أيضاً

المغني لإبن قدامة باب ما ينقض الطهارة

Abu Qasim [Al-Khiraqi] said: That which annuls a state of purity [*tahara*] is what comes out of one's front part or rear part.

Everything that comes out from the two passages [*al-sabilain*; i.e. the front and the rear] can be summed up into two categories: first, what is commonplace, such as urine, feces, semen, pre-ejaculate, prostatic secretion, and gas; all of these invalidate one's ablution. Ibn Al-Mundhir said: Scholars are in unanimous agreement that feces coming out of one's rear, urine coming out of a man's penis or a woman's front part, pre-ejaculate coming out, and gas coming out of one's rear, are all bodily occurrences [*hadath*]; each of these annuls a state of purity and makes ablution necessary. Moreover blood from vaginal bleeding annuls a state of purity according to the general opinion of scholars, except that of Rabi'a. The second category are things that are uncommon, such as blood, worms, stones, and hair; these also invalidate ablution.

*Ibn Qudama, Al-mughni, Chapter: Things that annul a state of purity*

عن بسرة بنت صفوان إحدى نساء بني كنانة أنها قالت يا رسول الله كيف ترى في إحدانا تمس فرجها والرجل يمس ذكره بعدما يتوضأ فقال لها رسول الله ﷺ توضأ يا بسرة بنت صفوان

السنن الكبرى للبيهقي كتاب الطهارة باب الوضوء من مس المرأة فرجها

Busrah bint Safwan, one of the women of the Banu Kinana, related that she said: Oh Messenger of Allah (SAW), what do you think if one of us touches her vagina, or a man touches his penis, after performing ablution? And the Messenger of Allah (SAW) said to her: You should do ablution again, oh Busrah bint Sufwan.

*Al-Bayhaqi, Al-sunan Al-kubra, The book of purity, Section: ablution for if a woman touches her vagina*

عن ابي هريرة قال من مس فرجه فليتوضأ ومن مسه يعني من وراء الثوب فليس عليه وضوء

السنن الكبرى للبيهقي كتاب الطهارة باب ترك الوضوء من مس الفرج بظهر ألكف

From Abu Huraira, who said: Whoever touches his crotch must perform ablution, but whoever touches it – here he means through a garment – is not obligated to perform ablution.

*Al-Bayhaqi, Al-sunan Al-kubra, The book of purity, Section: annulment of ablution from touching the crotch with the back of the hand*

عن بسرة بنت صفوان قالت سمعت رسول الله ﷺ يقول من مس ذكره أو أنثييه أو رفغه فليتوضأ وفي رواية الطوسي أو رفغيه فليتوضأ وضوءه للصلاة

السنن الكبرى للبيهقي كتاب الطهارة باب في مس الانثيين

Busra bint Safwan related that she said: I heard the Messenger of Allah (SAW) say: Whoever touches his penis or his testicles or his groin must perform ablution. In a narrative from Al-Tusi: ... or both his groins, must perform ablution as he does for prayer.

*Al-Bayhaqi, Al-sunan Al-kubra, The book of purity, Section: regarding touching the testicles*

عن إبن عمر قال إذا توضأ الرجل ومس ابطه أعاد الوضوء

السنن الكبرى للبيهقي كتاب الطهارة باب في مس الإبط

From Ibn 'Umar, who said: Whenever a man performs ablution but then touches his armpit, he should repeat the ablution.

*Al-Bayhaqi, Al-sunan Al-kubra, The book of purity, Section: regarding touching the armpits*

عن المغيرة بن شعبة أن رسول الله ﷺ رأى رجلاً طويل الشارب فدعا بسواك وشفرة فوضع السواك تحت الشارب فقص عليه

السنن الكبرى للبيهقي كتاب الطهارة باب كيف الأخذ من الشارب

Mughira ibn Shu'ba related that the Messenger of Allah (SAW) saw a certain man with a long mustache, so He called for a tooth-cleaning stick [*siwak*] and a blade, He put the *siwak* under his mustache, and He cut over it.

*Al-Bayhaqi, Al-sunan Al-kubra, The book of purity, Section: how much of the mustache is to be taken*

عن أنس بن مالك عن النبي ﷺ قال من توضأ فقال أشهد أن لا إله إلا الله وحده لا شريك له وأشهد أن محمداً عبده ورسوله ثلاث مرات فُتحت له ثمانية أبواب الجنة يدخل من أيها شاء

المصنف لإبن ابي شيبة كتاب الطهارة

Anas ibn Malik related from the Prophet (SAW) who said: Anyone who performs ablution and says three times "I bear witness that there is no god but Allah, Him alone, nothing associated with Him, and I bear witness that Muhammad is His servant and His Messenger"*, eight gates of *Jannah* will be opened to him, for him to enter through whichever he wishes. *["*Ashhadu an la ilaha illa Allah, wahdahu, la sharika lahu, wa-ashhadu anna Muhammadan 'abduhu wa-rasuluhu*"].

*Ibn Abi Shayba, Al-musannaf, The book of purity*

عن أنس أن النبي ﷺ كان إذا توضأ يخلّل لحيته

المصنف لإبن ابي شيبة كتاب الطهارة

Anas related that the Prophet (SAW), whenever He performed ablution, would run his fingers through his beard [with water].

*Ibn Abi Shayba, Al-musannaf, The book of purity*

عن صالح بن أبي حساب قال سمعت سعيد بن المسيب يقول إن الله طيّبٌ يحب الطيّب نظيفٌ يحب النظافة
كريمٌ يحب الكَرَم جوادٌ يحب الجود فنظّفوا أُراه قال أفنيتَكم ولا تَشبّهوا باليهود

جامع الترمذي كتاب الأدب

From Al-Salih ibn Abi Hassab, who said: I heard Sa'id ibn Al-Musayyab say: Indeed Allah is good, and loves goodness; clean, and loves cleanliness; generous, and loves generosity; kind, and loves kindness; so cleanse – it seems to me that he said – your courtyards, and do not be like the Jews.

*Sunan Al-Tirmidhi, The book of manners*

وأما نظافة جسمه وطيب ريحه وعرقه ونزاهته عن الأقذار وعورات الجسد فكان قد خصّه الله تعالى في
ذلك بخصائص لم توجد في غيره ثم تمّمها بنظافة الشرع وخصال الفطرة العشر وقال بُني الدين على النظافة

الشفا للقاضي عياض اليحصبي القسم الأول في تعظيم العلي الأعلى لقدر النبي المصطفى ﷺ قولاً وفعلاً

As regards cleanliness of his body, the pleasantness of his scent and sweat, his being free from impurities and bodily imperfections, Allah Most High favored him in this with qualities found in no one else, then perfected them with cleanliness in the law of Islam [*shar'*] and the ten traits of innate disposition [*fitrah*]. And He said: The religion [*deen*] is built upon cleanliness.

*Al-qadi 'Iyad Al-Yahsubi, Al-shifa, Part One: Regarding the exaltation of the High and Most High to the eminence of the chosen Prophet (SAW) in word and in deed*

عن ربيح بن عبد الرحمن بن أبي سعيد الخدري عن أبيه عن جده قال قال رسول الله ﷺ لا صلاة لمن لا
وضوء له ولا وضوء لمن لم يذكر إسم الله عليه

السنن الكبرى للبيهقي كتاب الطهارة باب التسمية على الوضوء

Rubaih ibn 'Abd Al-Rahman ibn Abi Sa'id Al-Khudri related from his father, from his grandfather, who said: The Messenger of Allah (SAW) said: There can be no prayer for someone who has not performed ablution, and there can be no ablution for someone who has not made remembrance of the name of Allah over it.

*Al-Bayhaqi, Al-sunan Al-kubra, The book of purity, Section: invoking the name of Allah for ablution*

عن سفيان بن الحكم أو الحكم بن سفيان أن رسول الله ﷺ كان إذا توضّأ وفرغ أخذ كفّاً من ماء فنضح به فرجه

المصنف لعبد الرزاق كتاب الطهارة

Sufyan ibn Al-Hakam (or Al-Hakam ibn Sufyan) related that the Messenger of Allah (SAW), whenever He performed ablution and finished, would take a handful of water and sprinkle his crotch with it.

*'Abd Al-Razzaq, the Musannaf, The book of purity*

عن الحسن بن عبيد الله قال سمعت مسلم بن صبيح يقول رأيت إبن عمر توضأ ثم أخذ غرفة من ماء فصبّها بين إزاره وبطنه على فرجه

المصنف لعبد الرزاق كتاب الطهارة

From Al-Hasan ibn 'Ubaid Allah, who said: I heard Muslim ibn Subaih say: I saw Ibn 'Umar perform ablution, then scoop up a handful of water and pour it between his waist wrap and his stomach, over his crotch.

*'Abd Al-Razzaq, the Musannaf, The book of purity*

عن طلحة عن أبيه عن جده قال دخلتُ يعني على النبي ﷺ وهو يتوضأ والماء يسيل من وجهه ولحيته على صدره فرأيته يفصِل بين المضمضة والإستنشاق

سنن أبي داود كتاب الطهارة

Talha related from his father, from his grandfather, who said: I went in to see him – that is, the Prophet (SAW) – when He was performing ablution, and the water was running down his face and beard onto his chest, and I saw him rinsing out his mouth [*madmadah*] and inhaling water up through his nose [*istinshaq*] separately.

*Sunan Abu Dawud, The book of purity*

عن عائشة أنّ النبي ﷺ كان يغسل مقعدته ثلاثاً. قال إبن عمر: فعلناه فوجدناه دواءً وطهوراً

سنن إبن ماجة كتاب الطهارة وسننها

'Aishah related that the Prophet (SAW) used to wash his backside three times. Ibn 'Umar said: We did this and found it to be healing and purifying.

*Sunan Ibn Majah, The book of purity and its sunnah*

عن بُسرة بنت صفوان أن النبي ﷺ قال من مسّ ذكره فلا يصلِّ حتى يتوضأ

جامع الترمذي كتاب الطهارة

Busrah bint Safwan related that the Prophet (SAW) said: Whoever has touched his penis must not pray until he performs ablution [*wudu'*].

*Sunan Al-Tirmidhi, The book of purity*

عن بسرة بنت صفوان أنها سمعت النبي ﷺ يقول إذا مسّ أحدكم ذكره فليتوضأ

صحيح إبن خزيمة كتاب الوضوء

Busrah bint Safwan related that she heard the Prophet (SAW) say: Whenever any of you touches his penis he should perform ablution.

*Sahih Ibn Khuzaima, The book of ablution*

عن قيس بن طلق بن علي عن أبيه قال خرجنا وفداً حتى قدمنا على رسول الله ﷺ فبايعناه وصلينا معه فلما قضى الصلاة جاء رجل كأنه بدوي فقال يا رسول الله ما ترى في رجل مس ذكره في الصلاة قال وهل هو إلا مُضغة منك أو بَضعة منك

سنن النسائي كتاب الطهارة

Qais ibn Talq ibn 'Ali related from his father, who said: We set out as a delegation until we came to the Messenger of Allah (SAW), and we made our pledge to him, and prayed with him; and when he had finished prayer, a certain man came by, seemingly a Bedouin, and said: Oh Messenger of Allah, what do you think about a man who touches his penis during prayer? He said: Is it not but a little morsel on you? (or "a little piece of you").

*Sunan Al-Nasa'i, The book of purity*

عن قيس بن طلق عن أبيه قال قدمنا على نبي الله ﷺ فجاء رجل كأنه بدوي فقال يا نبي الله ما ترى في مس الرجل ذكره بعد ما يتوضأ فقال هل هو إلا مضغة منه

سنن أبي داود كتاب الطهارة

Qais ibn Talq related from his father, who said: We came to the Prophet of Allah (SAW), and a man came along, seemingly a Bedouin, and he said: Oh Prophet of Allah, what do you think about a man touching his penis after he has performed ablution? And He said: Is it not but a little morsel on him?

*Sunan Abu Dawud, The book of purity*

عن عبدالله بن ابي قتادة عن أبيه أن النبي ﷺ نهى أن يمس الرجل ذكره بيمينه

جامع الترمذي كتاب الطهارة

Abdullah ibn Abi Qatada related from his father that the Prophet (SAW) forbade a man to touch his penis with his right hand.

*Sunan Al-Tirmidhi, The book of purity*

قيس بن طلق الحنفي عن أبيه قال سمعت رسول الله ﷺ سئل عن مس الذكر فقال ليس فيه وضوء إنما هو منك

سنن إبن ماجه كتاب الطهارة وسننها

Qais ibn Talq Al-Hanafi related that his father said: I heard the Messenger of Allah (SAW) being asked about touching the penis, and He said: There is no ablution regarding it, for indeed it is part of you.

*Sunan Ibn Majah, The book of purity and its sunnah*

عن رجل من بني غفار من أصحاب النبي ﷺ قال نهى رسول الله ﷺ أن يتوضأ الرجل بفضل طهور المرأة

المصنف لإبن أبي شيبة كتاب الطهارة

A certain man of the Banu Ghifar, from among the Companions of the Prophet (SAW), said: The Messenger of Allah (SAW) forbade a man to perform ablution with what is left over from a woman's purification.

*Ibn Abi Shayba, Al-musannaf, The book of purity*

عن علي قال توضأ فمضمض ثلاثاً وإستنشق ثلاثاً من كفٍّ واحدة وقال هكذا وضوء نبيكم ﷺ

المصنف لإبن أبي شيبة كتاب الطهارة

'Ali performed ablution, rinsed his mouth out three times, and inhaled water up into his nose three times out of one hand, and he said: This is how your Prophet (SAW) performed ablution.

*Ibn Abi Shayba, Al-musannaf, The book of purity*

عن عطاء فيمن نسي المضمضة في الوضوء أو الإستنشاق قال يُمضمض ويستنشق ويعيد الصلاة

المصنف لإبن أبي شيبة كتاب الطهارة

'Ataa related regarding someone who forgets to rinse out their mouth or draw water up into their nose; he said: They should rinse out their mouth, draw water up into their nose, and repeat the prayer.

*Ibn Abi Shayba, Al-musannaf, The book of purity*

عن ابي هريرة أن النبي ﷺ قال إذا إستيقظ أحدكم من نومه فلا يغمس يده في الإناء حتى يغسلها ثلاثاً فإنه لا يدري أين باتت يده

صحيح مسلم كتاب الطهارة

Abu Huraira related that the Prophet (SAW) said: Whenever any of you awakens from his sleep, he should not put his hand into the vessel until he washes it three times, for indeed he does not know where his hand has spent the night.

*Sahih Muslim, The book of purity*

أين باتت يده كناية عن وقوعها على دبره أو ذكره أو نجاسة أو غير ذلك من القذر

شرح سنن أبي داود للعيني باب الوضوء من آية الصُفر

"Where his hand has spent the night" : an allusion to it sliding onto his rear or his penis, or uncleanliness at all, or any other kind of filth.

*Badr Al-deen Al-'Aini, Sharh Sunan Abi Dawud, Chapter: Ablution from brass vessels*


عن زيد إبن أسلم أن تفسير هذه الآية ﴿ يا أيها الذين آمنوا إذا قمتم إلى الصلاة فاغسلوا وجوهكم وأيديكم إلى المرافق وامسحوا برؤوسكم وأرجلكم إلى الكعبين ﴾ أن ذلك إذا قمتم من المضاجع يعني النوم قال يحيى قال مالك الأمر عندنا أنه لا يتوضأ من رُعاف ولا من دم ولا من قيح يسيل من الجسد ولا يتوضأ إلا من حدث يخرج من ذكر أو دبر أو نوم

موطأ مالك كتاب الطهارة

Zaid ibn Aslam related that the explanation of this verse { Oh you who have believed, whenever you get up to go to prayer, wash your faces and your arms up to the elbows and wipe your heads and your feet up to the ankles } [Al-ma'ida 6] is that whenever you get up from your beds, that is, from sleeping. Yahya said that Malik said: The situation with us is that one does not perform ablution from a nosebleed, nor from blood, nor from pus that flows from the body; one does not perform ablution except from an occurrence [hadath] that comes from his penis or his rear, or from sleep.

*Muwatta Malik, The book of purity*


عن عروة عن عائشة أن النبي ﷺ قبَّل بعض نسائه ثم خرج إلى الصلاة ولم يتوضأ قال قلتُ من هي إلا إنتِ قال فضحكت

جامع الترمذي كتاب الطهارة

'Urwa related from 'Aishah, who said that the Prophet (SAW) kissed one of his women, and then went out to prayer without having performed ablution. 'Urwa said: Who could it have been but you? And she laughed.

*Sunan Al-Tirmidhi, The book of purity*


عن عاصم بن لقيط بن صبرة عن أبيه قال قلت يا رسول الله ﷺ أخبرني عن الوضوء فقال أسبغ الوضوء وخلل بين الأصابع وبالغ في الإستنشاق إلا أن تكون صائماً

تفسير إبن كثير المائدة ٦

'Asim ibn Laqit ibn Sabra related from his father, who said: I said: Oh Messenger of Allah, tell me about ablution. He said: Perform ablution thoroughly, go between your fingers, and really go at it when you draw water up through your nose [*istinshaq*], unless you are fasting.

*Tafsir Ibn Kathir (Al-Ma'ida 6)*

عن جابر أخبرني عمر بن الخطاب أن رجلاً توضأ فترك موضع ظُفُرٍ على قدمه فأبصره النبي ﷺ فقال إرجع فأحسن وضوءك فرجع ثم صلى

صحيح مسلم كتاب الطهارة

Jabir said: 'Umar ibn Al-Khattab related to me that a certain man performed ablution, but left a spot the size of a fingernail on his foot, and the Prophet (SAW) noticed it, and He said: Go back and perform ablution right. So the man went back, and then he prayed.

*Sahih Muslim, The book of purity*

عن عقبة بن عامر الجهني أن رسول الله ﷺ قال ما من أحد يتوضأ فيُحسن الوضوء ويصلي ركعتين يُقبل بقلبه ووجهه عليهما إلا وجب له الجنة

سنن ابي داود كتاب الصلاة

'Uqba ibn 'Amir Al-Juhani related that the Messenger of Allah (SAW) said: Anyone who performs ablution, and performs ablution well, and prays two sequences, giving full attention to it with his heart and his countenance, *Jannah* is indispensably his.

*Sunan Abu Dawud, The book of purity*

عن مغيرة عن ابراهيم قال سألته عن قُبلة الصبي بعد الوضوء فقال إنما تلك رحمةٌ لا وضوء فيها

المصنف لإبن ابي شيبة كتاب الطهارة

Mughira related from Ibrahim, saying: I asked him about kissing young boys after having performed ablution, and he said: Indeed that is gentle affection; there is no ablution necessary from it.

*Ibn Abi Shayba, Al-musannaf, The book of purity*

عن عامر والحكم قالا لا بأس بالوضوء بالثَّلج

المصنف لإبن ابي شيبة كتاب الطهارة

From 'Amir and Al-Hakam, who said: There is nothing wrong with performing ablution with snow.

*Ibn Abi Shayba, Al-musannaf, The book of purity*

عن الزهري في المريض لا يستطيع أن يتوضأ قال يتيمم

المصنف لإبن أبي شيبة كتاب الطهارة

Al-Zuhri related regarding someone who is sick and can not perform ablution; he said: He should wipe with dust [*tayammum*].

*Ibn Abi Shayba, Al-musannaf, The book of purity*


وينبغي أن تعلم أن جمهور العلماء أوجبوا الوضوء من زوال العقل بأي نوع كان من قبل إغماء أو جنون أو سكر

بداية المجتهد ونهاية المقتصد لإبن رشد كتاب الطهارة من الحدث

And you should know that the majority of scholars made ablution obligatory in the case of loss of one's faculties for any reason, primarily from loss of consciousness, insanity, or intoxication.

*Ibn Rushd, Bidaya Al-mujtahid wa Nihaya Al-Muqtasid, The book of purification from bodily occurrences [hadath]*


عن إبن عمر قال كان الرجال والنساء يتوضؤن في زمان رسول الله ﷺ جميعاً

سنن النسائي كتاب المياه

From Ibn 'Umar who said: During the time of Allah's Messenger (SAW), men and women would perform *wudu'* together.

*Sunan Al-Nasa'i, The book of water*


وهي سبعة اسياء الأول خروج الخارج من السبيلين طاهراً كان كالريح أو نجساً كالبول والثاني خروج النجاسات من بقية البدن فإن كانت بولاً أو عَذِرة فالقليل كالكبير في النقض وإن كانت غير ذلك نقض كثيرها وهو ما يفحش في النفس والثالث مس الفرج قبلاً كان أو دبراً والموضع الذي ينتقض وضوء المرأة بمسه هو القبل ما بين الشفرين سواء كان مخرج البول أو مخرج الحيض لأن الشفرين يجريان مجري الإليتين من الدبر والانثيين من الذكر والرابع لمس النساء وفي نقض وضوء الملموس روايتان والخامس زوال العقل إلا بالنوم اليسير جالساً أو قائماً أو راكعاً أو ساجداً والسادس أكل لحم الجزور والسابع غسل الميت

أحكام النساء لإبن الجوزي الباب العاشر ذكر نواقض الوضوء

There are seven things [that invalidate ablution]; the first is if anything comes out of the two passages [i.e. the front or the rear], whether it is clean, such as gas, or impure, such as urine. The second is if impurities come out of the rest of the body, whether urine or defecation; a little invalidates just as much as a lot; if it is something else, a lot of it annuls, this being an amount that causes one to feel repugnance. The third is touching the crotch, whether the front or the rear; the location that invalidates a woman's ablution from touching it is in the front between the two labia, whether this is where urine comes out or where menstrual blood comes out, since the two labia are like the two buttocks in the rear or the testicles of a male. The fourth is touching women; regarding invalidation of the ablution of the one who is touched, there are two accounts. The fifth is the loss of one's faculties, except in the case of a light sleep, sitting down or standing up, kneeling or prostrating. The sixth is eating the meat of a camel that is to be slaughtered. The seventh is washing a dead person.

*Ibn Al-Jawzi, Ahkam Al-nisaa, Chapter ten: mention of the things that invalidate ablution*

عن ابي العالية قال كان النبي ﷺ يصلي بأصحابه يوماً فجاء رجل ضرير البصر فوقع في ركية فيها ماء فضحك بعض أصحاب النبي ﷺ فلما إنصرف رسول الله ﷺ قال من ضحك فليُعد وضوءه ثم ليعد صلاته

المصنف لعبد الرزاق كتاب الصلاة

From Abu Al-'Aliya, who said: One day the Prophet (SAW) was leading his Companions in prayer, and a blind man came along and fell into a well with water in it, and some of the Prophet's (SAW) Companions laughed. And when the Messenger of Allah (SAW) departed, He said: Whoever laughs is to repeat his ablution, then repeat his prayer.

*'Abd Al-Razzaq, the Musannaf, The book of prayer*

وأما أنواع النجاسات فإن العلماء اتفقوا من أعيانها على أربعة ميتة الحيوان ذي الدم الذي ليس بمائي وعلى لحم الخنزير بأي سبب إتفق أن تذهب حياته وعلى الدم نفسه من الحيوان الذي ليس بمائي إنفصل من الحي أو الميت إذا كان مسفوحاً أعني كثيراً وعلى بول إبن آدم ورجيعه وأكثرهم على نجاسة الخمر وفي ذلك خلاف عن بعض المحدثين واختلفوا في غير ذلك

بداية المجتهد ونهاية المقتصد لإبن رشد كتاب الطهارة من الحدث

Regarding different kinds of impurities, scholars agree on four specific instances: non-aquatic dead animals that carry blood; pig meat for any reason that happens by which its life has left it; the blood itself of non-aquatic animals, whether it has come out of live or dead ones, whenever it is spilled – by this I mean a large amount; and the urine and excrement of humans. Most of them also agree that fermented beverage [khamr] is impure, although regarding this there is disagreement among some of the compilers of hadith. They disagree on everything else.

*Ibn Rushd, Bidaya Al-mujtahid wa Nihaya Al-Muqtasid, The book of purification from bodily occurrences [hadath]*

ومن الآداب غسل الفرج بالماء البارد عقيب الجماع ويجب تعجيله على الرجل وعلى المرأة فإن الماء البارد
يقوي الإحليل ويضيق الرحم ويُحذر الماء الحار لأنه يرخي الإحليل ويضعفه ويمنعه من القدرة على المعاودة

النزهة الاصحاب في معاشرة الأحباب لإبن يحيى المغربي ومن آداب الجماع الواجبة على المرأة

It is part of proper conduct to wash the private parts with cold water following sex, and
this must be done hastily by the man and the woman; for indeed cold water invigorates
the member and constricts the womb. One is warned against hot water, since it relaxes
the member, weakens it, and prevents it from being able to resume.

*Ibn Yahya, Nuzhat Al-ashab fi Mu'asharat Al-ahbab, Section: mandatory sexual conduct for women*


عن ابي هريرة قال قال رسول الله ﷺ طهور إناء أحدكم إذا ولغ فيه الكلب أن يغسله سبع مرات أولاهن بالتراب

صحيح مسلم كتاب الطهارة

From Abu Huraira who said: The Messenger of Allah (SAW) said: The cleansing of
the vessel of any one of you, whenever a dog has lapped in it, is to wash it seven
times, the first of these being with dirt.

*Sahih Muslim, The book of purity*


عن عبدالله بن المغفل أن رسول الله ﷺ أمر بقتل الكلاب ورخَّص في كلب الصيد والغنم وقال إذا ولغ
الكلب في الإناء فاغسلوه سبع مرات وعفِّروه الثامنة بالتراب

سنن النسائي كتاب الطهارة

Abdullah ibn Al-Mughaffal related that the Messenger of Allah (SAW) ordered dogs
to be killed, although he allowed hunting and herding dogs. And he said: Whenever a
dog laps in a vessel, wash it seven times, and sprinkle it with dirt on the eighth time.

*Sunan Al-Nasa'i, The book of purity*


قال أبو موسى دعا النبي ﷺ بقدح فيه ماء فغسل يديه ووجهه فيه وبجّ فيه ثم قال لهما يعني أبا موسى وبلالا
اشربا منه وافرغا على وجوهكما ونحوركما

صحيح البخاري كتاب الوضوء

Abu Musa said: The Prophet (SAW) called for a bowl with water in it, washed his
hands and face in it, spit out into it, and then said to the two of them (Abu Musa and
Bilal): Drink from it and pour some over your faces and chests.

*Sahih Al-Bukhari, The book of ablution*

المغيرة بن أبي بردة وهو من بني عبد الدار أخرجه أنه سمع أبا هريرة يقول سأل رجلٌ النبي ﷺ فقال يا رسول الله إنا نركب البحر ونحمل معنا القليل من الماء فإن توضأنا به عطشنا أفنتوضأ بماء البحر فقال رسول الله ﷺ هو الطهور ماؤه الحِلّ مَيْتته

سنن أبي داود كتاب الطهارة

Al-Mughira ibn Abi Burda, from the Banu 'Abd Al-Dar, related that he heard Abu Huraira say: A certain man came to the Messenger of Allah (SAW) and said: Oh Messenger of Allah, indeed we journey at sea and carry with us only a small amount of water, and if we perform ablution with it, we will be thirsty; can we perform ablution with seawater? And the Messenger of Allah (SAW) said: Its water is pure, and its dead creatures permissible.

*Sunan Abu Dawud, The book of purity*

عن حميدة بنت أبي عبيدة بن فروة عن خالتها كبشة بنت كعب بن مالك وكانت تحت إبن أبي قتادة الأنصاري أنها أخبرتها أن أبا قتادة دخل عليها فسكبت له وضوءاً فجاءت هرةٌ لتشرب منه فأصغى لها الإناء حتى شربت قالت كبشة فرآني أنظر إليه فقال أتعجبين يا إبنة أخي قلت فقلت نعم فقال إن رسول الله ﷺ قال إنها ليست بنجس إنما هي من الطوافين عليكم أو الطوافات

قال يحيى قال مالك لا بأس به إلا أن يُرى على فيها نجاسة

موطأ مالك كتاب الطهارة

Humaidah bint Abi 'Ubaida ibn Farwa related from her aunt Kabshah bint Ka'b ibn Malik, who was under [i.e. married to] the son of Abu Qatada Al-Ansari, that she told her that Abu Qatada had gone in to see her, and she poured him some water for ablution. Then a cat came to drink from it, and he inclined the vessel towards it so it could drink. And Kabshah said: He saw that I was looking at him, and he said: Do you find this strange, oh niece of mine? She said: Yes. And he said: Truly the Messenger of Allah (SAW) said: Indeed it is not filthy; surely it is one of the things that go around among you.

Yahya said that Malik said: There is no issue with this except if you see something filthy in its mouth.

*Muwatta Malik, The book of purity*

عن نافع أن عبدالله بن عمر كان يأخذ الماء بأصبُعَيه لأذنيه

موطأ مالك كتاب الطهارة

Nafi' related that 'Abdullah ibn 'Umar would take the water up to his ears with two fingers.

*Muwatta Malik, The book of purity*

عن مالك أنه بلغه أن جابر بن عبدالله الأنصاري سئل عن المسح على العمامة فقال لا حتى يُمسح الشعر بالماء

موطأ مالك كتاب الطهارة

Malik related that he had become aware that Jabir ibn 'Abdillah Al-Ansari was asked about wiping over one's turban, and he said: not until the hair has been wiped over with water.

*Muwatta Malik, The book of purity*


أبو هريرة يقول قال رسول الله ﷺ لا عدوى ولا طيرة ولا هامة ولا صفر وفِرّ من المجذوم كما تفر من الأسد

صحيح البخاري كتاب الطب

Abu Huraira said: The Messenger of Allah (SAW) said: There are no contagious diseases, no evil omens, no birds that go around graveyards at night [*hama*], and no intestinal worms that cause hunger [*safar*]; and run away from lepers like you would run away from a lion.

*Sahih Al-Bukhari, The book of medicine*


عن سالم أن إبن عمر كان يقول من قبل امرأته وهو على وضوء أعاد الوضوء

المصنف لعبد الرزاق كتاب الطهارة

Salim related that Ibn 'Umar said that anyone who kisses his woman, having performed ablution [*wudu'*], must repeat the ablution.

*'Abd Al-Razzaq, the Musannaf, The book of purity*


عن عائشة أن النبي ﷺ كان يقبل بعد الوضوء ولا يعيد أو قالت ثم يصلي

المصنف لعبد الرزاق كتاب الطهارة

'Aishah related that the Prophet (SAW) would kiss after ablution but not repeat the ablution; or she said: Then He would pray.

*'Abd Al-Razzaq, the Musannaf, The book of purity*


عن قتادة في الدود يخرج من الانسان مثل حَبّ القَرع قال ليس عليه منه وضوء

المصنف لعبد الرزاق كتاب الطهارة

From Qatada, regarding worms that come out of a man, like gourd seeds; he said: he does not need to perform any ablution from it.

*'Abd Al-Razzaq, the Musannaf, The book of purity*

عن عبدالله بن مسعود قال لما كانت ليلة الجن تخلف منهم رجلان فقالا نشهد الفجر معك يا رسول الله فقال
النبي ﷺ معك ماءٌ قلت ليس معي ماء ولكن معي إداوة فيها نبيذ فقال النبي ﷺ ثمرةٌ طيبة وماء طهور فتوضأ
المصنف لعبد الرزاق كتاب الطهارة

From Abdullah ibn Mas'ud, who said: On the night of the genies [*jinn*], two men from
among them remained behind and said: We'll witness daybreak with you, oh Messenger
of Allah. And the Prophet (SAW) said: Do you have any water? I said: I don't have any
water, but I have a small leather bottle with some wine [*nabidh*] in it. And the Prophet
(SAW) said: Wholesome dates and pure water. And He performed ablution.

*'Abd Al-Razzaq, the Musannaf, The book of purity*


عن عطاء أنه كره الوضوء باللبن والنبيذ وقال إن التيمم أعجب إلي منه
سنن أبي داود كتاب الطهارة

'Ataa related that he disliked performing ablution with milk or wine, and said: Indeed
wiping with dust [*tayammum*] is more to my liking than that.

*Sunan Abu Dawud, The book of purity*


﴿ يا نساء النبي لستن كأحد من النساء إن اتقيتن فلا تخضعن بالقول فيطمع الذي في قلبه مرض وقلن قولاً معروفاً
وقرن في بيوتكن ولا تبرجن تبرج الجاهلية الأولى وأقمن الصلاة وآتين الزكاة وأطعن الله ورسوله إنما يريد الله
ليذهب عنكم الرجس أهل البيت ويطهركم تطهيراً ﴾ الأحزاب ٣٢-٣٣

{ *Oh women of the Prophet! You all are not like other women; if you
are devout, do not be aquiescent in speaking, such that someone with
sickness in their heart might be enticed; but speak that which is right.
Remain in your houses, and do not display your charms like people did
in the former age of ignorance; and observe prayer, and give zakat, and
obey Allah and His Messenger; indeed Allah wants to remove the filth
from all of you, those of the household, and to thoroughly purify you* }
*Al-ahzab 32-33*

﴿ وَأَقِمْنَ الصلواة وآتِينَ الزكاة وأطعن الله ورسوله انما يريد الله ليذهب عنكم الرجس ﴾ الاثم يا ﴿ أهل البيت ﴾ أي نساء النبي ﷺ

تفسير الجلالين

{ And observe prayer, and give zakat, and obey Allah and His Messenger; indeed Allah wants to remove the filth from all of you } : the sin, oh { those of the household } , that is, the women of the Prophet (SAW).

*Tafsir Al-Jalalain*

أراد بالرجس الإثم الذي نهى الله النساء عنه قاله مقاتل

تفسير البغوي

By "filth" He means the sin that Allah forbade to women; Muqatil said this.

*Tafsir Al-Baghawi*

﴿ الرجس ﴾ إسم يقع على الاثم وعلى العذاب وعلى النجاسات والنقائص فاذهب الله جميع ذلك عن ﴿ أهل البيت ﴾

تفسير إبن عطية

{ Filth } : a word that encompasses sin, punishment, impurities, and imperfections; Allah removed all of this from { those of the household } .

*Tafsir Ibn 'Atiyya*

عن عائشة رضي الله عهن قالت خرج رسول الله ﷺ غداة وعليه مرط مرجل من شعر أسود لجاء الحسن والحسين رضي الله عنهما معه فأدخلهما معه ثم جاء علي فأدخله معه ثم قال ﴿ انما يريد الله ليذهب عنكم الرجس أهل البيت ويطهركم تطهيراً ﴾

الدر المنثور للسيوطي

From 'Aishah (may Allah be pleased with her), who said: The Messenger of Allah (SAW) went out early one morning wearing a women's wrap [*mirt*] made of groomed black fleece [or black fleece decorated with pictures of men], then Hasan and Husain (may Allah be pleased with them both) came, and He made them get in with him, then 'Ali came, and He made him get in with him, then He said: { Indeed Allah wants to remove the filth from all of you, those of the household, and to thoroughly purify you } .

*Al-Suyuti, Al-durr Al-manthur*

•     •     •

عن حذيفة قال قال رسول الله ﷺ فضلت على الناس بثلاث جعلت صفوفنا كصفوف الملائكة وجعلت لنا الأرض كلها مسجداً وجعلت تربتها لنا طهوراً وذكر خصلة أخرى

السنن الكبرى للبيهقي كتاب الطهارة باب الدليل على أن الصعيد الطيب هو التراب

From Hudhaifa, who said: The Messenger of Allah (SAW) said: I have been favored over everyone else in three things: Our ranks have been made like the ranks of the angels, the whole earth has been made a mosque for us [*masjid*, i.e. place of worship], and its dust has been made pure for us. And He mentioned one other attribute.

*Al-Bayhaqi, Al-sunan Al-kubra, The book of purity, Section: evidence that "clean earth" is dirt*

عن محمد بن الحنفية أنه سمع علي بن ابي طالب يقول قال رسول الله ﷺ أعطيت ما لم يعط أحد من الأنبياء فقلنا ما هو يا رسول الله فقال نصرت بالرعب واعطيت مفاتيح الأرض وسميت أحمد وجعلت لي التراب طهوراً وجعلت أمتي خير الامم

السنن الكبرى للبيهقي كتاب الطهارة باب الدليل على أن الصعيد الطيب هو التراب

Muhammad ibn Al-Hanafiyya related that he heard 'Ali ibn Abi Talib say: The Messenger of Allah (SAW) said: I have been given what has not been given to any of the prophets. And we asked: What is that, oh Messenger of Allah? He said: I have been made victorious by terror, I have been given the keys to the earth, I have been called "Ahmad", dirt has been made pure for me, and my people [*ummah*] have been made the best of people.

*Al-Bayhaqi, Al-sunan Al-kubra, The book of purity, Section: evidence that "clean earth" is dirt*

عن إبن طاوس عن أبيه قال إذا حككت شيئاً من جسدك وأنت على وضوء فمسحته بالبُصاق فإغسل ذلك المكان بالماء

المصنف لعبد الرزاق كتاب الطهارة

Ibn Tawus related from his father, who said: Whenever you scrape off something from your body, having already performed ablution, and you wipe it clean with spit, wash the location with water.

*'Abd Al-Razzaq, the Musannaf, The book of purity*

الأول ما يجتمع في شعر الرأس من الدَرَن والقمل فالتنظيف عنه مستحب بالغسل والترجيل والتدهين إزالةً للشعث عنه وكان ﷺ يدهن الشعر ويرجِّله غبّاً ويأمر به ويقول عليه الصلاة والسلام ادّهنوا غبّاً وقال عليه الصلاة والسلام من كان له شعرةٌ فليكرمها أي ليصنها عن الأوساخ ودخل عليه رجل ثائر الرأس أشعث اللحية فقال أما كان لهذا دُهن يسكن به شعره ثم قال يدخل علي أحدكم كأنه شيطان

الثاني ما يجتمع من الوسخ في معاطف الأذن والمسح يزيل ما يظهر منه وما يجتمع في قعر الصماخ فينبغي أن ينظَّف برفق عند الخروج من الحمام فإن كثرة ذلك ربما تضر بالسمع

الثالث ما يجتمع في داخل الأنف من الرطوبات المنعقدة الملتصقة بجوانبه ويزيلها الإستنشاق والإستنثار

الرابع ما يجتمع على الأسنان وأطراف اللسان من القَلَح ويزيله السواك والمضمضة وقد ذكرناهما

الخامس ما يجتمع في اللحية من الوسخ والقمل إذا لم يتعهد ويستحب إزالة ذلك بالغسل والتسريح بالمُشط وفي الخبر المشهور أنه ﷺ كان لا يفارقه المشط والمدرى والمرآة في سفر ولا حضر وهي سنة العرب وفي خبر غريب أنه ﷺ كان يسرّح لحيته في اليوم مرتين وكان ﷺ كثَّ اللحية وكذلك كان أبو بكر وكان عثمان طويل اللحية رقيقها وكان علي عريض اللحية قد ملأت ما بين منكبيه وفي حديث أغرب منه قالت عائشة رضي الله عنها إجتمع قوم بباب رسول الله ﷺ نخرج إليهم فرأيته يطلع في الحُبّ يسوّي من رأسه ولحيته فقلت أوتفعل ذلك يا رسول الله فقال نعم إن الله يحب من عبده أن يتجمل لاخوانه إذا خرج اليهم

السادس وسخ البراجم وهي معاطف ظهور الأنامل كانت العرب لا تكثر غسل ذلك لتركها غسل اليد عقيب الطعام فيجتمع في تلك الغضون وسخٌ فأمرهم رسول الله ﷺ بغسل البراجم

السابع تنظيف الرواجب أمر رسول الله ﷺ العرب بتنظيفها وهي رؤوس الأنامل وما تحت الأظفار من الوسخ لأنها كانت لا يحضرها المقراض في كل وقت فتجتمع فيها أوساخٌ فوقّت لهم رسول الله ﷺ قلم الأظفار ونتف الإبط وحلق العانة أربعين يوماً لكنه ﷺ أمر بتنظيف ما تحت الأظفار وجاء في الأثر أن النبي ﷺ استبطأ الوحي فلما هبط عليه جبريل عليه السلام قال له كيف ننزل عليكم وأنتم لا تغسلون براجمكم ولا تنظّفون رواجبكم وقُلحاً لا تستاكون مِنْ أمتك بذلك والأقّ وسخ الظفر وأُتُفّ وسخ الأذن وقوله عز وجل ﴿ فلا تقل لهما أفّ ﴾ أي لا تعبْهما بما تحت الظفر من الوسخ وقيل لا تتأذّ بهما كما تتأذى بما تحت الظفر

الثامن الدرن الذي يجتمع على جميع البدن برشح العرَق وغبار الطريق وذلك يزيله الحمام ولا بأس بدخول الحمام دخل أصحاب رسول الله ﷺ حمامات الشام

إحياء علوم الدين للغزالي كتاب أسرار الطهارة ومهماتها القسم الثالث من النظافة التنظيف عن الفضلات الظاهرة النوع الأول الأوساخ والرطوبات المترشحة وهي ثمانية

The first [kind of filthiness and fluids] is the filth and lice that accumulate in the hair on the head; cleansing this is desirable by washing, grooming, and oiling in order to remove the untidiness and matted hair. He (SAW) would oil his hair and groom it regularly, and He prescribed this; He (prayer and peace upon him) said: Oil yourselves regularly. And He (prayer and peace upon him) said: Whoever has hair, let him honor it; that is, let him keep it from getting filthy. A certain man with an unkempt head and a matted beard once came in to see him, and He said: Does this man not have any oil with which to tame his hair? Then He said: Would any of you all come to see me looking like a devil?!

The second: filth that accumulates in the crooks of the ears – wiping removes what is visible of it; and that which collects inside the ear canal – this ought to be cleaned gently upon exiting the bath, for indeed too much may damage the hearing.

The third: thick and sticky fluids which accumulate inside the sides of the nose. Inhaling water up through the nose [*istinshaq*] and rinsing out the nose [*istinthar*] remove this.

The fourth: plaque which accumulates on the teeth and the edges of the tongue. The teeth-cleaning stick [*siwak*] and rinsing the mouth remove this; we have mentioned both of these.

The fifth: filth and lice which accumulate in the beard whenever one does not look after this; it is desirable to remove this by washing and combing it through. There is a well-known account that He (SAW) always had a comb, a hair rake, and a mirror on journeys where there were few towns and inhabitants; this was the way of life of the Arabs. A *gharib* account relates that He (SAW) would comb through his beard twice a day; and He (SAW) had a thick beard. Abu Bakr was similar, and 'Uthman had a long and delicate beard, and 'Ali had a broad beard that filled the space between his shoulders. In another hadith even more *gharib* than this, 'Aishah (may Allah be pleased with her), said: Some people gathered around the Messenger of Allah's (SAW) door, and He went out to them, and I saw him rise out of a large vessel of water to level off his head and his beard; and I said: Do you really do that, oh Messenger of Allah?! He said: Yes; indeed Allah loves that a servant of His should make himself look good for his brothers whenever he goes out to see them.

The sixth: filth in the knuckles, that is, the crooks of the outside of the fingertips. The Arabs did not use to wash this often, leaving washing of the hands to after having eaten, so filth would accumulate in these creases. The Messenger of Allah (SAW) ordered them to wash their knuckles.

The seventh: cleansing the fingers. The Messenger of Allah (SAW) ordered the Arabs to clean them, including the tips of the fingers and any filth under the fingernails, since clippers can not always get there, and filth can accumulate there. The Messenger of Allah (SAW) fixed a period of time for them to clip their fingernails, pluck their armpits, and shave their pubic area – every forty days. But indeed He (SAW) ordered that under the fingernails be cleaned; it is related that the Prophet (SAW) found the divine inspiration to be slowing down, and when Jibril (peace be upon him) descended to him, he said to him: How can we send revelation to you all when you do not wash your knuckles nor clean your fingers nor use the *siwak* against any plaque on your teeth? Tell your people to do this. And "uff" refers to fingernail filth while "tuff" refers to filth in the ears. Regarding the word of the Mighty and Sublime { And do not say "uff" to either of them } [i.e. words of disrespect; Al-israa 23], that is, do not disgrace them by referring to the filth under the fingernails; it is said: Do not be repulsed by them as you are repulsed by what is under the fingernails.

The eighth: the filth that accumulates over the entire body from sweating and the dust of the road; a bath [hammam, i.e. the public bath] removes this. There is no problem with entering the hammam; the Messenger of Allah's (SAW) Companions used to enter the baths in Sham.

*Al-Ghazali, Ihyaa 'Ulum Al-din, The book of the foundations of purity [tahara] and its requirements, The third section on cleanliness: cleansing from external secretions; the first kind: filth and fluids that exude, there being eight kinds of these*

عن طلق بن حبيب قال رأى عمر بن الخطاب رجلاً حكَّ إبطه أو مسه فقال له قم فإغسل يديك أو تطهّر

المصنف لإبن ابي شيبة كتاب الطهارة

From Talq ibn Habib, who said: 'Umar ibn Al-Khattab saw a man scratching or touching his armpit, and he said to him: Get up and wash your hands (or cleanse yourself).

*Ibn Abi Shayba, Al-musannaf, The book of purity*

عن ابراهيم أنه كان يقول ما خرج من الجرح فهو بمنزلة الدم وفيه الوضوء ... عن الزهري قال سمعته يقول القَيح والدم سواءٌ

المصنف لإبن ابي شيبة كتاب الطهارة

Ibrahim related that he would say: Whatever comes out of a wound is on the same level as blood, and ablution is to be performed for it ... From Al-Zuhri, who said: I heard him say: Pus and blood are alike.

*Ibn Abi Shayba, Al-musannaf, The book of purity*

عن علي بن جعفر بن محمد بن علي عن أبيه عن جده أن رسول الله ﷺ قال كانت العنكبوت إمرأةً فسحرت زوجها فمسخها الله عنكبوتاً قال وكانت الأرنب إمرأة قذرة لا تغتسل من حيضٍ ولا من غير ذلك فمسخها الله أرنباً

أدب النساء لعبد الملك بن حبيب باب ما يكره للنساء من علاج مما يعرفن أنه يُحبِّبن إلى أزواجهن

'Ali ibn Ja'far ibn Muhammad ibn 'Ali related from his father, from his grandfather, that the Messenger of Allah (SAW) said: The spider used to be a woman; she cast a spell on her husband, so Allah turned her into a spider. He said: And the rabbit used to be a filthy woman who did not wash herself from menstruation or from anything else, so Allah turned her into a rabbit.

*'Abd Al-Malik ibn Habib, Adab Al-nisaa, Section: what is disapproved for women to remedy what they know endears them to their husbands*

وهو سبعة أشياء الأول خروج المني على وجه الدفق واللذة فإن خرج لمرض لم يوجب فأما خروج المني بالاحتلام فيوجب الغسل والثاني تغييب الحشفة في الفرج سواء كان قبلاً أو دبراً والثالث إسلام الكافر والرابع الموت وهذه الأربعة يشترك فيها الرجال والنساء وتختص النساء بثلاثة أشياء الحيض والنفاس والولادة على أحد الوجهين الوقت الذي يجب فيه الغسل من الحيض على المرأة خرج القطن ولا شيء عليه أو كان عليه بلة بيضاء

أحكام النساء لابن الجوزي الباب الحادي عشر في ذكر ما يوجب الغسل

There are seven things [that make bathing obligatory]. The first is when semen comes out in the manner of gushing and delight; if it comes out of someone who is sick, bathing is not obligatory; but when semen comes out from a wet dream, bathing is obligatory. The second is the concealment of the head of the penis in the vagina, whether from front or back. The third is when a disbeliever yields into Islam. The forth is death. Men and woman share these four, but women have three more things in particular: menstruation, postpartum bleeding, and childbirth, according to one of two opinions. The time at which washing from menstruation is obligatory for women is when a piece of cotton comes out with nothing on it, or just white moisture on it.

*Ibn Al-Jawzi, Ahkam Al-nisaa, Chapter eleven: mention of what makes bathing [ghusl] obligatory*

﴿ وَثِيَابَكَ فَطَهِّرْ ﴾ المدثر ٤

## { *And purify your garments* } Al-mudathir 4

﴿ وثيابك فطهر ﴾ عن النجاسة أو قصرها خلاف جرّ العرب ثيابهم خُيَلاء فربما اصابتها نجاسة

تفسير الجلالين

{ And purify your garments } : from filthiness; or shorten them, instead of how the Arabs would drag their garments out of vanity, since perhaps they might get filthy.

*Tafsir Al-Jalalain*

إبن عباس يقول ﴿ وثيابك فطهر ﴾ قال من الاثم ... عن قتادة قوله ﴿ وثيابك فطهر ﴾ يقول طهرها من المعاصي فكانت العرب تسمي الرجل إذا نكث ولم يف بعهد أنه دنِس الثياب وإذا وفى وأصلح قالوا مطهر الثياب ... عن محمد بن سيرين ﴿ وثيابك فطهر ﴾ قال اغسلها بالماء

تفسير الطبري

Ibn 'Abbas said, about { And purify your garments } ; he said: From sin. ... From Qatada, regarding His word { And purify your garments } ; he said: Purify them from sins; the Arabs, whenever someone would break and not honor a vow, would say that he had filthy garments; whenever someone honored and made it right, they said his garments were purified. ... From Muhammad ibn Sirin, of { And purify your garments } ; he said: Wash them with water.

*Tafsir Al-Tabari*

﴿ وثيابك فطهر ﴾ أمر بأن تكون ثيابه طاهرة من النجاسات لأن طهارة الثياب شرط في الصلاة لا تصح إلا بها وهي الأولى والأحب في غير الصلاة وقبيح بالمؤمن الطيب أن يحمل خبثاً

تفسير الزمخشري

{ And purify your garments } : He commands that his garments be pure from anything filthy, since cleanliness of garments is a condition for prayer, without which it is not valid, and it is most appropriate and desirable for things other than prayer; and it is loathsome for a wholesome Believer to harbor repulsive impurity [*khabath*].

*Tafsir Al-Zamakhshari*

﴿ وثيابك فطهر ﴾ يريد مالك أنه كنى عن الثياب بالدين

تفسير القرطبي

{ And purify your garments } : Malik was of the view that "garments" is an allusion to religion [*deen*].

*Tafsir Al-Qurtubi*

•     •     •

﴿ وبَشِّر الذين آمنوا وعملوا الصالحات أنَّ لهم جنات تجري من تحتها الأنهار كلما رُزِقوا منها من ثمرة رزقاً قالوا هذا الذي رُزِقنا من قبل وأُتوا به متشابهاً ولهم فيها أزواج مطهَّرة وهم فيها خالدون ﴾ البقرة ٢٥

{ *And give the good news to those who have believed, and done good deeds, that theirs are gardens below which rivers flow; every time they are favored with bounty of fruit from therein, they say: "This is what we have been favored with before", and similar things are brought to them; and there they have purified wives; and they will be there eternally* } *Al-baqara 25*

وأما قوله ﴿ مطهرة ﴾ فإن تأويله أنهن طهرن من كل أذى وقذى وريبة مما يكون في نساء أهل الدنيا من الحيض والنفاس والغائط والبول والمخاط والبصاق والمني وما أشبه ذلك من الأذى والأدناس والريب والمكاره

تفسير الطبري

Regarding His word { Purified } ; the interpretation of this is that the women are free of all harm, filth, and misgivings that are found in the women of this world, including menstruation, bleeding from childbirth, defecation, urine, mucus, spit, semen [*maniy*], and other similar harm, filthiness, concerns, and abominations.

*Tafsir Al-Tabari*

•  •  •

عن عائشة رضي الله عنها وكان عليه الصلاة والسلام إذا أمطرت السماء خلع ثيابه وتجرد حتى يصيبه المطر

تفسير القرطبي طه ٨٤

From 'Aishah (may Allah be pleased with her): Whenever it rained, He (prayers and peace upon him) would take off his clothes and be naked so He could get rained on.

*Tafsir Al-Qurtubi, Surah Taha 84*

عن حسن ﴿ انما المشركون نجس ﴾ قال لا تصافحوهم فمن صافحهم فليتوضأ

تفسير الطبري التوبة ٢٨

Hasan said, regarding { Truly the Idolaters are filthy } : Do not shake hands with them. Anyone who shakes hands with them should perform ablution.

*Tafsir Al-Tabari, Al-tawba 28*

وحكى الشيخ أبو محمد في الفروق أن بعض أصحابنا قال لو لف على اصبعه خرقة وادخلها في دبره وهو في الصلاة لم تبطل صلاته

المجموع شرح المهذب للنووي كتاب الطهارة باب الأحداث التي تنقض الوضوء

Sheikh Abu Muhammad [Al-Juwayni] recounted that some of our companions said: If someone wraps a cloth around his finger and inserts it into his rear while he is praying, his prayer is not invalidated.

*Al-Nawawi, Al-majmu' Sharh Al-muhadhab, The book of purity, Section: occurrences that annul ablution*

لو أخرجت دودة رأسها من أحد السبيلين ثم رجعت قبل انفصالها ففي انتقاض الوضوء وجهان حكاهما الماوردي والروياني والشاشي وغيرهم أصحهما ينتقض للخروج والثاني لا لعدم الإنفصال والله أعلم

المجموع شرح المهذب للنووي كتاب الطهارة باب الأحداث التي تنقض الوضوء

If a worm sticks out its head from one of the two passages [i.e. the front or the rear], and goes back in before detaching, there are two opinions regarding invalidation of ablution, related by Al-Mawardi, Al-Ruyani, Al-Shashi, and others; the more correct of the two is that it is invalidated by it coming out; the second is that it is not, since it did not detach; but Allah knows best.

*Al-Nawawi, Al-majmu' Sharh Al-muhadhab, The book of purity, Section: occurrences that annul ablution*

العناية بالجسم

*Body care*

عن عبد الرحمن بن ابي سعيد الخدري عن أبيه أن رسول الله ﷺ قال غسل يوم الجمعة على كل محتلم وسواك

ويمسُ من الطيب ما قدر عليه إلا أن بُكيراً لم يذكر عند الرحمن وقال في الطيب ولو من طيب المرأة

صحيح مسلم كتاب الجمعة

'Abd Al-Rahman ibn Abi Sa'id Al-Khudri related from his father that the Messenger of Allah (SAW) said: Bathing [ghusl] on Fridays is obligatory for everyone who has reached manhood [muhtalim; i.e. who has had a wet dream], and using the tooth-cleaning stick [siwak], and using some perfume as he is able. (Bukair, one of the narrators, did not mention 'Abd Al-Rahman.) And he said regarding perfume: Even if it is women's perfume.

*Sahih Muslim, The book of Fridays*


عن ابي سعيد الخدري رضي الله عنه أن رسول الله ﷺ قال غسل يرم الجمعة واجب على كل محتلم

صحيح البخاري كتاب الجمعة

Abu Sa'id Al-Khudri (may Allah be pleased with him), related that the Messenger of Allah (SAW) said: Bathing [ghusl] on Fridays is obligatory for everyone who has reached manhood [muhtalim].

*Sahih Al-Bukhari, The book of Friday assembly*


عن أنس بن مالك قال كان رسول الله ﷺ يُكثر دهن رأسه وتسريح لحيته ويكثر القناع حتى كأن ثوبه

ثوب زيات

الشمائل المحمدية للترمذي باب ما جاء في ترجل رسول الله ﷺ

Anas ibn Malik said: The Messenger of Allah (SAW) used a lot of oil on his head and for combing out his beard, and He covered his head a lot, to the point that his garment was like the garment of an oil vendor.

*Al-Tirmidhi, Al-shama'il al-Muhammadiya, The section concerning the grooming [tarajjul] of the Messenger of Allah (SAW)*


عن عائشة أنّ رسول الله ﷺ كان إذا أخذ مضجعه نفث في يديه وقرأ بالمعوّذات ومسح بهما جسده

صحيح البخاري كتاب الدعوات

'Aisha related that the Messenger of Allah (SAW), whenever He lay down to sleep, coughed out into his hands, recited the last three chapters of the Qur'an [Al-mu'awwidhat; the refuge surahs], and passed his hands over his body.

*Sahih Al-Bukhari, The book of supplications*

عن أبي هريرة رضي الله عنه قال قال النبي ﷺ إنّ اليهود والنصارى لا يصبغون نخالفوهم

صحيح البخاري كتاب اللباس

Abu Huraira (may Allah be pleased with him) related that the Prophet (SAW) said:
The Jews and the Christians do not dye their hair, so do things differently from them.

*Sahih Al-Bukhari, The book of dress*

عن أبي هريرة رواية الفطرة خمس الختان والاستحداد ونتف الإبط وتقليم الأظفار وقصّ الشارب

صحيح البخاري كتاب اللباس

Abu Huraira related the narration: "The innate disposition of man [*fitrah*] consists of
five things – circumcision, shaving the pubic hair, plucking the armpits, clipping the
nails, and trimming the mustache."

*Sahih Al-Bukhari, The book of dress*

عن طلق بن حبيب قال عشرةٌ من ألسنة السواك وقص الشارب والمضمضة والإستنشاق وتوفير اللحية وقص
الأظفار ونتف الابط والختان وحلق العانة وغسل الدبر

سنن النسائي كتاب الزينة والسنن

From Talq ibn Habib, who said: There are ten things to the *sunnah*: The tooth-
cleaning stick [*siwak*], trimming the mustache, rinsing out the mouth [*madmada*],
drawing water up into the nose to clean it [*istinshaq*], letting the beard grow out,
trimming the nails, plucking the armpits, circumcision, shaving the pubic area, and
washing one's rear.

*Sunan Al-Nasa'i, The book of adornment and lifestyle*

أنس بن مالك قال وقّت لنا رسول الله ﷺ في قصّ الشارب وتقليم الأظفار وحلق العانة ونتف الإبط أن لا
نترك أكثر من أربعين يوماً

جامع الترمذي كتاب الأدب

Anas Ibn Malik said: The messenger of Allah (SAW) fixed a time for us concerning
trimming the mustache, clipping the nails, shaving the pubic area, and plucking the
armpits – we were not to leave it more than forty days.

*Sunan Al-Tirmidhi, The book of manners*

شعر الشارب وقد قال ﷺ قُصّوا الشوارب وفي لفظ آخر جُزّوا الشوارب وفي لفظ آخر حُفّوا الشوارب وأعفوا اللِّحى أي اجعلوها حفاف الشفة وحفاف الشيء حوله ومنه قوله تعالى ﴿ وترى الملائكة حافين من حول العرش ﴾ وفي لفظ آخر أحفوا وهذا يشعر بالإستئصال وقوله حفوا يدل على ما دون ذلك قال الله عز وجل ﴿ إن يسألكموها فيُحفكم تبخلوا ﴾ أي يستقصي عليكم

إحياء علوم الدين للغزالي كتاب أسرار الطهارة ومهماتها

The hair of the mustache: He (SAW) said: Trim off your mustaches. In another wording: Clip off your mustaches. In another wording: Shave your mustaches and let your beards alone; that is, let them fill out on the borders and sides, that is, the part around them; the border of something is the part around it. Along these lines is the word of Allah Most High ⟨ And you will see the angels bordering around the Throne ⟩ [Al-zumar 75]. In another wording: Trim it down well; and this informs regarding plucking it out; his saying "Trim" indicates against anything less than this. Allah Mighty and Sublime has said ⟨ If He should ask it [your wealth] of you, and pressure you all ["trim you down"], you would be stingy ⟩ [Muhammad 37] ; that is, if He should examine and try to get to the bottom of you all.

*Al-Ghazali, Ihyaa 'Ulum Al-din, The book of the foundations of purity [tahara] and its requirements*

إبن ابي رواد قال أخبرني نافع أن إبن عمر كان يقلّم أظافيره في كل خمس عشرة ليلة ويستحدّ في كل شهر

الأدب المفرد للبخاري كتاب الختان

Ibn Abi Rawwad said: Nafi' told me that Ibn 'Umar cut his nails every fifteen nights and trimmed his pubic hair every month.

*Al-Bukhari, Al-adab Al-mufrad, The book of circumcision*

﴾ قيل لها ادخلي الصرح   فلما رأته حسبته لُجّةً وكشفت عن ساقيها قال إنه صرح ممرّد من قوارير قالت ربِّ إني ظلمتُ نفسي وأسلمتُ مع سليمان لله ربِّ العالمين ﴾ النمل ٤٤

{ It was said to her [the Queen of Sheba]: "Enter the pavilion"; but when she saw it, she took it to be a deep dark pool, and uncovered her shins. He [Suleiman] said: Indeed it is a well-built and smooth pavilion, of glass. She said: My Lord, truly I have wronged myself, but I will surrender along with Suleiman to Allah, Lord of the worlds. } Al-naml 44

عن عبدالله بن شداد قال ﴿ فلما رأته حسبته لُجّةً وكشفت عن ساقيها ﴾ الآية فإذا إمرأةٌ شعراء قال فقال سليمان ما يُذهب هذا قالوا النورة قال فجُعلت النورة يومئذٍ

المصنف لإبن أبي شيبة كتاب الطهارة

From Abdullah ibn Shaddad, who said: { But when she saw it, she took it to be a dark pool, and uncovered her shins } ; she was a hairy woman. Suleiman said: What can make this go away? They said: Depilatory cream. And so depilatory cream [nurah] came about on that day.

*Ibn Abi Shayba, Al-musannaf, The book of purity*

﴿ قيل لها ﴾ أيضاً ﴿ أدخلي الصرح ﴾ هو سطح من زجاج أبيض شفاف تحته ماء عذب جار فيه سمك اصطنعه سليمان لما قيل له إن ساقيها وقدميها كقدمي الحمار ﴿ فلما رأته حسبته لُجّةً ﴾ من الماء ﴿ وكشفت عن ساقيها ﴾ لتخوضه وكان سليمان على سريره في صدر الصرح فرأى ساقيها وقدميها حساناً ﴿ قال ﴾ لها ﴿ إنه صرحٌ ممرّد ﴾ مملس ﴿ من قوارير ﴾ أي زجاج ودعاها إلى الاسلام ﴿ قالت رب اني ظلمت نفسي بعبادة غيرك ﴿ وأسلمتُ ﴾ كائنة ﴿ مع سليمان لله رب العالمين ﴾ وأراد تزوّجها فكره شعر ساقيها فعملت له الشياطين النورة فأزالته فتزوجها وأحبها وأقرّها على ملكها

تفسير الجلالين

{ It was said to her } as well : { Enter the pavilion } : this being a transparent white crystal surface, with freshwater under it in which fish swam around, that Suleiman had fashioned, when he was told that her shins and her legs were like the legs of a donkey. { But when she saw it, she took it to be a deep dark pool } : of water, { and uncovered her shins } : to wade through it. And Suleiman was on his divan in the front of the pavilion, and he saw that her shins and her legs were fine; { He said } : to her { indeed it is a well-built and smooth pavilion } : smoothed over { of glass }

165

: that is, crystal; and he called her to Islam. { She said: My Lord, truly I have wronged myself } : by worshipping others besides you; { but I will surrender } : completely { along with Suleiman to Allah, Lord of the worlds } . And He desired to marry her, but disliked the hair on her shins, and so the devils [shayatin] made depilatory cream for him, and she got rid of it. Then he married her, and loved her, and allowed her to remain over her dominion.

*Tafsir Al-Jalalain*

عن عكرمة وابي صالح قالا لما تزوج سليمان بلقيس قالت له لم تمسني حديدة قط قال سليمان للشياطين انظروا ما يذهب الشعر قالوا النورة فكان أول من صنع النورة

تفسير الطبري

From 'Ikrama and Abu Salih, who said: When Suleiman married Bilqis, she said to him: Never has a razor ever touched me. Suleiman said to the devils: See about something that can remove hair. They said: Depilatory cream [*nurah*]. And so he was the first to prepare *nurah*.

*Tafsir Al-Tabari*

•     •     •

عن أم سلمة أن النبي ﷺ اطّلى وولِيَ عانته بيده

سنن إبن ماجه كتاب الأدب باب الإطّلاء بالنورة

Umm Salamah related that the Prophet (SAW) spread cream on Himself and took care of his pubic area with his hand.

*Sunan ibn Majah, The book of manners, Section: spreading depilatory cream*

عن أم سلمة أن النبي ﷺ كان إذا اطّلى بدأ بعورته فطلاها بالنورة وسائر جسده أهله

سنن إبن ماجه كتاب الأدب باب الإطّلاء بالنورة

Umm Salamah related that the Prophet (SAW), whenever He spread cream on Himself, He began with his private area ['*awrah*] and spread the depilatory cream on it; the women of His household would do the rest of His body.

*Sunan ibn Majah, The book of manners, Section: spreading depilatory cream*

سكين بن عبد العزيز بن قيس عن أبيه قال دخلت على عبدالله بن عمر وجارية تحلق عنه الشعر وقال النورة
تُرقّ الجلد

الأدب المفرد للبخاري كتاب المعرفة

Sukain ibn 'Abd Al-'Aziz ibn Qais related from his father, who said: I went in to see Abdullah ibn 'Umar, and a servant girl was removing his hair, and he said: Depilatory cream softens the skin.

*Al-Bukhari, Al-adab Al-mufrad, The book of learning*

عن إبن جريج قال قلت لعطاء رجلٌ إطّلى بنورة هل عليه وضوء قال أوليس مغتسلاً قال ولا بد له أن يمسّ
ذكره هو القائل قال قلت فطلى ساقَيه من وَجَع بهما وهو متوضّئٌ أُيعيد الوضوء قال ليست النورة بحدث

المصنف لعبد الرزاق كتاب الطهارة

From Ibn Juraij, who said: I asked 'Ataa about someone who applies depilatory cream on himself – must he perform ablution [*wudu*']? He said: If he has not completely washed? Ibn Juraij said: He inevitably touches his penis; then he applies it to both his legs feeling discomfort, having performed ablution; must he repeat ablution? 'Ataa said: Depilation is not a bodily occurrence [*hadath*].

*'Abd Al-Razzaq, the Musannaf, The book of purity*

وقيل لها الشعرة الطويلة خير أم القصيرة المحلوقة فقالت الشعرة الطويلة تبرد النفس وتطفئ الحرارة وتخل
بركن النيك وتطرد الشهوة والمحلوقة تهيج الشهوة وتضرم نارها وتشعل توقدها والتهابها وتسعر النيك وتشفي النهم

نواضر الأيك في معرفة النيك للسيوطي فصل في حظوة النساء

And it was said to her: Is long pubic hair better or short and shaved? She said: Long pubic hair chills a person and extinguishes heat, disrupts the grounds for fucking [*naik*], and drives away the desire. Shaved hair stirs up the desire and inflames its fire, fuels its blaze and its burning, kindles fucking, and cures excessive appetite.

*Al-Suyuti, Nawadir Al-aik fi Ma'rifa Al-naik, Section: high standing with women*

فقال آخر الشعرة الطويلة تطفئ شهوة النيك وتخمد نار الأير وتذبله وتصده عن الحر والمحلوقة تشد الفؤاد وتحيي
الشهوة وتشفط الأير وتنشطه

نواضر الأيك في معرفة النيك للسيوطي فصل في حظوة النساء

And someone else said: Long pubic hair extinguishes the passion of fucking, weakens the fire in the dick, causes it to dry up, and deters it from the vagina; but shaved hair charms the heart, enlivens the desire, and sucks up the dick and invigorates it.

*Al-Suyuti, Nawadir Al-aik fi Ma'rifa Al-naik, Section: high standing with women*

عن الهذيل بن الحكَم أن النبي ﷺ قال إن جزّ الشعر يزيد في الجماع

موسوعة الطب النبوي لابي نعيم الاصفهاني باب في ما يقوي الإيعاظ ويزيد في الباه

Al-Hudhail ibn Al-Hakam related that the Prophet (SAW) said: Indeed trimming the hair short boosts sex.

*Abu Nu'im Al-Asfahani, Mawsu'a Al-tibb Al-nabawi, Section: concerning that which strengthens discourse and increases coitus*

عن نافع عن إبن عمر عن النبي س قال خالفوا المشركين وفّروا اللحى وأحفوا الشوارب وكان إبن عمر إذا حجّ أو اعتمر قبض على لحيته فما فضل أخذه

صحي ح البخاري كتاب اللباس

Nafi' related from Ibn 'Umar who related from the Prophet (SAW), who said: Be different from the pagans – let the beard abound and keep the mustache trimmed. And Ibn 'Umar, whenever he went on the *hajj* or *'umrah* pilgrimage, would take hold of his beard, and cut off what was in excess of his grasp.

*Sahih Al-Bukhari, The book of dress*

عن عكرمة أن أناساً من أهل العراق جاءوا فقالوا يا إبن عباس أترى الغسل يوم الجمعة واجباً قال لا ولكنه أطهر وخيرٌ لمن إغتسل ومن لم يغتسل فليس عليه بواجب وسأخبركم كيف بدء الغسل كان الناس مجهودين يلبسون الصوف ويعملون على ظهورهم وكان مسجدهم ضيّقاً مقارب السقْف انما هو عريش نخرج رسول الله ﷺ في يوم حار وعرِق الناس في ذلك الصوف حتى ثارت منهم رياح آذى بعضهم بعضاً فلما وجد رسول الله ﷺ تلك الريح قال أيها الناس إذا كان هذا اليوم فاغتسلوا وليمسَّ أحدكُم أفضل ما يجد من دُهنه وطيبه قال إبن عباس ثم جاء الله بالخير ولبسوا غير الصوف وكُفوا العمل ووُسِّع مسجدهم وذهب بعض الذي كان يؤذي بعضهم بعضاً من العَرَق

سنن أبي داود كتاب الطهارة

'Ikrama related that some people from Iraq came and said: Oh Ibn 'Abbas, do you consider it obligatory to bathe [*ghusl*] on the day of the Friday assembly? He said: No, but it is purer and better for whoever bathes; although there is no obligation on whoever does not bathe. I will tell you all how bathing started: people used to work a great deal and wear fleece, and carry their work on their backs; and their mosque was tight with a low ceiling, just like a hut. The Messenger of Allah (SAW) came out on one hot day, and people were sweating in their fleeces, to the point that bad smells were breaking out from among them, causing harm to each other. And when the Messenger of Allah (SAW) perceived the smell, He said: Oh people! Whenever it is this day, bathe yourselves, and let each of you rub on the best oil and perfume he can find. Ibn 'Abbas said: Then Allah brought abundance, and people wore things other than fleece, they stopped working, their mosque was vastly expanded, and the sweating with which they had been harming each other went away.

*Sunan Abu Dawud, The book of purity*

عن ابي هريرة قال قال رسول الله ﷺ الوضوء مما مسّت النار ولو من ثور أقطٍ

جامع الترمذي كتاب الطهارة

Abu Huraira said: The Messenger of Allah (SAW) said: Ablution [*wudu'*] is required for whatever has touched fire, even a piece of *aqit* [cheese produced in part by thickening milk over heat].

*Sunan Al-Tirmidhi, The book of purity*

عن الأشعري قال قال رسول الله ﷺ أيّما إمرأة استعطرت فمرّت على قوم ليجدوا من ريحها فهي زانية

سنن النسائي كتاب الزينة

From Al-Ash'ari who said: The Messenger of Allah (SAW) said: Any woman who puts on perfume and then passes by people so they may perceive her scent – she is an adulteress [*zaniyah*].

*Sunan Al-Nasa'i, The book of adornment*

حميد بن عبد الرحمان قال لقيت رجلاً صحب النبي ﷺ كما صحبه أبو هريرة قال نهى رسول الله ﷺ أن يمتشط أحدنا كل يوم أو يبول في مغتسله

سنن ابي داود كتاب الطهارة

Humaid ibn 'Abd Al-Rahman said: I met a man who accompanied the Prophet (SAW) like Abu Huraira accompanied him and who said: The Messenger of Allah (SAW) forbade any of us to comb his hair every day or to urinate where he bathed.

*Sunan Abu Dawud, The book of purity*

عن عمرو بن شعيب عن أبيه عن جده قال قال رسول الله ﷺ لا تنتفوا الشيب ما من مسلمٍ يشيب شيبةً في الاسلام إلا كانت له نوراً يوم القيامة

سنن ابي داود كتاب الترجل

'Amr ibn Shu'aib related from his father, from his grandfather, who said: The Messenger of Allah (SAW) said: Do not pluck white hair; there is no Muslim who grows a white hair in Islam but that it will be light to him on the day of resurrection.

*Sunan Abu Dawud, The book of grooming*

عن إبن عمر قال قال رسول الله ﷺ ثلاث لا تُرَدُّ الوسائد والدُهن واللبن

جامع الترمذي كتاب الأدب

From Ibn 'Umar who said: The Messenger of Allah (SAW) said: Three things are not to be refused: cushions and body oil and milk.

*Sunan Al-Tirmidhi, The book of manners*

عن جابر بن عبدالله رضي الله عنهما أن النبي ﷺ قال إذا دخلت ليلاً فلا تدخل على أهلك حتى تستحدّ المغيبة وتمتشط الشعثة

صحيح البخاري كتاب النكاح

Jabir ibn 'Abdullah (may Allah be pleased with him) related that the Prophet (SAW) said: Whenever you come into town at night, do not enter in to see a woman of your household until the woman whose husband has been absent has trimmed her pubic hair and the unkempt woman has combed her hair.

*Sahih Al-Bukhari, The book of marital relations*

وحكى إبن خلّكان فيما نقل من خطّ الشيخ قُطب الدين اليونيني قال بلغنا أن رجلاً يدعى أبا سلامة من ناحية بُصرى كان فيه مجون وإستهتار فذُكِر عنده السواك وما فيه من الفضيلة فقال والله لا استاك إلا في المخرج يعني دبره فأخذ سواكاً فوضعه في مخرجه ثم أخرجه فمكث بعده تسعة أشهر فوضع ولداً على صفة الجرذان له أربعة قوائم ورأسه كرأس السمكة وله دبر كدبر الأرنب ولما وضعه صاح ذلك الحيوان ثلاث صيحات فقامت إبنة ذلك الرجل فرضّخت رأسه فمات وعاش ذلك الرجل بعد وضعه له يومين ومات في الثالث وكان يقول هذا الحيوان قتلني وقطّع امعائي

البداية والنهاية لإبن كثير فصل ثم دخلت سنة خمس وستين وستمائة

Ibn Khalikan related regarding what had been conveyed from what Sheikh Qutb Al-Deen Al-Yunini had written down; he said: It came to our awareness that there was a man called Abu Salama from the region of Busra, who was a reckless joker. The teeth-cleaning stick [*siwak*] and its merits were mentioned to him, and he said: "I swear by Allah, I don't use a *siwak* except in the exit"; he meant his rear end. And he took a *siwak*, put it in his exit, and then took it out. After this he remained for nine months, and then delivered a child that looked like a rat, having four limbs, a head like the head of a fish, and a rear end like the rear end of a rabbit. And when he delivered it, the animal shrieked three times; the man's daughter got up and smashed its head and it died. And the man lived two days after his delivery and died on the third; saying: "This animal has killed me and ripped up my intestines."

*Ibn Kathir, Al-bidaya wa Al-nihaya, Section: Entering then year six hundred sixty-five*

عن ابي أيوب قال قال رسول الله ﷺ أربع من سنن المرسلين ألحياء والتعطر والسواك والنكاح

جامع الترمذي كتاب النكاح

From Abu Ayub who said: The Messenger of Allah (SAW) said: There are four things to the way of life of the Messengers: modesty, perfuming oneself, the teeth-cleaning stick [*siwak*], and marital relations.

*Sunan Al-Tirmidhi, The book of marital relations*

صهيب الخير قال قال رسول الله ﷺ إن أحسن ما إختضبتم به لهذا السواد ارغب لنسائكم فيكم وأهيب لكم في صدور عدوكم

سنن إبن ماجه كتاب اللباس

Suhaib Al-Khair said: The Messenger of Allah (SAW) said: Indeed the best you can dye your hair with is black; it is more desirable to your women and makes you more intimidating in the hearts of your enemy.

*Sunan Ibn Majah, The book of dress*

عن ابي الزناد أخبرني إبن جرهد عن أبيه أن النبي ﷺ مر به وهو كاشف عن فخذه فقال النبي ﷺ غطِّ فخذك فانها من العورة

جامع الترمذي كتاب الأدب

From Abu Al-Zinad: Ibn Jarhad related to me from his father that the Prophet (SAW) passed by him when his thigh was exposed; and the Prophet (SAW) said: Cover your thigh, for indeed it is part of nakedness [*'awrah*].

*Sunan Al-Tirmidhi, The book of manners*

عن عبدالله بن مسعود أن نبي الله ﷺ كان يكره عشر خصال الصفرة يعني الخلوق وتغيير الشيب وجرّ الإزار والتختم بالذهب والضرب بالكعاب والتبرج بالزينة لغير محلّها والرقى إلا بالمعوذات وتعليق التمائم وعزل الماء بغير محلّه وإفساد الصبي

سنن النسائي كتاب الزينة من السنه

Abdullah ibn Mas'ud related that the Prophet of Allah (SAW) disliked ten practices: yellow dye [*al-sufrah*], that is, *khaluq* [a yellowish perfume], changing gray hair, dragging one's waist wrap, wearing gold rings, throwing dice, showing one's adornment to someone not permitted to see it, reciting incantations [*ruqyah*] except with the verses of seeking refuge [*al-mu'awadhat*], hanging up talismans, discharging semen other than where permitted, and harming a young boy [i.e. by intercourse with a nursing mother, which would damage her milk should she become pregnant, harming the boy].

*Sunan Al-Nasa'i, The book of adornment in the sunnah*

عن زيد بن أسلم قال رأيت إبن عمر يصفّر لحيته بالخَلوق فقلت يا أبا عبد الرحمن إنك تصفر لحيتك بالخلوق قال إني رأيت رسول الله ﷺ يصفر بها لحيته ولم يكن شيءٌ من الصِبغ أحبّ إليه منها ولقد كان يصبُغ بها ثيابه كلها حتى عِمامته

سنن النسائي كّاب الزينة من السنه

From Zaid ibn Aslam, who said: I saw Ibn 'Umar dye his beard yellow with *khaluq*, and I said: Oh Abu 'Abd Al-Rahman, indeed you dye your beard yellow with *khaluq*? He said: Indeed I saw the Messenger of Allah (SAW) dye his beard yellow with it, and there was no kind of dye that He loved more than it; He used to dye all his clothes with it, even his turban.

*Sunan Al-Nasa'i, The book of adornment in the sunnah*

وكان إبن عمر يلبس النعال السِبتية ويصبُغ بالصفرة إذ رأى النبي ﷺ يفعل نحو ذلك ﷺ

الشفا للقاضي عياض اليحصبي القسم الثاني فيما يجب على الأنام من حقوقه ﷺ فصل في علامة محبته ﷺ

Ibn 'Umar used to wear tanned leather sandals and use yellow dye [*al-sufrah*], since he saw the Prophet (SAW) doing something similar.

*Al-qadi 'Iyad Al-Yahsubi, Al-shifa, Part Two: Regarding the rights of His (SAW) that are due on all of creation, Section: regarding signs of love for Him (SAW)*

اغسلوا ثيابَكم وخذوا من شعوركم وإستاكوا وتزينوا وتنظفوا فإن بني إسرائيل لم يكونوا يفعلون كذلك فزنت نساؤهم (إبن عساكر عن علي)

كنز العمال للهندي حرف الزاي كّاب الزينة والتجمل الباب الأول الترغيب فيه

"Wash your garments, cut your hair back, use a *siwak* to clean your mouth and teeth, dress well, and clean yourselves, for indeed the People of Israel did not do these things, and their women committed adultery." (Related by Ibn 'Asakir from 'Ali)

*Al-Hindi, Kanz Al-'ummal. Section "Z", The book of grooming and adornment, Section one: regarding the desirability of it*

ومن الآداب المفترضة على المرأة ألا تزال يداها ناعمتين سالمتين من الخشونة وأن تكون أظفارها مقلمة مبرودة ناعمة لثلا تؤذي إحليل الرجل أو تخدشه

نزهة الاصحاب في معاشرة الأحباب لإبن يحيى المغربي ومن آداب الجماع الواجبة على المرأة

Part of the presumed proper conduct of a woman is that her hands always be smooth and free from roughness, and that her fingernails be trimmed, filed, and smooth; otherwise she may hurt the man's member or scratch it.

*Ibn Yahya, Nuzhat Al-ashab fi Mu'asharat Al-ahbab, Section: mandatory sexual conduct for women*

وقال بعض السلف ينبغي للرجل أن يتعاهد من نفسه ثلاثاً ينبغي أن لا يدع المشى فإن احتاج إليه يوماً قدر عليه وينبغي أن لا يدع الأكل فإن أمعاءه تضيق وينبغي أن لا يدع الجماع فإن البئر إذا لم تُنزح ذهب ماؤها

الطب النبوي لإبن قيّم

Some of those before us said: A man ought to pledge three things to himself: He ought to not give up walking, for indeed he needs it daily as is possible. And he ought to not give up eating, for indeed his bowels will become constrained. And he ought to not give up sex, for indeed whenever a well is not drained its water runs out.

*Ibn Qayyim, Al-tibb Al-nabawi*


اعلم يرحمك الله الرائحة الرديئة في الفرج والإبط من أكبر المصائب

الروض العاطر في نزهة الخاطر للشيخ النفزاوي الباب التاسع عشر فيما يزيل بخور الإبط والفرج ويضيفه

Know (may Allah have mercy on you) that bad smell in the armpits or vagina is among the greatest of calamities.

*Al-Nafzawi, Al-rawd Al-'atir fi Nuzha Al-khatir, Chapter nineteen: regarding what eliminates the scent of the armpits and the vagina and accomodates it*


وإستعمال الطيب للرجال والنساء يعين على النكاح

الروض العاطر في نزهة الخاطر للشيخ النفزاوي الباب الأول في المحمود من الرجال

The use of perfume among men and women aids in marital relations.

*Al-Nafzawi, Al-rawd Al-'atir fi Nuzha Al-khatir, Chapter one: regarding praiseworthy men*


اعلم يرحمك الله أيها الوزير أن هذا الباب لتغليظ الذكر نافع للرجال والنساء لأن الذكر الصغير تكرهه المرأة عند الجماع كما تكره اللين الضعيف المسترخي وإن لذة المرأة في الذكر الكبير فمن كان ذكره صغيراً وأراد أن يعظمه ويقويه على الجماع فليدلكه بالماء الفاتر وهو الحار حتى يحمر ويجري فيه الدم ويسخن ويغلظ ثم يمسحه بعسل الزنجبيل المربى ويتقدم حينئذ للجماع فإن المرأة تتلذذ به لذة عظيمة

الروض العاطر في نزهة الخاطر للشيخ النفزاوي الباب الثامن عشر فيما يكبر الذكر الصغير ويعظمه وهو ما يحتاج إليه جُلّ الناس

Know, Oh Vizier (may Allah have mercy on you), that this chapter for thickening the penis is useful to men and women, since women dislike a small penis during sex, just as they dislike a limp one, a weak one, or one that grows tired. For truly the delight of women is in a large penis. Whoever has a small penis and wishes to maximize and strengthen it for sex, let him rub it with lukewarm, almost hot water, until it reddens, the blood flows in it, it warms up, and thickens; let him then spread ginger honey on it liberally. Then he may proceed to sex, and the woman will delight in him with great delight.

*Al-Nafzawi, Al-rawd Al-'atir fi Nuzha Al-khatir, Chapter eighteen: concerning what enlarges and maximizes a small penis, and this is what most people need*

عن إبن عباس قال حدثتنا ميمونة قالت صببت للنبي ﷺ غسلاً فأفرغ بيمينه على يساره فغسلهما ثم غسل
فرجه ثم قال بيده الأرض فمسحها بالتراب ثم غسلها ثم تمضمض وإستنشق ثم غسل وجهه وأفاض على رأسه
ثم تنحى فغسل قدميه ثم اُتِيَ بمنديل فلم ينفض بها

صحيح البخاري كتاب الغسل

From Ibn 'Abbas, who said: Maimunah related to us saying: I poured bath water for the
Prophet (SAW); He poured it out with his right hand over his left, washing both, then
washed his crotch, then hit the ground with his hand and wiped it with dust, then washed
it, then rinsed out his mouth and drew water up into his nose, then washed his face and
poured water generously over his head, then moved aside and washed his feet; then a cloth
was brought to him but He did not dry off with it.

*Sahih Al-Bukhari, The book of washing*

عن عثمان بن عفان قال قال رسول الله ﷺ من توضأ فأحسن الوضوء خرجت خطاياه من جسده حتى
تخرج من تحت أظفاره

صحيح مسلم كتاب الطهارة

From 'Uthman ibn 'Affan, who said: The Messenger of Allah (SAW) said: Whoever
performs ablution and performs the ablution well, his sins leave his body to the point of
even coming out from underneath his fingernails.

*Sahih Muslim, The book of purity*

عن أنس بن مالك أن النبي ﷺ إضطجع على نطع فعرق فقامت أم سليم الى عرقه فنشّفته فجعلته في قارورة
فرآها النبي ﷺ قال ما هذا الذي تصنعين يا أم سليم قالت اجعل عرقك في طيبي فضحك النبي ﷺ

سنن النسائي كتاب الزينة من السنن

Anas ibn Malik related that the Prophet (SAW) lay down on a leather mat and sweated;
Umm Sulaim got up as He was sweating, wiped it, and put it in a bottle. And the Prophet
(SAW) saw her and said: What is this you are doing, oh Umm Sulaim? She said: I am
putting your sweat in my perfume. And the Prophet (SAW) laughed.

*Sunan Al-Nasa'i, The book of adornment in sunnah*

عن عون بن ابي جحيفة عن أبيه قال أتيت النبي ﷺ وهو في قبّة حمراء من أدم ورأيت بلالاً أخذ وضوء النبي
ﷺ والناس يبتدرون الوضوء فمن أصاب منه شيئاً تمسّح به ومن لم يُصب منه شيئاً أخذ من بلل يد صاحبه

صحيح البخاري كتاب اللباس

'Awn ibn Abi Juhaifa related from his father, who said: I came to the Prophet (SAW) while
He was in a small red tent made out of hide, and I saw Bilal take the Prophet's (SAW)

ablution water. And the people were rushing to get some of the water; whoever got some of it rubbed himself with it, and whoever did not get any would take some of the moisture off the hand of his companion.

*Sahih Al-Bukhari, The book of dress*

عن إبن عباس أن النبي ﷺ قال اكتحلوا بالإثمد فإنه يجلو البصر ويُنبت الشعر وزعم أن النبي ﷺ كانت له
مُكحُلة يكتحل بها كل ليلة ثلاثة في هذه وثلاثة في هذه
جامع الترمذي كتاب اللباس

Ibn 'Abbas related that the Prophet (SAW) said: Smear your eyelids with *kuhl* [ointment] made of *ithmid* [antimony, lead, or other mineral], for indeed it brightens the vision and makes the hair grow. And he alleged that the Prophet (SAW) had a *kuhl* stick that he would use to smear himself every night – three times on one and three times on the other.

*Sunan Al-Tirmidhi, The book of clothing*

عن زر قال سألت صفيان بن عسال عن المسح على الخفّين فقال كان رسول الله ﷺ يأمرنا إذا كنا مسافرين
أن نمسح على خِفافنا ولا ننزعها ثلاثة أيام من غائط وبول ونوم إلا من جنابة
سنن النسائي كتاب الطهارة

From Zirr, who said: I asked Safyan ibn 'Assal about wiping one's two slippers [*khuff*], and he said: The Messenger of Allah (SAW) ordered us, whenever we were travelling, to wipe over our slippers, but not take them off for three days, in the case of defecating, urinating, or sleeping; only in the case of sexual impurity.

*Sunan Al-Nasa'i, The book of purity*

الوشم لا يحل لأنه أذى لا فائدة فيه وفي الصحيح أن رسول الله ﷺ لعن الواشمة والمستوشمة قال أبو الوفاء
بن عقيل والنهي عن الوشم تنبيه على منع ثقب الآذان قال المصنف رحمه الله قلت وكثير من النساء يستجزن
هذا في حق البنات ويعللن بأنه يحسنهن وهذا لا يلتفت إليه لأنه تعجيل أذى لا فائدة منه فليعلم فاعل هذا
أنه آثم معاقب
أحكام النساء لإبن الجوزي الباب السادس في ذكر الختان للنساء

Getting a tattoo is not permitted since it is harm with no benefit. It is related in the *Sahih* collections that the Messenger of Allah (SAW) cursed women who give tattoos and women who get tattoos. Abu Al-Wafaa ibn 'Aqil said: The prohibition on tattooing is warning against piercing the ears. The author (may Allah have mercy on him) said: I have said that many women consider this permitted for girls, and they justify this on the basis that it makes them beautiful; but this is not to be heeded, since it is a hastening of harm with no benefit. Let anyone who does this know that it is a punishable sin.

*Ibn Al-Jawzi, Ahkam Al-nisaa, Chapter six: mention of circumcision for women*

عن شداد بن أوس قال قال رسول الله ﷺ الختان سنة للرجال ومكرمة للنساء

المعجم الكبير للطبراني شداد بن أوس الأنصاري

From Shadad ibn Aws who said: The Messenger of Allah (SAW) said: Circumcision is *sunnah* for men and a noble trait [*makrumah*] in women.

*Al-Tabarani, Al-mu'jam Al-kabir, Section on Shadad ibn Aws Al-Ansari*

فالختان واجب عند الشافعي وكثير من العلماء وسنة عند مالك وأكثر العلماء وهو عند الشافعي واجب على الرجال والنساء جميعاً ثم إن الواجب في الرجل أن يقطع جميع الجلدة التي تغطي الحشفة حتى ينكشف جميع الحشفة وفي المرأة يجب قطع أدنى جزء من الجلدة التي في أعلى الفرج والصحيح من مذهبنا الذي عليه جمهور أصحابنا أن الختان جائز في حال الصغر ليس بواجب ولنا وجه أنه يجب على الولي أن يختن الصغير قبل بلوغه

المنهاج في شرح صحيح مسلم للنووي كتاب الطهارة

Circumcision is obligatory for Al-Shafi'i and many scholars, and *sunnah* [model to be followed] for Malik and the majority of scholars, and for Al-Shafi'i it is obligatory for both men and women. The requirement then for men is that all of the skin covering the head of the penis be cut, so that the whole head of the penis is showing; and for women it is necessary to cut the outermost piece of skin found on the upper part of the genitals. The sound view in our school, on which most of our companions stand, is that circumcision is permissible at a young age, but this is not obligatory; however we hold the view that is obligatory for a guardian to circumcise young children before puberty.

*Al-Nawawi, Al-minhaj fi Sharh Sahih Muslim, The book of purity*

وسئل عن المرأة: هل تختتن أم لا فأجاب الحمد لله نعم تختتن وختانها أن تقطع أعلى الجلدة التي كعرف الديك، قال رسول الله ﷺ للخافضة - وهي الختانة - أشمّي ولا تنهكي فإنه أبهى للوجه وأحظى لها عند الزوج يعني لا تبالغي في القطع وذلك أن المقصود بختان الرجل تطهيره من النجاسة المحتقنة في القلفة، والمقصود من ختان المرأة تعديل شهوتها فإنها إذا كانت قلفاء كانت مغتلمة شديدة الشهوة ... وإذا حصلت المبالغة في الختان ضعفت الشهوة فلا يكمل مقصود الرجل فإذا قطع من غير مبالغة حصل المقصود باعتدال

مجموع فتاوى للشيخ ابن تيمية باب السؤال

He [Ibn Taymiyyah] was asked regarding women: Should they be circumcised or not? And he answered: Praise be to Allah, yes, they should be circumcised. Their circumcision is in cutting the topmost skin, the part like a rooster's comb. The Messenger of Allah (SAW) said to the "diminisher" [*al-khafidah*] – the woman who performed circumcisions: Leave a little and do not go all the way, for that is more pleasant for the face and more of a privilege for her with her husband. In other words, do not exaggerate in cutting, since the purpose of circumcision for a man is his purification from filth that becomes trapped in the foreskin, while the purpose of circumcision for a woman is to regulate her desire, for indeed if she is uncircumcised, she can be aroused to strong desire. ... If exaggeration in circumcision occurs, desire is weakened, and the man's intention is not attained, but if the cut is made without exaggerating, the intended moderation is accomplished.

*Ibn Taymiyyah, Majmu' Fatawa, Section: questions*

الختان واجب في حق الرجل والمرأة ومن أدب الخاتنة للمرأة ما رواه أبو داود في سننه من حديث أم عطية الأنصارية أن إمرأة كانت تختن بالمدينة فقال لها النبي ﷺ لا تُنهِكي فإن ذلك أحظى للمرأة وأحب إلى البعل وعن أنس رضي الله عنه أن النبي ﷺ قال لأم عطية إذا خفضت فاشمي ولا تنهكي فإنه أسرى للوجه وأحظى عند الزوج

وقال أبو عثمان البصري أصل الختان للنساء لم يحاول به الحسن دون إلتماس نقصان الشهوة ليكون العفاف مقصوراً عليهن فالذي أراد رسول الله ﷺ بقوله لا تنهكي أن ينقص من شهوة المرأة بقدر ما يردها إلى الإعتدال فإن شهوتها إذا قلّت ذهب التمتع ونقص حبّ الأزواج ومعلوم أن حب الأزواج قيد دون الفجور وقد كان بعض الأشراف يقول للخاتنة لا تعترضي إلا لما يظهر فقط وأكثر العفائف موعبات وإنما صار الزنا وطلب الرجال في نساء الهند والروم أعم لأن شهوتهن للرجل أشد وليس لذلك علة إلا وفارة القلفة ولما تعمق أهل الهند في توفير حظ الباه منعوا من الختان

أحكام النساء لإبن الجوزي الباب السادس في ذكر الختان للنساء

Circumcision is obligatory for men and women; and it is proper conduct of the woman who performs circumcision on women [*khatinah*] to observe what Abu Dawud narrated in his *Sunan* from a hadith of Umm 'Atiyya Al-Ansariya: A certain woman was circumcised in Medina, and the Prophet (SAW) told her [i.e. the *khatinah*]: Do not go all the way, for that is more of a privilege for the woman and more desirable for the husband. And Anas (may Allah be pleased with him) related that the Prophet (SAW) said to Umm 'Atiyya: Whenever you diminish [i.e. circumcise], leave a little and do not go all the way, for that is better-looking for the face and more of a privilege with the husband.

Abu 'Uthman Al-Basri said: The basis for circumcision for women is not an attempt at pleasantness without also seeking to reduce the sex drive, so that self-restraint is less burdensome for them. What the Messenger of Allah (SAW) meant in saying "Do not go all the way" was to decrease the woman's desire so to bring about just the right amount of moderation; for indeed if her desire is too low, enjoyment departs and spousal love diminishes; and it is known that spousal love is restraint from adultery.

And some of the nobility said to the women performing the circumcisions: Only go as far as what is visible; most of the abstinent women have been cut too completely;

indeed adultery has arisen, as well as men more commonly seeking out women from India or Rome, since the desire of these women for men is stronger, and there is no other reason for this but an excess of clitoral head, for once the people of India delved deeper into the richness of coitus, they forbade circumcision.

*Ibn Al-Jawzi, Ahkam Al-nisaa, Chapter six: mention of circumcision for women*

عن يحيى بن سعيد أنه كان يقول ختان المرأة سنة لا يتركها المسلمون قال وكان رسول الله ﷺ يقول أول ما
تُسأل المرأة عنه يوم القيامة الصلاة والثانية رضى زوجها والثالثة ختانها

أدب النساء لعبد الملك بن حبيب باب ما جاء في الختان

From Yahya ibn Sa'id, who said: Circumcision for women is *sunnah*, which Muslims must not neglect. He said: The Messenger of Allah (SAW) used to say: The first thing that women will be asked about on the day of resurrection is prayer, the second is the satisfaction of their husbands, and the third is their circumcision.

*'Abd Al-Malik ibn Habib, Adab Al-nisaa, Section: what is related regarding circumcision*

عن علي رضي الله عنه أنه كره للجارية أن تُخفض حتى تبلغ سبع سنين

أدب النساء لعبد الملك بن حبيب باب ما جاء في سنة النساء في الخفاض

It is related from 'Ali (may Allah be pleased with him) that he disliked for young girls to be diminished [i.e. circumcised] until they reached seven years of age.

*'Abd Al-Malik ibn Habib, Adab Al-nisaa, Section: what is said regarding sunnah for women in reduction [khifad, i.e. circumcision]*

عن أسماء بنت ابي بكر قالت لعن رسول الله ﷺ الواصلة والمستوصلة

صحيح البخاري كتاب اللباس

From Asmaa bint Abu Bakr who said: The Messenger of Allah (SAW) cursed women who do hair extensions and women who get hair extensions.

*Sahih Al-Bukhari, The book of dress*

عن أنس قال رخَّص النبي ﷺ للزبير وعبد الرحمن في لُبس الحرير لحِكَّة بهما

صحيح البخاري كتاب اللباس

From Anas, who said: The Prophet (SAW) allowed Zubair and 'Abd Al-Rahman to wear silk because of an itch that they had.

*Sahih Al-Bukhari, The book of dress*

عن ابي الدرداء قال سمعت رسول الله ﷺ يقول من إشتكى منكم شيئاً أو اشتكاه أخ له فليقل ربُّنا الله الذي
في السماء تقدَّس اسمك أمرُك في السماء والأرض كما رحمتك في السماء فاجعل رحمتك في الأرض إغفر
لنا حوبنا وخطايانا أنت رب الطيِّبين أنزل رحمةً من رحمتك وشفاءً من شفائك على هذا الوجع فيبرأ

سنن ابي داود كتاب الطب

From Abu Al-Dardaa, who said: I heard the Messenger of Allah (SAW) say: Whoever
of you suffers from anything, or his brother complains to him of suffering from
anything, let him say: Our Lord Allah who is in heaven, may your name be sanctified,
may your command be in heaven and earth as is your mercy in heaven, send your
mercy to earth, forgive us our wrongdoing and our sins, you, Lord of those who are
good, send down mercy from your mercy, and healing from your healing upon this
ailment, and may it be healed.

*Sunan Abu Dawud, The book of medicine*

عن عائشة أم المؤمنين رضي الله عنها قالت مدت إمرأة من وراء الستر بيدها كتاباً إلى رسول الله ﷺ فقبض
رسول الله ﷺ يده قال ما أدري أيد رجل أو يد إمرأة فقالت بل يد إمرأة فقال لو كنتِ إمرأة غيرتِ
أظفارك بالحناء
وعنها رضي الله عنها قالت سمعت رسول الله ﷺ يقول إني لأبغض المرأة أن تكون سلتاء مرهاء لا تكون في
عينها كحل ولا في يدها خضاب

أحكام النساء لإبن الجوزي الباب الثالث والسبعون في إستحباب الخضاب بالحناء للنساء

From 'Aishah, mother of the believers (may Allah be pleased with her), who said: A
certain woman extended her hand to the Messenger of Allah (SAW) from behind the
curtain with a letter, but the Messenger of Allah (SAW) held back his hand and said:
I don't know if this is a man's hand or a woman's hand. She said: Well, a woman's
hand. And He said: If you were a woman you would do your nails with henna.

And she (may Allah be pleased with her) said: I heard the Messenger of Allah (SAW)
say: Truly I hate for women to be uncolored and unmarked, with no eyeliner on their
eyes and no color on their hands.

*Ibn Al-Jawzi, Ahkam Al-nisaa, Chapter seventy-three: regarding the desirability for women to use henna coloring*

عن كريمة بنت همام قالت سمعت عائشة تقول يا معشر النساء إياكن وقشر الوجه فسألتها إمرأة عن الخضاب
فقالت لا بأس بالخضاب ولكني أكرهه لأن حبيبي ﷺ كان يكره ريحه

مسند الإمام أحمد مسند عائشة

From Karimah bint Hammam who said: I heard 'Aishah say: Oh womenfolk, do
not use face peels. A woman asked her about dyeing hair, and she said: There is
nothing wrong with dying hair, but I dislike it because my beloved (SAW) disliked
the smell of it.

*Musnad Ahmad, Narrations from 'Aishah*

عن جابر بن عبدالله قال أتانا رسول الله ﷺ فرأى رجلاً شَعِثاً قد تفرق شعرة فقال أما كان يجد هذا ما
يسكّن به شعره ورأى رجلاً آخر وعليه ثياب وسخة فقال أما كان هذا يجد ماءً يغسل به ثوبه

سنن أبي داود كتاب اللباس

From Jabir ibn Abdullah, who said: The Messenger of Allah (SAW) came to see us, and
He saw a unkempt man whose hair was in all directions. And He said: Could this man
not find something to tame his hair with? Then He saw another man wearing a dirty
garment, and He said: Could this man not find some water to clean his garment with?

*Sunan Abu Dawud, The book of clothing*

عن ابي هريرة أن رسول الله ﷺ قال من كان له شعر فليكرمه

سنن أبي داود كتاب الترجل

Abu Huraira related that the Messenger of Allah (SAW) said: Whoever has hair, let
him honor it.

*Sunan Abu Dawud, The book of grooming*

عن زيد بن أسلم أن عطاء بن يسار أخبره قال كان رسول الله ﷺ في المسجد فدخل رجل ثائر الرأس واللحية
فأشار إليه رسول الله ﷺ بيده أن أخرجْ كأنه يعني إصلاح شعر رأسه ولحيته ففعل الرجل ثم رجع فقال
رسول الله ﷺ أليس هذا خيراً من أن يأتي أحدكم ثائر الرأس كأنه شيطانٌ

موطأ مالك كتاب الطهارة

Zaid ibn Aslam related that 'Ataa ibn Yasar related to him, saying: The Messenger of
Allah (SAW) was in the mosque, and a man with an unkempt head and beard came
in; the Messenger of Allah (SAW) motioned to him with his hand – "Get out" –
seeming to mean that he should fix the hair on his head and his beard. The man did
so, then returned. And the Messenger of Allah (SAW) said: Is this not better than any
of you coming with an unkempt head, as if he were a devil?

*Muwatta Malik, The book of purity*

عن الحسن قال إذا خرج من دبر الانسان الدود أو الدودة فعليه الوضوء

المصنف لإبن أبي شيبة كتاب الطهارة

From Al-Hasan, who said: If a worm or worms come out of a man's rear, then it is obligatory for him to perform ablution.

*Ibn Abi Shayba, Al-musannaf, The book of purity*

أنس بن مالك يقول كان النبي ﷺ يدخل على أم حرام إبنة ملحان فتُطعمه وكانت تحت عبادة بن الصامت فأطعمته وجعلت تفلي رأسه ثم إستيقظ فنام ثم إستيقظ يضحك

الأدب المفرد للبخاري كتاب الحركات

Anas ibn Malik said: The Prophet (SAW) used to go in to see Umm Haram, the daughter of Milhan, and she would feed him. She was under [married to] 'Ubada ibn Al-Samit. She fed him and began to look for lice in his head, and he fell asleep and then woke up chuckling.

*Al-Bukhari, Al-adab Al-mufrad, The book of gestures*

قيل لعائشة ماذا كان يعمل رسول الله ﷺ في بيته قالت كان بشراً من البشر يفلي ثوبه ويحلُب شاته ويخدُم نفسه

الشمائل المحمدية للترمذي ما جاء في تواضع رسول الله ﷺ

'Aishah was asked: What did the Messenger of Allah (SAW) do in his house? She said: He was a man among men [i.e. an ordinary man] – He would look for lice in his garment, milk his young ewe, and take care of himself.

*Al-Tirmidhi, Al-shama'il al-Muhammadiya, The section concerning the Messenger of Allah's (SAW) modesty*

عن كعب هو إبن عجرة قال أتى علي النبي ﷺ زمن الحديبية وأنا أوقِد تحت بُرمةٍ والقمل يتناثر عن رأسي فقال أيؤذيك هوامُّك قلت نعم قال فاحلِق وصُم ثلاثة أيام أو أطعِم ستة أو أنسُك نسيكة

صحيح البخاري كتاب الطب

Ka'b ibn 'Ujra said: During the time of Hudaibiyya the Prophet (SAW) came to me while I was lighting a fire under a cooking pot and lice were falling off my head. He said: Are your pests harming you? I said: Yes. He said: Shave your head and fast for three days, or feed six people or slaughter a sacrifice to draw near to Allah [*nasikah*].

*Sahih Al-Bukhari, The book of medicine*

عن عبدالله قال العن الله الواشمات والمستوشمات والنامصات والمتنمّصات والمتفلّجات لحُسن المغيّرات خَلْق الله

صحيح مسلم كتاب اللباس والزينة

From Abdullah, who said: Allah curses women who do tattoos and women who get tattooed, women who pluck hair and women who pluck the hair on their brows, and women who make gaps between their teeth to look nice, those who change what Allah has created.

*Sahih Muslim, The book of clothing and adornment*

ومن حقها على الوالدين تعليمها حسن المعاشرة وآداب العشرة مع الزوج كما روي أن أسماء بنت خارجة الفزاري قالت لابنتها عند التزوج إنك خرجت من العش الذي فيه درجت فصرت إلى فراش لم تعرفيه وقرين لم تألفيه فكوني له أرضاً يكن لك سماء وكوني له مهاداً يكن لك عماداً وكوني له أمة يكن لك عبداً لا تلحقي به فيقلاك ولا تباعدي عنه فينساك إن دنا منك فاقربي منه وإن نأى فأبعدي عنه واحفظي أنفه وسمعه وعينه فلا يشمن منك إلا طيباً ولا يسمع إلا حسناً ولا ينظر إلا جميلاً

إحياء علوم الدين للغزالي كتاب آداب النكاح الباب الثالث في آداب المعاشرة وما يجري في دوام النكاح والنظر فيما على الزوج وفيما على الزوجة القسم الثاني النظر في حقوق الزوج عليها

Between both parents, it is a woman's duty that she give instruction in agreeable intimate contact and proper conduct in intimacy with the husband, as has been related that Asmaa bint Kharija Al-Fazari said to her daughter when she got married: Indeed you have left the nest that you have grown in, and you have gone to a bed that you have not known before, and to a companion that you have not been accustomed to; so be to him like the earth and may he be to you as the sky; and be to him as level ground and may he be to you as a pillar; and be to him as a servant girl and may he be to you as a servant; do not cling to him that he should abhor you, nor be distant from him that he should forget you; if he approaches you, draw near to him, and if he moves away, stay far from him; and protect his nose, his hearing, and his eyes; let him not ever smell anything from you but perfume, and not hear but what is pleasant, and not see but what is beautiful.

*Al-Ghazali, Ihyaa 'Ulum Al-din, The book of proper conduct in marital relations, Section three: concerning proper conduct in intimacy, what should be observed for the duration of marital relations, and consideration of the obligations of the husband and the obligations of the wife, Part two: consideration of the husband's rights over her*

# الشتيمة والإهانة

*Insult and offense*

﴿ وَإِن نَّكَثُوا أَيْمَانَهُم مِّن بَعْدِ عَهْدِهِمْ وَطَعَنُوا فِي دِينِكُمْ فَقَاتِلُوا أَئِمَّةَ الْكُفْرِ إِنَّهُمْ لَا أَيْمَانَ لَهُمْ لَعَلَّهُمْ يَنتَهُونَ ﴾

التوبة ١٢

*{ And if they break their oaths after having made their covenant, and defame your religion, then fight the leaders of disbelief – for indeed they have no oaths – that perhaps they might cease }* Al-tawba 12

يقول تعالى وإن نكث المشركون الذين عاهدتموهم على مدة معينة أيمانهم أي عهودهم ومواثيقهم ﴿ وطعنوا في دينكم ﴾ أي عابوه وإنتقصوه ومن ههنا أخذ قتل من سب الرسول صلوات الله وسلامه عليه أو من طعن في دين الاسلام

تفسير إبن كثير

The Most High is saying that if the Idolaters, those with whom you made covenant for a specific period, break their oaths, their covenants, or their agreements, { and defame your religion } , that is, slander it and undermine it. From this it can be taken that whoever slanders the Messenger (may the prayers and peace of Allah be upon him), or whoever defames the religion of Islam, is to be killed.

*Tafsir Ibn Kathir, Al-tawba 12*

﴿ وطعنوا في دينكم ﴾ يقول وقدحوا في دينكم الاسلام فثلبوه وعابوه ﴿ فقاتلوا أئمة الكفر ﴾ يقول فقاتلوا رؤساء الكفر بالله ﴿ إنهم لا أيمان لهم ﴾ يقول إن رؤساء الكفر لا عهد لهم ﴿ لعلهم ينتهون ﴾ لكي ينتهوا عن الطعن في دينكم والمظاهرة عليكم

تفسير الطبري

{ And defame your religion } ; He is saying: And vilify Islam, your religion [*deen*], and defile it, and slander it; { then fight the leaders of disbelief } ; He is saying: Fight the heads of disbelief in Allah; { for indeed they have no oaths } ; He is saying: Indeed the heads of disbelief have no covenant; { that perhaps they might cease } : so that they will stop defaming your religion and manifesting against you.

*Tafsir Al-Tabari*

﴿ وطعنوا في دينكم ﴾ يقال طعنه بالرمح يطعنه وطعن بالقول السيء يطعن قال الليث وبعضهم يقول يطعن
بالرمح ويطعن بالقول فيفرق بينهما والمعنى أنهم عابوا دينكم وقدحوا فيه ثم قال ﴿ فقاتلوا أئمة الكفر ﴾ أي
متى فعلوا ذلك فافعلوا هذا

تفسير الرازي

{ And defame [*ta'anu*, i.e. stab] your religion } ; it can be said that someone "stabs"
with a spear, and also "stabs" with malicious speech. Al-Laith said: Some of them said
stabs with a spear or stabs in speech, and distinguishes between the two; but the
meaning is that they slander your religion and vilify ["pierce"] it. Then He says: { Then
fight the leaders of disbelief } : that is, when they do that, do this.

*Tafsir Al-Razi*

استدلّ بعض العلماء بهذه الآية على وجوب قتل كل من طعن في ألدين إذ هو كافر والطعن أن ينسب إليه
ما لا يليق به أو يعترض بالإستخفاف على ما هو من الدين لما ثبت من الدليل القطعي على صحة أصوله
وإستقامة فروعه

تفسير القرطبي

Some scholars have reached the conclusion from this verse that it is obligatory to kill
anyone who defames the religion, as he is a Disbeliever [*Kafir*]. And defaming
["stabbing"] means attributing to it what is not befitting of it, or raising frivolous
objections against matters of the religion, when the veracity of their foundation and
the integrity of their rulings have been affirmed by definitive evidence.

*Tafsir Al-Qurtubi*

•   •   •

{ *You will not find people who believe in Allah and the last day to be affectionate towards anyone who opposes Allah and His Messenger.* }

*Al-mujadilah 22*

قوله عز وجل ﴿ لا تجد قوماً يؤمنون بالله واليوم الآخر يوادون من حاد الله ورسوله ... ﴾ أخبر أن إيمان المؤمنين يفسد بموادة الكفار وأن من كان مؤمناً لا يوالي من كفر

تفسير البغوي

The word of the Mighty and Sublime { You will not find people who believe in Allah and the last day to be affectionate towards anyone who opposes Allah and His Messenger ... } . He is making known that the faith of a Believer is spoiled by affection with Disbelievers [*Kuffar*], and that anyone who is a Believer is not close with anyone who has disbelieved.

*Tafsir Al-Baghawi, Al-mujadilah 22*

قال إبن جريج حُدثت أن أبا قحافة سب النبي ﷺ فصكه أبو بكر صكة شديدة سقط منها ثم ذكر ذلك للنبي ﷺ قال أو فعلت قال نعم قال فلا تعد إليه فقال أبو بكر والله لو كان السيف قريباً لقتلته فأنزل الله تبارك وتعالى هذه الآية

اسباب التزول للواحدي

Ibn Juraij said: It is reported that Abu Quhafa insulted the Prophet (SAW), so Abu Bakr hit him so hard that he fell down from it. Then he mentioned this to the Prophet (SAW), and He said: Did you really do that? He said: Yes. He said: Don't go back to him. And Abu Bakr said: I swear by Allah if there was a sword nearby I would have killed him. Then Allah Blessed and Exalted sent down this verse.

*Al-Wahidi, Asbab Al-nuzul*

قال السدي نزلت في عبدالله بن عبدالله بن أبيّ جلس إلى النبي ﷺ فشرب النبي ﷺ ماء فقال له بالله يا
رسول الله ما أبقيت من سرابك فضلةً أسقيها ابي لعل الله يطهّر بها قلبه فأفضل له فأتاه بها فقال له عبدالله
ما هذا فقال هي فضلة من شراب النبي ﷺ جئتك بها تشربها لعل الله يطهر قلبك بها فقال له أبوه فهلا جئتني
ببول أمك فإن أطهر منها فغضب وجاء إلى النبي ﷺ وقال يا رسول الله أما أذنت لي في قتل ابي فقال النبي
ﷺ بل ترفق به وتحسن إليه

تفسير القرطبي

Al-Suddi said: This came down concerning Abdullah, the son of Abdullah ibn Ubayy; he went and sat with the Prophet (SAW), and the Prophet (SAW) drank some water, and Abdullah said to him: I swear by Allah oh Messenger of Allah, if I could only get what is left over from your drink, to give it to my father to drink so that perhaps Allah might cleanse his heart with it. So He gave him what was left over, and he brought it to his father. And Abdullah said to him: What is this? He said: It is what is left over from the Prophet's (SAW) drink; I brought it to you to drink that perhaps Allah might cleanse your heart with it. But his father said to him: Why didn't you just bring me your mother's urine; indeed that is cleaner than this! And Abdullah became enraged and went to the Prophet (SAW) and said: Oh Messenger of Allah, will you not give me permission to kill my father? But the Prophet (SAW) said: Rather you should be nice to him and treat him well.

*Tafsir Al-Qurtubi*

•     •     •

﴿ إِنَّ الَّذِينَ يُؤْذُونَ اللَّهَ وَرَسُولَهُ لَعَنَهُمُ اللَّهُ فِي الدُّنْيَا وَالْآخِرَةِ وَأَعَدَّ لَهُمْ عَذَابًا مُهِينًا وَالَّذِينَ يُؤْذُونَ الْمُؤْمِنِينَ وَالْمُؤْمِنَاتِ بِغَيْرِ مَا اكْتَسَبُوا فَقَدِ احْتَمَلُوا بُهْتَانًا وَإِثْمًا مُبِينًا ﴾ الأحزاب ٥٧-٥٨

*{ Indeed those who harm Allah and His Messenger, Allah will curse them in this world and the next, and He has prepared for them an impressive punishment. And those who harm the believing men and believing women, without them deserving it, bear the responsibility of defamation and manifest wrongdoing }* Al-ahzab 57-58

يقول تعالى متهدداً ومتوعداً من آذاه بمخالفة أوامره وإرتكاب زواجره وإصراره على ذلك وإيذاء رسوله بعيب أو بنقص عياذاً بالله من ذلك

تفسير ابن كثير

The Most High says this as intimidation and as a threat to whoever harms him by going against his orders, by committing the things He has restricted, by persisting in this, and by harming His Messenger, ascribing to him defects and imperfections – may Allah save us from this!

*Tafsir Ibn Kathir*

عن إبن عباس في قوله ﴿ إن الذين يؤذون الله ورسوله لعنهم الله في الدنيا والآخرة وأعد لهم عذاباً مهيناً ﴾ قال نزلت في الذين طعنوا على النبي ﷺ حين إتخذ صفية بنت حيي بن أخطب ... عن قتادة ﴿ والذين يؤذون المؤمنين والمؤمنات بغير ما اكتسبوا فقد إحتملوا بهتاناً وإثماً مبيناً ﴾ فإياكم وأذى المؤمن فإن الله يحوطه ويغضب له

تفسير الطبري

Ibn 'Abbas, concerning His word { Indeed those who harm Allah and His Messenger, Allah will curse them in this world in the next, and He has prepared for them an impressive punishment } , said: This came down regarding those who defamed the Prophet (SAW) when He took Safiyah bint Huyay ibn Akhtab ... From Qatada, concerning { And those who harm the believing men and believing women, without them deserving it, bear the responsibility of defamation and manifest wrongdoing } : So be careful of harming any Believer! For indeed Allah surrounds and protects him, and will stand up for him.

*Tafsir Al-Tabari*

﴿ يؤذون الله ورسوله ﴾ فيه وجهان احدهما أن يعبر بإيذائهما عن فعل ما يكرهانه ولا يرضيانه من الكفر والمعاصي وإنكار النبوة ومخالفة الشريعة

تفسير الزمخشري

{ Who harm Allah and His Messenger } : there are two points of view regarding this; one of them is that their "harm" refers to the disbelief [*kufr*] and sins that both of them dislike and that both of them are not pleased by: denying the prophethood and going against ordained laws [*shari'a*].

*Tafsir Al-Zamakhshari*

قوله عز وجل ﴿ إن الذين يؤذون الله ورسوله لعنهم الله في الدنيا والآخرة واعد لهم عذاباً مهيناً ﴾ قال ابن عباس هم اليهود والنصارى والمشركون فأما اليهود فقالوا عزير ابن الله ويد الله مغلولة وقالوا إن الله فقير وأما النصارى فقالوا المسيح ابن الله وثالث ثلاثة وأما المشركون فقالوا الملائكة بنات الله والأصنام شركاؤه ... ﴿ والذين يؤذون المؤمنين والمؤمنات بغير ما اكتسبوا ﴾ من غير أن عملوا ما أوجب أذاهم وقال مجاهد يقعون فيهم ويرمونهم بغير جرم ﴿ فقد احتملوا بهتاناً وإثماً مبيناً ﴾ وقال مقاتل نزلت في علي بن ابي طالب وذلك أن ناساً من المنافقين كانوا يؤذونه ويشتمونه وقيل نزلت في شأن عائشة وقال الضحاك والكلبي نزلت في الزناة الذين كانوا يمشون في طرق المدينة يتبعون النساء إذا برزن بالليل لقضاء حوائجهن

تفسير البغوي

The word of the Mighty and Sublime { Indeed those who harm Allah and His Messenger, Allah will curse them in this world and the next, and He has prepared for them an impressive punishment } . Ibn 'Abbas said: These are the Jews, the Christians, and the Idolaters; the Jews say that 'Uzair is the son of Allah and that Allah's hand is bound and that Allah is poor; the Christians say that the Messiah is the son of Allah and the third of three; and the Idolaters say that the angels are the daughters of Allah and that the idols are His associates. ... { And those who harm the believing men and believing women, without them deserving it } : without them having done anything to warrant harming them. Mujahid said: They would insult them and accuse them of nonexistent crimes. { Bear the responsibility of defamation and manifest wrongdoing } : Muqatil said that this came down regarding 'Ali ibn Abi Talib; some of the hypocrites would harm him and slander him. It is also said that this came down regarding the issue of 'Aishah. Al-Dahhak and Al-Kalbi said: This came down regarding the fornicators who would walk around the streets of Medina pursuing women whenever they went out to fulfill their needs.

*Tafsir Al-Baghawi*

قوله سبحانه ﴿ إن الذين يؤذون الله ورسوله لعنهم الله في الدنيا والآخرة ﴾ وهذه الآية توجب قتل من آذى الله ورسوله

الصارم المسلول على شاتم الرسول لإبن تيمية المسألة الاولى أن من سب النبي س من مسلم أو كافر فإنه يجب قتله

The word of the Exalted { Indeed those who harm Allah and His Messenger, Allah will curse them in this world and the next } ; this verse makes it obligatory to kill whoever harms Allah and His Messenger.

*Ibn Taymiyya, Al-sarim Al-maslul, The first issue: That any Muslim or Disbeliever who slanders the Prophet (SAW) must indeed be killed.*

•   •   •

﴿ يا أيها الذين آمنوا لا تدخلوا بيوت النبي إلا أن يؤذن لكم إلى طعام غير ناظرين إناه ولكن إذا دعيتم فادخلوا فإذا طعمتم فانتشروا ولا مستأنسين لحديث إن ذلكم كان يؤذي النبي فيستحي منكم والله لا يستحي من الحق وإذا سألتموهن متاعاً فاسألوهن من وراء حجاب ذلكم أطهر لقلوبكم وقلوبهن وما كان لكم أن تؤذوا رسول الله ولا أن تنكحوا أزواجه من بعده أبداً إن ذلكم كان عند الله عظيماً ﴾ الأحزاب ٥٣

{ Oh you who have believed! Do not enter the Prophet's houses unless you have been given permission, to have a meal, without watching as the time approaches; but whenever you are invited, then enter, and when you have eaten, disperse and do not hang around to be sociable; indeed that harms the Prophet, and He is ashamed around you; but Allah is not ashamed of the truth. And whenever you ask the women for something, ask them from behind a veil; that is purer for your hearts and theirs; and it is not for you to harm the Messenger of Allah, nor to ever have marital relations with his wives after him; indeed that would be terrible in the sight of Allah. } Al-ahzab 53

﴿ كان يؤذي النبي ﴾ لتضييق المنزل عليه وعلى أهله واشغاله بما لا يعنيه ... ﴿ وما كان لكم ﴾ وما صح لكم
﴿ أن تؤذون رسول الله ﴾ أن تفعلوا ما يكرهه

تفسير البيضاوي

{ That harms the Prophet } : due to space in the house getting tight for him and
those of his household, and by taking up space in it with what does not interest
him. ... { And it is not for you } : it is not right for you { to harm the Messenger of
Allah } : to do that which He dislikes.

*Tafsir Al-Baydawi*

﴿ إن ذلكم كان يؤذي النبي ﴾ يقول إن دخولكم بيوت النبي من غير أن يؤذن لكم وجلوسكم فيها مستأنسين
للحديث بعد فراغكم من أكل الطعام الذي دعيتم له كان يؤذي النبي

تفسير الطبري

{ Indeed that harms the Prophet } ; He is saying: Indeed when you all enter the
Prophet's (SAW) houses without having been given permission, and sit in them to
hang around and talk after you have finished eating the meal to which you have been
invited; this harms the Prophet.

*Tafsir Al-Tabari*

عن إبن عباس في قوله تعالى ﴿ وما كان لكم أن يؤذوا رسول الله ﴾ قال نزلت في رجل هم أن يتزوج بعض
نساء النبي ﷺ بعده قال رجل لسفيان أهي عائشة قال قد ذكروا ذلك وكذا قال مقاتل بن حيان وعبد الرحمن
بن زيد بن أسلم وذكر بسنده عن السدي أن الذي عزم على ذلك طلحة بن عبيد الله رضي الله عنه حتى نزل
التنبيه على تحريم ذلك ولهذا أجمع العلماء قاطبة على أن من توفي عنها رسول الله ﷺ من أزواجه أنه يحرم على
غيره تزوجها من بعده لانهن أزواجه في الدنيا والآخرة وأمهات المؤمنين

تفسير إبن كثير

Ibn 'Abbas, regarding the word of the Most High { It is not for you to harm the
Messenger of Allah } , said: This came down regarding a certain man who was intent
on marrying one of the Prophet's (SAW) women after him. Someone said to Sufyan:
Was it 'Aishah? He said: That's what they say. Muqatil ibn Hayyan and 'Abd Al-
Rahman ibn Zaid ibn Aslam said this as well. It is mentioned by way of his chain of
narration from Al-Suddi, that the one who had this in mind was Talha ibn 'Ubaid
Allah (may Allah be pleased with him), until the warning came down regarding the
prohibition of this. For this reason all scholars have come together in agreement that
whichever wives of the Messenger of Allah (SAW) that He dies and leaves behind, it
is forbidden for anyone else to marry them after him, since they are his wives in this
world and the next, and they are the mothers of the Believers.

*Tafsir Ibn Kathir*

•   •   •

﴿ ومنهم الذين يؤذون النبي ويقولون هو أذن قل أذن خير لكم يؤمن بالله ويؤمن للمؤمنين ورحمة للذين آمنوا منكم والذين يؤذون رسول الله لهم عذاب أليم ﴾ التوبة ٦١

{ *Among them are those who harm the Prophet and say that He is an ear; say: "An ear of good to you; He believes in Allah and He believes the Believers, and a mercy to those of you who have believed". And there is painful punishment for those who harm the Messenger of Allah* }

*Al-tawba 61*

يقول تعالى ومن المنافقين قوم يؤذون رسول الله ﷺ بالكلام فيه

تفسير إبن كثير

The Most High is saying: Among the hypocrites are people who harm the Messenger of Allah (SAW) by saying things about him.

*Tafsir Ibn Kathir*

يقول تعالى ذكره ومن هؤلاء المنافقين جماعة يؤذون رسول الله ﷺ ويعيبونه ويقولون هو أذن سامعة يسمع من كل أحد ما يقول فيقبله ويصدّقه

تفسير الطبري

He (may his remembrance be exalted) is saying: There is a group of these hypocrites who harm the Messenger of Allah (SAW), shame him, and say that He is a hearing ear, who hears from everyone whatever they say, and accepts it and believes it.

*Tafsir Al-Tabari*

قوله تعالى ﴿ ومنهم الذين يؤذون النبي ويقولون هو أذن ﴾ الآية نزلت في جماعة من المنافقين كانوا يؤذون الرسول ويقولون فيه ما لا ينبغي قال بعضهم لا تفعلوا فإنا نخاف أن يبلغه ما تقولون فيقع بنا فقال الجلاس بن سويد نقول ما شئنا ثم نأتيه بما نقول فيصدقنا بما نقول فإنما محمد أذن سامعة فأنزل الله تعالى هذه الآية

اسباب النزول للواحدي

The word of the Most High: { Among them are those who harm the Prophet and say that He is an ear }, and the rest of the verse. This came down regarding a group of hypocrites who would harm the Messenger and say things about him that ought not to be said. Some of them said: Don't do that; indeed we fear that He might find out what you all are saying and come down on us. But Al-Julas ibn Suwaid said: We say whatever we want, then we come to him, and He believes whatever we say, for indeed Muhammad is just an ear that hears. And So Allah Most High sent down this verse.

*Al-Wahidi, Asbab Al-nuzul*

•   •   •

﴿ ومن يُشَاقِق اللّهَ ورسولَه فإن اللّهَ شديدُ العقاب ﴾ الأنفال ١٣

{ *And whoever antagonizes Allah and His Messenger – indeed Allah is* *severe in punishment* } *Al-anfal* 13

﴿ ومن يشاقق الله ورسوله ﴾ ومن يخالف أمر الله وأمر رسوله وفارق طاعتهما

تفسير الطبري

{ And whoever antagonizes Allah and His Messenger } : whoever goes against the command of Allah and the command of His Messenger, and ceases to obey them.

*Tafsir Al-Tabari*

﴿ ومن يشاقق الله ورسوله فإن الله شديد العقاب ﴾ أي هو الطالب الغالب لمن خالفه وناوأه لا يفوته شيء ولا يقوم لغضبه شيء تبارك وتعالى

تفسير ابن كثير

{ And whoever antagonizes Allah and His Messenger – indeed Allah is severe in punishment } : that is, He seeks and prevails over anyone who goes against Him or acts in hostility towards Him; nothing can surpass Him nor can anything stand against His wrath, Blessed and Exalted is He.

*Tafsir Ibn Kathir*

·    ·    ·

اعلم وفّقنا الله وإياك أن جميع من سب النبي ﷺ أو عابَه أو ألحقَ به نقصاً في نفسه أو نسبه أو دينه أو خصلةٍ من خصاله أو عرّض به أو شبّهه على طريق ألسب له أو الإزراء عليه أو التصغير لشأنه أو الغضّ منه والعيب له فهو سابّ له والحُكم فيه حكم السابّ يقتل كما نبيّنه ولا نستثني فصلاً من فصول هذا الباب على هذا المقصد ولا نمتري فيه تصريحاً كان أو تلويحاً وكذلك من لعنه أو دعا عليه أو تمنّى مَضَرّة له أو نسب إليه ما لا يليق بمنصبه على طريق الذَمّ أو عبِث في جهته العزيزة بسُخف من الكلام وهُجر ومنكَر من القول وزور

195

أو عيّره بشيء مما جرى من البلاء والمحنة عليه أو غمصه ببعض العوارض البشرية الجائزة والمعهودة لديه وهذا

كله إجماع من العلماء وأئمة الفتوى من لَدُن الصحابة رضوان الله عليهم إلى هَلُمّ جرّاً

الشفا للقاضي عياض اليحصبي القسم الرابع في تصرف وجوه الأحكام فيمن تنقّصه أو سبّ عليه الصلاة والسلام الباب الأول في

بيان ما هو في حقه ﷺ سب أو نقص من تعريض أو نص

Know – may Allah grant us success and you as well – that all those who slander the Prophet (SAW), or defame him, or attribute flaws to him concerning his person, his lineage, his religion, or any of his features, or put him in a bad light, or compare him to anything else as a means of slandering him, contempt for him, belittling his state of affairs, degrading him, or shaming him – they slander him, and the ruling for them is the ruling for slanderers; they are to be killed, as we make clear; and we make no exceptions in any of the judgments of this chapter in this intent, and we have no reservations, either in stating clearly or making allusions. Similarly for anyone who curses him, or makes invocations against him, or wishes harm on him, or unduly attributes anything to his position as a means of defiling him, or abuses his honorable authority with foolish remarks, obscenities, reprehensible speech, and falsehood, or dishonors him with any of the distress and trials that came upon him, or holds him in contempt for any of the conceivable and commonplace natural human features he may have had. All of this is the univeral consensus of the scholars and imams dictating legal opinions [fatwa] from among the Companions (may the pleasure of Allah be upon them in perpetuity).

*Al-qadi 'Iyad Al-Yahsubi, Al-shifa, Part Four: regarding disposition of the aspects of legal rulings for those who slander Him or insult Him (prayers and peace be upon him), Chapter One: Declaration of what is in His (SAW) right in being slandered or slighted, either insinuated or openly*

وقد فرض الله تعالى توقيره وبرّه وفي المبسوط عن عثمان بن كنانة من كان من شتم النبي ﷺ من المسلمين قُتل أو

صلب حياً ولم يُستتب والامام مخيّر في صلبه حياً أو قتله

الشفا للقاضي عياض اليحصبي القسم الرابع في تصرف وجوه الأحكام فيمن تنقّصه أو سبّ عليه الصلاة والسلام الباب الأول في

بيان ما هو في حقه ﷺ سب أو نقص من تعريض أو نص

Allah Most High has made it obligatory to venerate him and show loyalty to him; in the *Mabsut* [legal manual by Al-Sarakhsi] it is narrated from 'Uthman ibn Kinana: Any Muslim who insults the Prophet (SAW) is either killed or crucified alive; repentance is not sought from him. The Imam is given the choice to crucify him alive or kill him.

*Al-qadi 'Iyad Al-Yahsubi, Al-shifa, Part Four: regarding disposition of the aspects of legal rulings for those who slander Him or insult Him (prayers and peace be upon him), Chapter One: Declaration of what is in His (SAW) right in being slandered or slighted, either insinuated or openly*

وقال حبيب بن ربيع القروي مذهب مالك وأصحابه أن من قال فيه ﷺ ما فيه نقص قتل دون استتابة وقال إبن
عتاب الكتّاب والسنة موجبان أنّ من قصد النبي ﷺ بأذى أو نقص معرّضاً أو مصرّحاً وإن قلّ قتله واجب

الشفا للقاضي عياض اليحصبي القسم الرابع في تصرف وجوه الأحكام فيمن تنقّصه أو سبّ عليه الصلاة والسلام الباب الأول في
بيان ما هو في حقه ﷺ سب أو نقص من تعريض أو نص

Habib ibn Rabi' Al-Qawari said: The doctrine of Malik and his companions is that
whoever says anything of Him (SAW) in which there is any slighting, is to be killed
without seeking his repentance. Ibn 'Attab said: The Book and the *sunnah* both make
it obligatory that whoever intends to harm or slight the Prophet (SAW), insinuating
or openly, even just a little, must be killed.

*Al-qadi 'Iyad Al-Yahsubi, Al-shifa, Part Four: regarding disposition of the aspects of legal rulings for those who
slander Him or insult Him (prayers and peace be upon him), Chapter One: Declaration of what is in His (SAW)
right in being slandered or slighted, either insinuated or openly*

وكذلك أقول حكم من غمصه أو عيره برعاية الغنم أو الشهو أو النسيان أو السحر أو ما أصابه من جرح أو هزيمة
لبعض جيوشه أو أذى من عدوه أو شدة من زمنه أو بالميل إلى نسائه فكم هذا كله لمن قصد به نقصه القتل

الشفا للقاضي عياض اليحصبي القسم الرابع في تصرف وجوه الأحكام فيمن تنقّصه أو سبّ عليه الصلاة والسلام الباب الأول في
بيان ما هو في حقه ﷺ سب أو نقص من تعريض أو نص

And similarly I say that the ruling for whoever holds him in contempt or shames
him for shepherding flocks, or having cravings, or being forgetful, or being
bewitched, or for the injuries that befell him or the defeat of some of his troops,
or harm from his enemy, or the difficulties of his time, or his inclination towards
his women; the ruling for all of this, for anyone who intends to slight him, is that
he be killed.

*Al-qadi 'Iyad Al-Yahsubi, Al-shifa, Part Four: regarding disposition of the aspects of legal rulings for those who
slander Him or insult Him (prayers and peace be upon him), Chapter One: Declaration of what is in His (SAW)
right in being slandered or slighted, either insinuated or openly*

عن سماك بن الفضل قال أخبرني عروة بن محمد عن رجلٍ من بلقين أن إمرأة كانت تَسُبّ النبي ﷺ فقال
النبي ﷺ من يكفيني عدوي نخرج إليها خالد بن الوليد فقتلها

المصنف لعبد الرزاق كتاب الجهاد

From Simak ibn Al-Fadl, who said: 'Urwa ibn Muhammad related to me from a man
of Balqin, that a certain woman used to insult the Prophet (SAW); and so the Prophet
(SAW) asked: Who can deal with my enemy for me? So Khalid ibn Al-Walid set out
to find her, and killed her.

*Abd Al-Razzaq, the Musannaf, The book of jihad*

هذا مذهبٌ عليه عامة أهل العلم قال إبن المنذر أجمع عوام أهل العلم على أن حد من سب النبي ﷺ القتل
ومن قاله مالك والليث وأحمد وإسحاق وهو مذهب الشافعي ... وقد حكى أبو بكر الفارسي من أصحاب الشافعي
إجماع المسلمين على أنّ حد من سب النبي س القتل كما أن حد من سب غيره الجلد ... وتحرير القول فيه أن
الساب إن كان مسلماً فإنه يُكفّر ويقتل بغير خلاف وهو مذهب الأئمة الأربعة وغيرهم ... وإن كان ذمياً
فإنه يقتل أيضاً في مذهب مالك وأهل المدينة

الصارم المسلول على شاتم الرسول لإبن تيمية المسألة الاولى أن من سب النبي س من مسلم أو كافر فإنه يجب قتله

This is a tenet which scholars generally hold. Ibn Al-Mundhir said: Scholars in general
agree that the punishment for someone who slanders the Prophet (SAW) is death;
among those who said this are Malik, Al-Laith, Ahmad, and Ishaq, and it is a tenet of
Al-Shafi'i. ... Abu Bakr Al-Farisi recounted – from the companions of Al-Shafi'i –
the agreement among Muslims that the punishment for someone who slanders the
Prophet (SAW) is death, just as the punishment for someone who slanders anyone
else is whipping. ... Drawing up what is said regarding this: the one who slanders, if
he is a Muslim, is indeed declared a Disbeliever and is killed without dispute; this is
the view of the four Imams as well as others. ... If he is a *dhimmi*, then indeed he also
is to be killed according to the doctrine of Malik and the people of Medina.

*Ibn Taymiyya, Al-sarim Al-maslul, The first issue: That any Muslim or Disbeliever who slanders the Prophet (SAW)*
*must indeed be killed.*

وروي عن مالك من سبّ أبا بكر جُلد ومن سب عائشة قُتل قيل له لِمَ قال من رماها فقد خالف القرآن ...
وذكر تعالى ما نسبه المنافقون إلى عائشة فقال ﴿ ولو لا إذ سمعتموه قلتم ما يكون لنا أن نتكلم بهذا سبحانك
هذا بُهتان عظيم ﴾ سبّح نفسه في تنزيهها من السوء كما سبح نفسه في تبرئته عز وجل من السوء وهذا يشهد
لقول مالك في قتل من سب عائشة ومعنى هذا والله أعلم أن الله تعالى لما عظّم سبّها كما عظم سبه وكان سبها
سباً لنبيّه عليه السلام وقرن سب نبيه عليه السلام واذاه باذاه تعالى وكان حكم مؤذيه مؤذي القتل كان مؤذي
نبيه كذلك كما قدمناه

الشفا للقاضي عياض اليحصبي القسم الرابع في تصرف وجوه الأحكام فيمن تنقّصه أو سبّه عليه الصلاة والسلام فصل وسب آل بيته
وأزواجه وأصحابه عليه الصلاة والسلام وتنقصهم حرام ملعون فاعله

It is narrated from Malik: Whoever insults Abu Bakr is to be flogged, and whoever
insults 'Aishah is to be killed. He was asked: Why? He said: Whoever casts things at
her has opposed the Qur'an. ... Allah Most High made mention of the accusations of
the hypocrites against 'Aishah, and said { Were it not, when you heard it, for you to
say: It is not for us to talk of this. Exalted are You! This is great slander } [*Al-nur*
16]. He praised himself for absolving her from evil, just as He praised himself for
absolving himself, Mighty and Sublime, from evil. And this bears witness to what

Malik said regarding killing someone who insults 'Aishah. The meaning here – but Allah knows better – is that Allah Most High made it a grave offense to insult her, just as He made it a grave offense to insult Him [the Prophet]; and an insult to her is an insult to Him (peace be upon him). And He made insulting His Prophet (peace be upon him) and harming him equivalent to harming Himself Most High. The judgment for someone who harms Him Most High is to be killed; for someone who harms His Prophet, the same, as we have presented.

*Al-qadi 'Iyad Al-Yahsubi, Al-shifa, Part Four: regarding disposition of the aspects of legal rulings for those who slander Him or insult Him (prayers and peace be upon him), Section: insulting those of His (prayers and peace be upon him) house, His wives, and His Companions; it is forbidden to slander them, and he who does this is accursed.*

قال أبو حنيفة وأصحابه من برئ من محمد أو كذب به فهو مرتد حلال الدم إلا أن يرجع

الشفا للقاضي عياض اليحصبي القسم الرابع في تصرف وجوه الأحكام فيمن تنقصه أو سبّ عليه الصلاة والسلام

Abu Hanifa and his companions said: Whoever absolves himself from Muhammad or refutes him is an apostate, whose blood is permissible unless he comes back around.

*Al-qadi 'Iyad Al-Yahsubi, Al-shifa, Part Four: regarding disposition of the aspects of legal rulings for those who slander Him or insult Him (prayers and peace be upon him)*

وكان ﷺ يداري الكفار والمنافقين ويُجمل صُحبتهم ويُغضي عنهم ويحتمل من أذاهم ويصبر على جفائهم ما لا يجوز لنا اليوم الصبر لهم عليه وكان يُرفقهم بالعطاء والاحسان وبذلك أمره الله تعالى فقال تعالى ﴿ ولا تزال تطّلع على خائنة منهم إلا قليلاً منهم فاعفُ عنهم واصفح إن الله يحب المحسنين ﴾ وقال تعالى ﴿ إدفع بالتي هي أحسن فإذا الذي بينك وبينه عداوة كأنه ولي حميم ﴾ وذلك لحاجة الناس للتأّلف أول الاسلام وجمع الكلمة عليه فلما إستقرّ وأظهره الله على الدين كله قتل من قدر عليه وإشتهر أمرُه

الشفا للقاضي عياض اليحصبي القسم الرابع في تصرف وجوه الأحكام فيمن تنقصه أو سبّ عليه الصلاة والسلام الباب الأول في بيان ما هو في حقه ﷺ سب أو نقص من تعريض أو نص

He (SAW) used to flatter the Disbelievers [*Kuffar*] and the hypocrites, act nicely towards them in companionship, overlook their faults, put up with their hurtfulness, and patiently endure their coarseness, such as would not be possible for us to endure from them nowadays. And He would treat them kindly with gifts and favors; Allah Most High ordered this for him; the Most High said: { You will never cease to discover some treachery on their part, except a few of them, but forgive them, and be forbearing; indeed Allah loves those who do good } [*Al-ma'ida* 13]. And the Most High said: { Push back with what is better, so that he who is at enmity with you may be as an intimate associate } [*Fussilat* 34]. This was because people needed to come together in the beginning of Islam, and for anything that was said to agree on it. But when it was firmly established, and Allah made it victorious over all religion, He killed whoever He could, and became notorious.

*Al-qadi 'Iyad Al-Yahsubi, Al-shifa, Part Four: regarding disposition of the aspects of legal rulings for those who slander Him or insult Him (prayers and peace be upon him), Chapter One: Declaration of what is in His (SAW) right in being slandered or slighted, either insinuated or openly*


وقال أحمد بن ابي سليمان صاحب سحنون من قال إن النبي ﷺ أسود قتل لم يكن النبي ﷺ بأسود وقال نحوه أبو عثمان الحداد قال لو قال إنه مات قبل أن يلتحي أو أنه كان بتاهرت ولم يكن بتهامة قتل لأن هذا نفيٌ

الشفا للقاضي عياض اليحصبي القسم الرابع في تصرف وجوه الأحكام فيمن تنقّصه أو سبّه عليه الصلاة والسلام

Ahmad ibn Abi Sulaiman, the companion of Sahnun, said: Whoever says that the Prophet (SAW) was black is to be killed; the Prophet (SAW) was not black. Abu 'Uthman Al-Haddad said something similar; he said: If anyone says that He died before his beard grew out, or that He was in Tahert, and was not in Tihama, he is to be killed, because this is denying the truth.

*Al-qadi 'Iyad Al-Yahsubi, Al-shifa, Part Four: regarding disposition of the aspects of legal rulings for those who slander Him or insult Him (prayers and peace be upon him)*


عن ابي برزة قال غضب أبو بكر على رجلٍ غضباً شديداً حتى تغير لونه قلت يا خليفة رسول الله ﷺ لئن أمرتني لأضربن عنقه فكأنما صُبَّ عليه ماءٌ بارد فذهب غضبه عن الرجل وقال ثَكِلَتْكَ أمك أبا برزة إنها لم تكن لأحد بعد رسول الله ﷺ

السنن الكبرى للنسائي كتاب المحاربة الحكم فيمن سب النبي ﷺ

From Abu Barza, who said: Abu Bakr became so intensely angry with a certain man, to the point that his color changed. I said: Oh caliph of the Messenger of Allah (SAW), if you order me to, I'll decapitate him! And it was like someone poured cold water over him, and his anger towards the man subsided, and he said: May your mother be deprived of you, Abu Barza! Truly that was not for anyone besides the Messenger of Allah (SAW).

*Al-Nasa'i, Al-sunan Al-kubra, The book of warfare, Section: the ruling for those who insult the Prophet (SAW)*

عن عمرو بن ميمون عن عبدالله قال بينما رسول الله ﷺ قائم يصلي عند الكعبة وجَمْع قريش في مجالسهم إذ قال قائل منهم ألا تنظرون إلى هذا المُرائي أَيّكم يقوم إلى جزور آل فلان فيعمد إلى فرثها ودمها وسلاها فيجيء به ثم يُمهله حتى إذا سجد وضعه بين كتفيه فإنبعث أشقاهم فلما سجد رسول الله ﷺ وضعه بين كتفيه وثبت النبي ﷺ ساجداً فضحكوا حتى مال بعضهم إلى بعض من الضحك فإنطلق منطلق إلى فاطمة عليها السلام وهي جُوَيرية أقبلت تسعى وثبت النبي ﷺ ساجداً حتى ألقته عنه وأقبلت عليهم تَسُبُّهم فلما قضى رسول الله ﷺ الصلاة قال اللهم عليك بقريش اللهم عليك بقريش اللهم عليك بقريش ثم سمى اللهم عليك بعمرو بن هشام وعتبة بن ربيعة وشيبة بن ربيعة والوليد بن عتبة وأمية بن خلف وعقبة بن أبي معيط وعمارة بن الوليد قال عبدالله فوالله لقد رأيتهم صرعى يوم بدر ثم سُحبوا إلى القليب قليب بدر ثم قال رسول الله ﷺ وأُتبع أصحاب القليب لعنةً

صحيح البخاري كتّاب الصلاة باب تطرح المرأة عن المصلي شيئاً من الأذى

'Amr ibn Maymun related from Abdullah, who said: While the Messenger of Allah (SAW) was praying at the Ka'ba, and a group of the Quraish was seated around in a gathering, one of them said: Do you all not see this show-off? Which of you would get up and go to the camel that's about to be slaughtered from the family of so-and-so, carry out its feces, its blood, and its placenta, bring it, and then wait for him until he prostrates and put it between his shoulders? So the most miserable one among them was sent out, and when the Messenger of Allah (SAW) prostrated, this man put it between his shoulders. The Prophet (SAW) remained prostrated, and they laughed until they were rolling over each other from laughing. Then someone set out to tell Fatimah (peace be upon her), who at the time was a little girl. She came out running intently, while the Prophet (SAW) was still prostrating, and threw it off of him, faced them, and cursed them. And when the Messenger of Allah (SAW) finished prayer, He said: Oh Allah! Deal with Quraish, Oh Allah! Deal with Quraish, Oh Allah! Deal with Quraish. Then he called out: Oh Allah! Deal with 'Amr ibn Hisham, and 'Utba ibn Rabi'a, and Shayba ibn Rabi'a, and Al-Walid ibn 'Utba, and Umayya ibn Khalaf, and 'Utba ibn Abi Mu'ait, and 'Umara ibn Al-Walid. Abdullah said: And I swear by Allah, I saw them struck down on the day of Badr, then they were dragged out to the well, the well at Badr. Then the Messenger of Allah (SAW) said: Those of the well were pursued by a curse.

*Sahih Al-Bukhari, The book of prayer, Section: A woman may get rid of anything harmful from someone who is praying*

عن جابر بن عبدالله رضي الله عنهما أن النبي ﷺ قال من لكعب بن الأشرف فإنه قد آذى الله ورسوله قال محمد بن مسلمة أتحب أن أقتله يا رسول الله قال نعم قال فأتاه فقال إن هذا يعني النبي ﷺ قد عنّانا وسألنا الصدقة قال وأيضاً والله قال فإنا قد اتبعناه فنكره أن ندعه حتى ننظر إلى ما يصير أمره قال فلم يزَل يكلّمه حتى استمكن منه فقتله

صحيح البخاري كتاب الجهاد والسير

Jabir ibn Abdullah (may Allah be pleased with them both) related that the Prophet (SAW) said: Who can take care of Ka'b ibn Al-Ashraf? For indeed he has harmed Allah and His Messenger. Muhammad ibn Maslama said: Would you like me to kill him, Oh Messenger of Allah? He said: Yes. So he went to him and said: Indeed this man – referring to the Prophet (SAW) – has burdened us and asked us to give charity. Ka'b said: You'll see about that, by Allah. He said: Indeed we have followed him, and we don't really want to leave him until we see what will become of him. And he kept on talking to him until he saw a chance, then he killed him.

*Sahih Al-Bukhari, The book of jihad and campaigns*


عن ابي جبيرة بن الضحاك قال كان الرجل منا يكون له الاسمين والثلاثة فيُدعى ببعضها فعسى أن يكره قال فنزلت هذه الآية ﴿ ولا تنابزوا بالالقاب ﴾

جامع الترمذي كتاب تفسير القرآن

From Abu Jabira ibn Al-Dahhak, who said: Men among us would have two names or even a third, and would be called by one of them, although perhaps they disliked it; so this verse was sent down: { Do not call each other offensive nicknames } [Al-hujarat 11].

*Sunan Al-Tirmidhi, The book of tafsir*


عن عبدالله بن مغفل قال قال رسول الله ﷺ الله الله في أصحابي الله الله في أصحابي لا تتَّخذوهم غرَضاً بعدي فمن أحبَّهم فبحُبي أحبهم ومن أبغضهم فببُغضي أبغضهم ومن آذاهم فقد آذاني ومن آذاني فقد آذى الله ومن آذى الله فيوشك أن يأخذه

جامع الترمذي كتاب المناقب

From Abdullah ibn Mughaffal, who said: The Messenger of Allah (SAW) said: Allah, Allah about my Companions! Allah, Allah about my Companions! Do not make them your targets after me; for whoever loves them, loves them out of love for me; and whoever hates them, hates them out of hatred for me; and whoever harms them has harmed me; and whoever harms me has harmed Allah; and whoever harms Allah, Allah will get him soon.

*Sunan Al-Tirmidhi, The book of virtuous traits*

ينبغي للمرأة العاقلة إذا وجدت زوجاً صالحاً يلائمها أن تجتهد في مرضاته وتجتنب كل ما يؤذيه فإنها متى آذته أو تعرضت لما يكره أوجب ذلك ملالته وبقي ذلك في نفسه فربما وجد فرصة فتركها أو آثر غيرها فإنه قد يجد وقد لا تجد هي ومعلوم أن الملل للمستحسن قد يقع فكيف للمكروه

أحكام النساء لإبن الجوزي الباب الرابع والستون في وجوب طاعة الزوج وحقه على المرأة

A rational woman, if she finds a good husband suitable for her, ought to strive to please him and avoid everything that harms him; for indeed when she harms him or gets into things that he dislikes, this necessarily irritates him and sticks in his mind. And perhaps he may find the opportunity and leave her or prefer someone other than her, and indeed perhaps he will find this but she will not. It is well-known that it is possible to grow weary from something agreeable, so how much more from something disagreeable.

*Ibn Al-Jawzi, Ahkam Al-nisaa, Chapter sixty-four: regarding the duty to obey the husband, and his rights over the woman*

عن عبدالله بن عباس قال قال رسول الله ﷺ ألا أخبركم بنسائكم من أهل الجنة الودود الولود العؤود على زوجها التي إذا آذت أو أوذيت جاءت حتى تأخذ بيد زوجها ثم تقول والله لا أذوق غمضاً حتى ترضى

السنن الكبرى للنسائي كتاب عشرة النساء

From Abdullah ibn 'Abbas who said: The Messenger of Allah (SAW) said: Shall I not tell you all about your women from among the people of *Jannah*? The docile and the fertile, accustomed to her husband, the one who, whenever she does harm or is harmed, comes to take the hand of her husband and says: I swear by Allah I will not even taste closing my eyes to sleep until you are pleased.

*Al-Nasa'i, Al-sunan Al-kubra, The book of intimacy with women*

عن ابي هريرة قال قال رجلٌ يا رسول الله إن لي جاراً يؤذيني فقال إنطلق فأخرج متاعك إلى الطريق فإنطلق فأخرج متاعه فإجتمع الناس عليه فقالوا ما شأنك قال لي جارٌ يؤذيني فذكرت للنبي ﷺ فقال إنطلق فأخرج متاعك إلى الطريق فجعلوا يقولون اللهم العنه اللهم أخزِه فبلغه فأتاه فقال إرجع إلى منزلك فوالله لا أؤذيك

الأدب المفرد للبخاري كتاب الجار

From Abu Huraira, who said: A certain man said: Oh Messenger of Allah, indeed I have a neighbor who harms me. He said: Go and put your belongings out on the street. So the man went and put his belongings out on the street. The people gathered around him and said: What is going on with you? He said: I have a neighbor who harms me, and I mentioned it to the Prophet (SAW), and He said go and put your belongings out on the street. Then the people began to say "Oh Allah, curse him! Oh Allah, disgrace him!" And this reached the neighbor, so he went to the man and said: Go back to your house; I swear by Allah I won't harm you.

*Al-Bukhari, Al-adab Al-mufrad, The book of neighbors*

وبلغ المهاجر بن أبي أمية أمير اليمن لأبي بكر رضي الله عنه أن امرأةً هناك في الردة غنّت بسبّ النبي ﷺ
فقطع يدها ونزع ثنيّتها فبلغ أبا بكر رضي الله عنه ذلك فقال له لو لا ما فعلتَ لأمرتُك بقتلها لأن حد الأنبياء
ليس يُشبه الحدود

الشفا للقاضي عياض اليحصبي القاسم الرابع في تصرف وجوه الأحكام فيمن تنقصه أو سبّ عليه الصلاة والسلام فصل في
إيجاب قتل من سبه أو عانه ﷺ

Muhajir ibn Abi Umayya, the chief of Yemen, informed Abu Bakr (may Allah be pleased with him) that a certain woman there had apostatized and sang insulting songs about the Prophet (SAW), so he had cut off her hand and took out her front tooth. The news reached Abu Bakr (may Allah be pleased with him), and he said to him: Were it not for what you have already done, I would have ordered you to kill her, for punishment regarding the prophets is unlike the normal punishments.

*Al-qadi 'Iyad Al-Yahsubi, Al-shifa, Part Four: regarding disposition of the aspects of legal rulings for those who slander Him or insult Him (prayers and peace be upon him), Section: regarding affirmation of the necessity to kill whoever insults or dishonors Him (SAW)*


عن علي رضي الله عنه أن يهودية كانت تشتِم النبي ﷺ وتقع فيه نخنقها رجلٌ حتى ماتت فأبطل رسول الله ﷺ دمها

سنن أبي داود كتاب الحدود

'Ali (may Allah be pleased with him) related that a certain Jewish woman used to insult the Prophet (SAW) and slander him, so a man strangled her until she died. And the Messenger of Allah (SAW) released any liability for her blood.

*Sunan Abu Dawud, The book of legal punishments [hudud]*


عن علي بن أبي طالب رضي الله عنه قال قال رسول الله ﷺ من سب نبياً قتل ومن سب أصحابه جلد
رواه أبو محمد الخلال وابو القاسم الأزجي ورواه أبو ذر الهروي ولفظه من سب نبياً فاقتلوه ومن سب
أصحابي فإجلدوه

الصارم المسلول على شاتم الرسول لإبن تيمية المسألة الأولى أن من سب النبي س من مسلم أو كافر فإنه يجب قتله

From 'Ali ibn Abi Talib (may Allah be pleased with him), who said: The Messenger of Allah (SAW) said: Whoever slanders a prophet is to be killed, and whoever slanders his companions is to be whipped. Abu Muhammad Al-Khallal and Abu Al-Qasim Al-Azji narrated this. Abu Dharr Al-Harawi also narrated this as follows: Whoever slanders a prophet, kill him; and whoever slanders my companions, whip him.

*Ibn Taymiyya, Al-sarim Al-maslul, The first issue: That any Muslim or Disbeliever who slanders the Prophet (SAW) must indeed be killed.*

﴾ يا أيها الذين آمنوا لا تكونوا كالذين آذوا موسى فبرأه الله مما قالوا وكان عند الله وجيهاً ﴿
الأحزاب ٦٩

{ *Oh you who have believed! Do not be like those who harmed Musa,
then Allah absolved him of what they had said; and he was
distinguished in the sight of Allah* } *Al-ahzab* 69

إختلف أهل التأويل في الأذى الذي أوذي به موسى الذي ذكره الله في هذا الموضع فقال بعضهم رموه بأنه آدر
تفسير الطبري

The expositors differ regarding the harm that Musa was harmed by, which Allah
mentions here; some of them say that people accused him of having swollen
testicles [*adar*].

*Tafsir Al-Tabari*

﴾ يا أيها الذين آمنوا لا يكونوا ﴿ مع نبيكم ﴾ كالذين آذوا موسى ﴿ بقولهم مثلاً ما يمنعه معنى
إلا أنه آدر ﴾ فبرّأه الله مما قالوا ﴿ بأن وضع ثوبه على حجر ليغتسل ففرّ الحجر به حتى وقف بين ملأ من
بني إسرائيل فأدركه موسى فأخذ ثوبه فإستتر به فرأوه ولا أُدرة به وهي نفخة في الخصية ﴾ وكان عند الله
وجيهاً ﴿ ذا جاه ومما أوذي به نبينا ﷺ أنه قسم قسماً فقال رجل هذه قسمة ما أريد بها وجه الله تعالى
فغضب النبي ﷺ من ذلك وقال يرحم الله موسى لقد أوذي بأكثر من هذا فصبر رواه البخاري
تفسير الجلالين

{ Oh you who have believed! Do not be } : with your Prophet, { like those who harmed
Musa } : by the things they said, for example "What is keeping him from bathing with
us except that he has swollen testicles." } Then Allah absolved him of what they had
said } : he put his garment on a rock in order to bathe, but the rock darted off with
it until it stopped among a group of the children of Israel. And Musa caught up with
it, grabbed his garment, and covered himself with it; and they saw that he did not
have swollen testicles; { and he was distinguished in the sight of Allah } : a man of
distinction } . One of the things by which our Prophet (SAW) was harmed was when
He was dividing up some spoils, and a certain man said: These are spoils in which I
do not seek the face of Allah Most High. And the Prophet (SAW) became upset at
this, and said: May Allah have mercy on Musa; he was harmed by greater things than
this but he was forbearing. (Narrated by Al-Bukhari.)

*Tafsir Al-Jalalain*

وحديث إيذاء موسى مختلف فيه قال بعضهم هو إيذاؤهم إياه بنسبته إلى عيب في بدنه وقال بعضهم إن قارون
قرر مع إمرأة فاحشة حتى تقول عند نبي إسرائيل إن موسى زنى بي

تفسير الرازي

There is disagreement regarding the hadith of Musa's harm; some say that it was people harming him regarding a defect in his body; others say that Qarun imposed on a certain loose woman until she said to the children of Israel: Indeed Musa adulterated with me.

*Tafsir Al-Razi*

•　　•　　•

﴿ ولا تطع الكافرين والمنافقين ودع أذاهم وتوكل على الله وكفى بالله وكيلاً ﴾ الأحزاب ٤٨

*{ Do not obey the Disbelievers and the hypocrites, and do not worry about their harm, and trust in Allah; Allah is sufficient a guardian }*

Al-ahzab 48

﴿ ودع أذاهم ﴾ يقول وأعرض عن أذاهم لك واصبر عليه ولا يمنعك ذلك عن القيام بأمر الله في عباده
والنفوذ لما كلّفك

تفسير الطبري

{ And do not worry about their harm } : He is saying: Turn away from their harm towards you, and be forbearing with it, and do not let it keep you from fulfilling what Allah has ordered concerning His servants and from carrying out what He has required of you.

*Tafsir Al-Tabari*

﴿ ودع أذاهم ﴾ أي دعه إلى الله فإنه يعذبهم بأيديكم وبالنار ويبين هذا قوله تعالى ﴿ وتوكل على الله وكفى بالله وكيلاً ﴾ أي الله كاف عبده

تفسير الرازي

{ And do not worry about their harm } : that is, leave it to Allah, for indeed He will torment them by your hands and by hellfire; the word of the Most High makes this clear: { Trust in Allah; Allah is sufficient a guardian } : that is, Allah is sufficient for His servants.

*Tafsir Al-Razi*

﴿ أذاهم ﴾ يحتمل اضافته إلى الفاعل والمفعول يعني ودع أن تؤذيهم بضرر أو قتل وخذ بظاهرهم وحسابهم على الله في باطنهم أو ودع ما يؤذونك به ولا تجازهم عليه حتى يؤمر وعن إبن عباس رضي الله عنهما هي منسوخة بآية السيف

تفسير الزمخشري

{ Their harm } : This wording can refer to either doing or receiving; that is, let up from harming them by injury or killing, and just go by what is evident from them on the outside; their reckoning is with Allah for what they hold inside. Or: Do not worry about what they harm you with, and do not go beyond it with them until you are commanded to. Ibn 'Abbas (may Allah be pleased with him) related that this is abrogated by the verse of the sword.

*Tafsir Al-Zamakhshari*

•     •     •

﴿ وَاصْبِرْ عَلَى مَا يَقُولُونَ وَاهْجُرْهُمْ هَجْرًا جَمِيلًا ﴾ المزمل ١٠

## { *Be forbearing with what they say, and refrain from them nicely* }

*Al-muzzammil* 10

﴿ وَاصْبِرْ عَلَى مَا يَقُولُونَ ﴾ أي كفار مكة من أذاهم ﴿ وَأَهْجُرْهُمْ هَجْرًا جَمِيلًا ﴾ لا جذع فيه وهذا قبل الأمر بقتالهم

تفسير الجلالين

{ Be forbearing with what they say } : that is, the Disbelievers [*Kuffar*] of Mecca, from their harm; { and refrain from them nicely } : without worrying about it. But this was before the command to fight them.

*Tafsir Al-Jalalain, Al-muzzammil* 10

﴿ وَاصْبِرْ عَلَى مَا يَقُولُونَ وَأَهْجُرْهُمْ هَجْرًا جَمِيلًا ﴾ براءة نسخت ما ههنا أمر بقتالهم حتى يشهدوا أن لا إله إلا الله وأن محمداً رسول الله لا يقبل منهم غيرها

تفسير الطبري

{ Be forbearing with what they say, and refrain from them nicely } ; an absolution that abrogates what is here is the command to fight them until they bear witness that there is no god but Allah, and that Muhammad is the Messenger of Allah; nothing is to be accepted from them other than this.

*Tafsir Al-Tabari, Al-muzzammil* 10

•     •     •

عن ابي بكرة أن نبي الله ﷺ مرّ برجل ساجد وهو ينطلق إلى الصلاة فقضى الصلاة ورجع عليه وهو ساجد فقام النبي ﷺ فقال من يقتل هذا فقام رجل لحسر عن يديه فاخترط سيفه وهزّه وقال يا نبي الله بأبي أنت وأمي كيف اقتل رجلاً ساجداً يشهد أن لا إله إلا الله وأن محمداً عبده ورسوله ثم قال من يقتل هذا فقال رجل فقال أنا لحسر عن ذراعيه واخترط سيفه فهزه حتى أُرعِدت يده فقال يا رسول الله كيف اقتل رجلاً ساجداً يشهد أن لا إله إلا الله وأن محمداً عبده ورسوله فقال النبي ﷺ والذي نفسي بيده لو قتلتموه لكان أول فتنة وآخرها

رواه أحمد والطبراني من غير بيان شاف ورجال أحمد رجال الصحيح

مجمع الزوائد ومنبع الفوائد للهيثمي كتاب قتال أهل البغي

Abu Bakra narrated that the Prophet of Allah (SAW) was headed to prayer and passed by a certain man who was bowed down in prostration. He finished prayer and went back past the same man, and he was still prostrating. And the Prophet (SAW) got up and said: Who will kill this guy? A man got up, took out his hands, drew his sword and shook it around, and said: Oh Prophet of Allah! I would give my father and mother for you – but how can I kill a man who is bowed down, who bears witness that there is no god but Allah and that Muhammad is His servant and His messenger? So He said again: Who will kill this guy? Another man said: Me! And he took out his arms, drew his sword and shook it around until his hand began to tremble, but said: Oh Messenger of Allah, how can I kill a man who is bowed down, who bears witness that there is no god but Allah and that Muhammad is His servant and His messenger? The Prophet (SAW) said: I swear by Him who holds my soul, if you all would have killed him, it would have been the beginning and the end of all ordeals [*fitnah*].

(Ahmad and Al-Tabarani related this narrative without clear articulation, but the men in Ahmad's chain of narration are men of veracity [*sahih*].)

*Al-Haythami, Majma' Al-zawa'id wa Manba' Al-fawa'id, The book of fighting those who offend and commit aggression*

عن ابي سعيد الخدري أن أبا بكر جاء إلى رسول الله ﷺ فقال يا رسول الله إني مررت بوادي كذا وكذا فإذا رجل متخشع حسن الهيئة يصلي فقال له النبي ﷺ إذهب إليه فأقتله قال فذهب إليه أبو بكر فلما رآه على تلك الحال كره أن يقتله فرجع إلى رسول الله ﷺ قال فقال النبي ﷺ لعمر إذهب فأقتله فذهب عمر فرآه على تلك الحال التي رآه أبو بكر قال فكره أن يقتله قال فرجع فقال يا رسول الله اني رأيته يصلي متخشعاً فكرهت أن أقتله قال يا علي إذهب فأقتله فذهب علي فلم يره فرجع علي فقال يا رسول الله إنه لم يره قال

فقال النبي ﷺ إن هذا وأصحابه يقرؤون القرآن لا يجاوز تراقيهم يمرقون من الدين كما يمرق السهم من الرمية
ثم لا يعودون فيه حتى يعود السهم في فُوقه فاقتلوهم هم شر البرية

مسند الإمام أحمد مسند أبي سعيد الخدري رضي الله عنه

Abu Sa'id Al-Khudri related that Abu Bakr came to the Messenger of Allah (SAW) and said: Oh Messenger of Allah, indeed I was passing through such-and-such valley, and there was a humbly submissive, well-groomed man there praying. The Prophet (SAW) said to him: Go to him and kill him. And Abu Bakr went to him, but when he saw him in that position, he really didn't want to kill him. So he returned to the Messenger of Allah (SAW). And the Prophet (SAW) said to 'Umar: Go and kill him. So 'Umar went, and saw him in the same position that Abu Bakr had seen him, and he really didn't want to kill him either. So he returned, and said: Oh Messenger of Allah, indeed I saw him praying humbly and submissive, and I really didn't want to kill him. Then He said: Oh 'Ali! Go kill him. And 'Ali went, but could not find him. So 'Ali returned and said: Oh Messenger of Allah, indeed he couldn't find him. And the Messenger of Allah (SAW) said: Truly this man and his companions recite the Qur'an without it going past their throats, they pass through and out of the *deen* like an arrow passes through and out of its target, and until the arrow returns to its bowstring they will not return to the *deen*; so kill them; they are the worst of creatures.

*Musnad Ahmad, Narrations from Abu Sa'id Al-Khudri (may Allah be pleased with him)*

عن الحسن في النصراني يقذف المسلم قال يُجلد ثمانين

عن هشام بن عروة عن أبيه قال إذا قذف النصراني المسلم جُلد الحد

عن الزهري قال في أهل الذمة يجلدون في الفِرية على المسلمين

عن عامر قال أتاني مسلم وجرمقاني قد إفترى كل واحد منهما على صاحبه فجلدتُ الجرمقاني وتركت المسلم فأتى عمر بن عبدالعزيز فذكر ذلك له فقال أحسن

عن عاصم قال شهدت الشعبي وضرب نصرانياً قذف مسلماً فقال إضرب ولا يرى ابطك

عن عكرمة مولى إبن عباس عن إبن عباس في المملوك يقذف الحر قال يجلد أربعين

عن يحيى بن سعيد قال جلد أبو بكر بن محمد بن عمرو بن حزم عبداً قذف حراً ثمانين

المصنف لإبن أبي شيبة كتاب الحدود

From Hasan regarding a Christian [*Nasrani*] who slanders a Muslim; he said: He is to be whipped eighty times.

Hisham ibn 'Urwa related from his father, who said: If a Christian slanders a Muslim, whipping is the punishment.

From Al-Zuhri, who said regarding those held under safeguard [*dhimmis*]: They are to be whipped for defaming Muslims.

From 'Amir, who said: A Muslim and Jarmaqani came to me, each of them having fabricated lies about the other; so I whipped Al-Jarmaqani and I left the Muslim alone. And 'Amr ibn 'Abd Al-'Aziz came, and he mentioned it to him, and he said: That's the way!

From 'Asim, who said: I saw Al-Sha'bi having beaten a Christian who had slandered a Muslim. And he ['Asim] said: Beat him! So you can't even see your armpit!

'Ikrama, the freed slave of Ibn 'Abbas, related from Ibn 'Abbas regarding a slave who slanders a free person; he said: He is to be whipped forty times.

From Yahya ibn Sa'id, who said: Abu Bakr ibn Muhammad ibn 'Amr ibn Hazm whipped a slave, who had slandered a free person, eighty times.

*Ibn Abi Shayba, Al-musannaf, The book of legal punishments [hudud]*

# Scholars and sources

### 'Abd Al-Malik ibn Habib

أبو مروان عبد الملك بن حبيب بن سليمان بن هارون بن جاهمة بن العباس بن مرداس السلمي, *Abu Marwan 'Abd Al-Malik ibn Habib ibn Sulaiman ibn Harun ibn Jahima ibn Al-'Abbas ibn Mirdas Al-Sulami.* Poet and genealogist from Andalusia who wrote on law, history, language, and medicine. Wrote *Adab Al-nisaa Al-mawsum bi Kitab Al-ghaya wa Al-nihaya* [Manners of Women, designated as The Book of the Utmost and the End]. Died 238 A.H./853 A.D.

### 'Abd Al-Razzaq

أبو بكر عبد الرزاق بن همام الصنعاني, *Abu Bakr 'Abd Al-Razzaq ibn Hammam Al-San'ani.* Hadith scholar from Yemen. He wrote the extensive *Musannaf* [Categorized Collection], one of the earliest compilations of hadith and therefore rich in narrations directly from the Prophet (SAW) and Companions. Died 211 A.H./826 A.D.

### Abu Dawud

أبو داود سليمان بن الاشعث بن إسحاق بن بشير الازدي السجستاني, *Abu Dawud Sulaiman ibn Al-Ash'ath ibn Ishaq ibn Bashir Al-Azdi Al-Sajistani.* From Sajistan (Sistan; Persia/Afghanistan) and later Basra (Iraq). Compiled *Sunan Abi Dawud*, one of the six leading Sunni hadith collections. Died 275 A.H./888 A.D.

### Abu Nu'im Al-Asfahani

أبو نُعيم أحمد بن عبد الله بن أحمد بن إسحاق بن موسى ابن مهران الاصفهاني, *Abu Nu'im Ahmad ibn Abdillah ibn Ahmad ibn Ishaq ibn Musa Ibn Mahran Al-Asfahani.* Historian and compiler of hadith from Isfahan (Persia), of the Shafi'i school and early Sufi scholar. Wrote *Mawsu'a Al-tibb Al-nabawi* [Encyclopedia of medicine of the Prophet (SAW)]. Died 430 A.H./1038 A.D.

### Ahmad

أبو عبدالله أحمد بن محمد بن حنبل الشيباني, *Abu Abdillah Ahmad ibn Muhammad ibn Hanbal Al-Shaybani* or simply *Ahmad ibn Hanbal.* From Baghdad. Revered figure in Islamic history and founder of the Hanbali school of law, most known for his extensive hadith collection the *Musnad.* Died 241 A.H./855 A.D.

## Al-Baghawi

أبو محمد الحسين بن مسعود بن محمد الفراء البغوي, *Abu Muhammad Al-Husain ibn Mas'ud ibn Muhammad Al-Farra' Al-Baghawi*. Hadith scholar from Central Asia and Shafi'i jurist most known for his well-respected commentary on the Qur'an *Ma'alim Al-tanzil* [Guideposts to the Revelation] or *Tafsir Al-Baghawi*. Died 516 A.H./1122 A.D.

## Al-Baydawi

ناصر الدين أبو الخير عبدالله بن ابي القاسم عمر بن محمد بن ابي الحسن علي البيضاوي, *Nasr Al-din Abu Al-Khair Abdullah bn Abi Al-Qasim 'Umar ibn Muhammad ibn Abi Al-Hasan 'Ali Al-Baydawi*. Persian theologian and judge. His major work is the commentary on the Qur'an *Anwar Al-tanzil wa Asrar Al-ta'wil* [Lights of Revelation and Secrets of Interpretation], a standard tafsir and one of the most important and popular. Died 685 A.H./1286 A.D.

## Al-Bayhaqi

أبو بكر أحمد بن الحسين بن علي بن موسى الخسروجردي الخراساني البيهقي, *Abu Bakr Ahmad ibn Al-Husain ibn 'Ali ibn Musa Al-Khusrawjirdi Al-Khurasani Al-Bayhaqi*. Persian and of the Shafi'i school; well-known scholar of hadith and prolific writer, among whose works are *Al-sunan Al-kubra* [The Larger Compilation of Sunnah] also known as *Sunan Al-Bayhaqi*. Died 458 A.H./1066 A.D.

## Al-Bukhari

أبو عبدالله محمد بن إسماعيل بن ابراهيم بن المغيرة بن بردزبة الجعفي البخاري, *Abu Abdillah Muhammad ibn Isma'il ibn Ibrahim ibn Al-Mughira ibn Bardizba Al-Ju'fi Al-Bukhari*. From Bukhara (now Uzbekistan). Compiled *Sahih Al-Bukhari*, one of the six leading Sunni hadith collections and one of the two most highly regarded compilations (along with *Sahih Muslim*); also compiled *Al-adab Al-mufrad* [Exemplary Manners], a collection of hadith concerning the behavior and morals of the Prophet (SAW). Died 256 A.H./870 A.D.

## Al-Ghazali

أبو حامد محمد الغزّالي الطوسي النيسابوري, *Abu Hamid Muhammad Al-Ghazali Al-Tusi Al-Nisaburi*. Prominent jurist, theologian, and philosopher, Shafi'i and Sufi, from Tus (Persia). Given many titles, the most well-known of them حجة الإسلام, The Case for Islam. His celebrated work is *Ihyaa 'Ulum Al-din* [Revival of the Religious Sciences]. Died 505 A.H./1111 A.D.

## Al-Hakim Al-Tirmidhi

أبو عبد الله محمد بن علي بن الحسين الترمذي, *Abu Abdillah Muhammad ibn 'Ali ibn Al-Husain Al-Tirmidhi*, known as الحكيم الترمذي, The Wise Al-Tirmidhi. From Termez (now Uzbekistan); jurist and well-known among the early authors in Sufism. Wrote *Nawadir Al-usul fi Ahadith Al-Rusul* [Anecdotes of the foundations of the hadith of the Messenger (SAW)]. Died 320 A.H./932 A.D.

## Al-Haythami

أبو الحسن علي بن ابي بكر بن سليمان الهيثمي, *Abu Al-Hasan 'Ali ibn Abi Bakr ibn Sulaiman Al-Haythami*, known as نور الدين, Light of the *Deen*. Hadith scholar and author of *Majma' Al-zawa'id wa Manba' Al-fawa'id* [Collection of Unique Hadith and Wellspring of Benefits]. Died 807 A.H./1405 A.D.

## Al-Hindi

علاء الدين علي بن حسام الدين إبن قاضي خان القادري الشاذلي الهندي البرهانفري المكي, *'Ulaa Al-din 'Ali ibn Husam Al-din ibn Qadi Khan Al-Qadiri Al-Shadhili Al-Hindi Al-Burhanfuri Al-Makki*, known as المتقي الهندي, The God-fearing Indian. From Burhanpur, India. Legal scholar of the Hanafi school and collector of hadith; his most well-known work is *Kanz Al-'ummal fi Sunan Al-aqwal wa Al-af'al* [Treasures of the Workers in the *Sunnah* of Speech and Action]. Died 975 A.H./1567 A.D.

## Al-Munawi

محمد عبد الرؤوف بن تاج العارفين بن علي بن زين العابدين الحدادي المناوي القاهري, *Muhammad 'Abd Al-Ru'uf ibn Taj Al-'Arifin ibn 'Ali ibn Zain Al-'Abidin Al-Haddadi Al-Munawi Al-Qahiri*. Given the title زين الدين, Adornment of the *Deen*. From Cairo. Among the greatest scholars of religion and the arts. Author of many works, the most well-known being *Faid Al-Qadir* [The Outpouring of the Almighty], a commentary on the hadith collection *Al-jami' Al-saghir* of Al-Suyuti. Died 1031 A.H./1621 A.D.

## Al-Nafzawi

أبو عبد الله محمد بن محمد النفزاوي, *Abu Abdillah Muhammad ibn Muhammad Al-Nafzawi*. From Tunisia. Wrote the sex manual and treatise *Al-rawd Al-'atir fi Nuzha Al-khatir* [The Perfumed Garden along the Stroll of the Desirous]. Early to mid-15th century.

## Al-Nasa'i

أبو عبد الرحمن أحمد بن شعيب بن علي بن سنان بن بحر بن دينار النسائي, *Abu 'Abd Al-Rahman Ahmad ibn Shu'aib ibn 'Ali ibn Sinan ibn Bahr ibn Dinar Al-Nasa'i*. From Nisa (now

Turkmenistan), later Palestine. Judge and compiler of several collections of hadith, including *Al-sunan al-kubra* [The Greater *Sunan*], and *Al-sunan Al-sughra* [The Lesser *Sunan*], also called *Sunan Al-Nasa'i*, one of the leading Sunni hadith collections. Died 303 A.H./915 A.D.

## Al-Nawawi

أبو زكريا يحيى بن شرف الحزامي النووي, *Abu Zakariya Yahya ibn Sharaf Al-Hizami Al-Nawawi.* Scholar of hadith, theology, law, and lexicology, and one of the foremost in the Shafi'i school. From Nawa (now Syria). Author of many works, including *Kitab Al-majmu' Sharh Al-muhadhab* [Compilation on Exposition of the *Muhadhab*] (The *Muhadhab* or "The Cultivated One" is a Book of Law by Ibn Ishaq Al-Shirazi); *Al-minhaj fi Sharh Sahih Muslim* [Open Path to Exposition of Sahih Muslim], also called *Sahih Muslim bi Sharh Al-Nawawi* [Al-Nawawi's Commentary on Sahih Muslim], one of the most regarded commentaries on Sahih Muslim; and *Al-tibyan fi Adab Hamala Al-Qur'an* [Exposition on the Conduct of those who Convey the Qur'an]. Died 676 A.H./1277 A.D.

## Al-qadi 'Iyad Al-Yahsubi

أبو الفضل عياض بن موسى بن عياض بن عمرو بن موسى بن عياض السبتي اليحصبي, *Abu Al-Fadl 'Iyad ibn Musa ibn 'Iyad ibn 'Amr ibn Musa ibn 'Iyad Al-Sabti Al-Yahsubi.* Scholar and judge (*qadi*) from Andalusia and later Morocco, well-known in the Maliki school. Wrote *Kitab Al-shifaa bi Ta'rif Huquq Al-Mustafa* [The Book of Healing by Making Known the Rights of the Chosen One], a well-admired and referenced compilation of the life, attributes, and acts of the Prophet (SAW). Died 544 A.H./1149 A.D.

## Al-Qastalani

شهاب الدين القسطلاني, *Shihab Al-deen Al-Qastalani.* Scholar of hadith, jurist and historian from Cairo. Compiled *Al-mawahib Al-laduniyya bi Al-minah Al-Muhammadiyya* [Mystic Gifts from the Divine Favors of Muhammad], a biography of the Prophet (SAW). Died 923 A.H./1517 A.D.

## Al-Qurtubi

محمد بن أحمد بن ابي بكر بن فرح الأنصاري القرطبي, *Muhammad ibn Ahmad ibn Abi Bakr ibn Farh Al-Ansari Al-Qurtubi*; شمس الدين, Sun of the *Deen*. From Cordoba (Andalusia) and later lived in Egypt. Scholar of hadith, law, and commentary, of the Maliki school, most known for his important commentary on the Qur'an *Al-jami' Li-Ahkam Al-Qur'an* [Collection of Rulings of the Qur'an] or *Tafsir Al-Qurtubi*. Died 671 A.H./1273 A.D.

## Al-Raghib Al-Asfahani

أبو القاسم الحسين بن محمد بن المفضل الاصفهاني, *Abu Al-Qasim Al-Husain ibn Muhammad ibn Al-Mufaddal Al-Asfahani*, known as الراغب, *Al-raghib* [the desirous]. Scholar of literature and exegesis from Isfahan (Persia), of debated association (Sunni or Shia). Wrote *Muhadarat Al-udabaa wa Muhawarat Al-shu'raa wa Al-bulaghaa* [Lectures of the Writers of Prose and Reasonings of the Poets and the Eloquent of Expression]. Died 502 A.H./1108 A.D.


## Al-Razi

أبو عبدالله محمد بن عمر بن الحسن بن الحسين بن علي الرازي, *Abu Abdillah Muhammad ibn 'Umar ibn Al-Hasan ibn Al-Husain ibn 'Ali Al-Razi*, given the title فخر الدين, Pride of the *Deen*. From Persia, later lived in Afghanistan. Wrote on ethics, medicine, history, law, and other subjects, and authored the extensive Qur'anic commentary *Mafatih Al-ghaib* [Keys to the Unseen] also called *Al-tafsir Al-kabir* [The Great Exegesis] or simply *Tafsir Al-Razi*. Died 604 A.H./1210 A.D.


## Al-Suyuti

عبد الرحمن بن كمال الدين ابي بكر بن محمد سابق الدين خضر الخضيري الأسيوطي, *'Abd Al-rahman ibn Kamal Al-din Abi Bakr ibn Muhammad Sabiq Al-din Khadar Al-Khadiri Al-Asyuti*; known by the honorary title جلال الدين, Majesty of the *Deen*. Prolific comentator, historian, and scholar of hadith from Egypt. Compiled the popular exegesis of the Qur'an *Tafsir Al-Jalalain* with his mentor *Jalal Al-Din Al-Mahalli*. Among his other works are the authoritative Qur'anic exegesis based on direct narrations *Al-durr Al-manthur fi Al-tafsir Al-ma'thur* [Scattered Pearls on the Transmitted Commentary], a Commentary on *Sunan Al-Nasa'i,* and *Nawadir Al-aik fi Ma'rifa Al-naik* [Fresh Blooms of the Forest in the Knowledge of Fucking]. Died 911 A.H./1505 A.D.


## Al-Tabarani

أبو القاسم سليمان بن أحمد بن أيوب بن مطير اللخمي الشامي الطبراني, *Abu Al-Qasim Sulaiman ibn Ahmad ibn Ayyub ibn Mutayyir Al-Lakhmi Al-Shami Al-Tabarani*. A well-known scholar and narrator of hadith from Palestine and later Persia; among his works is *Al-mu'jam Al-kabir* [The Large Compilation]. Died 360 A.H./971 A.D.


## Al-Tabari

أبو جعفر محمد بن جرير بن يزيد بن كثير بن غالب الطبري, *Abu Ja'far Muhammad ibn Jarir ibn Yazid ibn Kathir ibn Ghalib Al-Tabari*. Early commentator, historian, and jurist from Tabaristan (Persia), later Baghdad; given the title إمام المفسرين, Leader of the Commentators. His main and most influential work is his commentary on the Qur'an *Jami' Al-bayyan fi*

*Ta'wil Al-Qur'an* [Collection of Explanations on Interpretation of the Qur'an] also called *Tafsir Al-Tabari*, the earliest extant work among the well-known commentaries and often considered the most important. Died 310 A.H./923 A.D.

## Al-Tirmidhi

أبو عيسى محمد بن عيسى بن سورة بن موسى بن الضحاك السلمي الترمذي, *Abu 'Isa Muhammad ibn 'Isa ibn Sawra ibn Musa ibn Al-Dahhak Al-Sulami Al-Tirmidhi.* From Termez (now Uzbekistan). His collection *Jami' Al-Tirmidhi* or *Sunan Al-Tirmidhi* is one of the leading collections of Sunni hadith; he also compiled *Al-shama'il Al-muhamadiyya* [The Muhammadan Attributes], a collection of hadith concerning details of the Prophet's (SAW) appearance, mannerisms, and way of life. Died 279 A.H./892 A.D.

## Al-Wahidi

أبو الحسن علي بن أحمد بن محمد إبن علي الواحدي النيسابوري, *Abu Al-Hasan 'Ali ibn Ahmad ibn Muhammad ibn 'Ali Al-Wahidi Al-Nisaburi.* From Nishapur (Persia). The earliest of the scholars concerned with the context of revelation of the Qur'an. His most renowned work is *Asbab Al-nuzul* [Reasons for the Revelations], which presents known occasions and incidents related to the revelation of specific verses in the Qur'an. Died 468 A.H./1076 A.D.

## Al-Zamakhshari

أبو القاسم محمود بن عمر بن محمد بن عمر الخوارزمي الزمخشري, *Abu Al-Qasim Mahmud ibn 'Umar ibn Muhammad ibn 'Umar Al-Khawarzami Al-Zamakhshari*; given the title جار الله, Companion of Allah. From Turkmenistan. His most well-known work is the *tafsir Al-Kashaf 'an Haqa'iq Al-tanzil* [The Revealer of the True Meanings of the Revelation]. Died 538 A.H./1143 A.D.

## Badr Al-deen Al-'Aini

أبو محمد محمود بن أحمد بن موسى العيني, *Abu Muhammad Mahmud ibn Ahmad ibn Musa Al-'Aini*, known as بدر الدين, Full Moon of the *Deen*. Hanafi scholar from Antep (Turkey) and later Cairo. Most known for his large exposition *'Umdat Al-qari Sharh Sahih Al-Bukhari* [Support for the Scrutinizer: Commentary on *Sahih Al-Bukhari*]; also wrote *Sharh Sunan Abi Dawud* [Commentary on *Sunan Abi Dawud*]. Died 855 A.H./1451 A.D.

## Ibn Abi Hatim

أبو محمد عبد الرحمن بن محمد بن إدريس بن المنذر بن داود بن مهران التّميمي الحنظلي الرازي, *Abu Muhammad 'Abd Al-Rahman ibn Muhammad ibn Idris ibn Al-Mundhir ibn Dawud ibn*

*Mahran Al-Tamimi Al-Handhali Al-Razi,* more well-known as Ibn Abi Hatim. Scholar of hadith from Ray (Iran); author of *'Ilal Al-Hadith* [Occasions of the Hadith]. Died 327 A.H./938 A.D.

## Ibn Abi Shaybah

أبو بكر عبد الله بن محمد بن أبي شيبة إبراهيم بن عثمان بن خواستي العبسي مولاهم الكوفي, *Abu Bakr Abdullah ibn Muhammad ibn Abi Shaybah Ibrahim ibn 'Uthman ibn Khuwasti Al-'Abasi Mawlahim Al-Kufi.* Scholar of hadith from Kufa (Iraq) and among the most significant of early authors; his *Musannaf* [Categorized Collection] is one of the largest existing compilations of hadith. Died 235 A.H./849 A.D.

## Ibn 'Abidin

محمد أمين بن عمر بن عبد العزيز عابدين الدمشقي, *Muhammad Amin ibn 'Umar ibn 'Abd Al-'Aziz 'Abidin Al-Dimashqi.* Hanafi Jurist from Damascus. His legal manual *Radd Al-muhtar 'ala Al-dur Al-mukhtar* [Answer to the Perplexed over the Choicest Pearls] is an annotated commentary on Al-Haskafi's *Tanwir Al-Absar* [Illuminating the Gazes], and is the leading Hanafi legal manual. Died 1252 A.H./1836 A.D.

## Ibn Al-A'rabi

أحمد بن محمد بن زياد بن بشر بن درهم العنزي, *Ahmad ibn Muhammad ibn Ziyad ibn Bishr ibn Dirham Al-'Anzi,* known as Abu Sa'id Al-A'rabi. Historian who lived in Mecca. Among his works is the collection/lexicon *Kitab Al-Mu'jam.* Died 340 A.H./952 A.D.

## Ibn Al-Jawzi

أبو الفرج عبد الرحمن بن أبي الحسن علي بن محمد التيمي البكري, *Abu Al-Faraj 'Abd Al-Rahman ibn Abi Al-Hasan 'Ali ibn Muhammad Al-Taimi Al-Bakri,* known as إبن الجوزي, Ibn Al-Jawzi. Hanbali jurist, collector of hadith and historian; influential in his native Baghdad. One of the most copious writers in the history of Islam, he wrote extensively on many areas of study, including *Ahkam Al-nisaa* [Rulings on Women]. Died 597 A.H./1201 A.D.

## Ibn Al-Naqib Al-Misri

أبو العباس أحمد بن لؤلؤ بن عبد الله الرومي, *Abu Al-'Abbas Ahmad ibn Lu'lu' ibn Abdillah Al-Rumi,* known as شهاب الدين ابن النقيب المصري, Shining Star of the *Deen* Ibn Al-Naqib Al-Misri. From Cairo. Wrote the leading manual of Shafi'i law *'Umda Al-salik wa 'Udda Al-nasik* [Reliance of the Traveler and Instruments of the Devout]. Died 769 A.H./1368 A.D.

## Ibn 'Atiyya

أبو محمد عبد الحق بن غالب بن عطية الأندلسي, *Abu Muhammad 'Abd Al-Haqq ibn Ghalib ibn 'Atiyya Al-Andalusi*. Jurist and scholar of tafsir, legal decrees, and hadith, from Analusia. His large commentary on the Qur'an is *Al-muharrar Al-wajeez fi Tafsir Al-kitab Al-'aziz* [Concise Compilation in Exegesis of the Great Book]. Died 541 A.H./1148 A.D.

## Ibn Hajar Al-'Asqalani

أبو الفضل أحمد بن علي بن محمد بن محمد بن علي بن محمود بن أحمد بن أحمد الكناني العسقلاني, *Abu Al-fadl Ahmad ibn 'Ali ibn Muhammad ibn Muhammad ibn 'Ali ibn Mahmud ibn Ahmad ibn Ahmad Al-Kanani Al-'Asqalani*; given the title شهاب الدين, Flaming star of the *Deen*. Of the Shafi'i school, from Egypt. Compiled many works of hadith. Among his works is *Bulugh Al-maram min Adilla Al-Ahkam* [Attainment of the Goal in Affirmations of the Rulings]. Died 852 A.H./1449 A.D.

## Ibn Hazm Al-Andalusi

أبو محمد علي بن أحمد بن سعيد بن حزم بن غالب بن صالح بن خلف بن معدان بن سفيان بن يزيد الأندلسي القرطبي, *Abu Muhammad 'Ali ibn Ahmad ibn Sa'id ibn Hazm ibn Ghalib ibn Salih ibn Khalaf ibn Ma'dan ibn Sufyan ibn Yazid Al-Andalusi Al-Qurtubi*. From Andalusia; he is the greatest scholar (along with Al-Tabari and Al-Suyuti) in terms of authorship and compilation, writing much on law, theology, science, and other subjects. Wrote *Al-muhalla bi Al-athar* [Sweetened by the outcomes], highly esteemed as a legal encyclopedia. Died 456 A.H./1064 A.D.

## Ibn Hibban

أبو حاتم محمد بن حبان بن أحمد بن حبان بن معاذ بن معبد التيمي الدارمي البستي, *Abu Hatim Muhammad ibn Hibban ibn Ahmad ibn Hibban ibn Mu'adh ibn Ma'bad Al-Tamimi Al-Darimi Al-Busti*. Historian, collector of hadith, and judge in the Shafi'i school; from Afghanistan. His most influential work is the collection of hadith *Sahih Ibn Hibban*. Died 354 A.H./965 A.D.

## Ibn Kathir

أبو الفداء إسماعيل بن عمر بن كثير القريشي الحصلي البصروي الدمشقي, *Abu Al-fidaa Isma'il ibn 'Umar ibn Kathir ibn Al-Quraishi Al-Hasli Al-Busrawi Al-Dimashqi*; honorary title عماد الدين, Pillar of the *Deen*. Salient scholar from Syria in exegesis and law. Wrote *Tafsir Al-Qur'an Al-'adhim* [Exegesis of the Great Qur'an], one of the most esteemed *tafsir*, and *Al-bidaya wa Al-nihaya* [The beginning and the End], a highly regarded universal history of the world. Died 774 A.H./1373 A.D.

## Ibn Khuzaima

أبو بكر محمد بن إسحاق بن خزيمة, *Abu Bakr Muhammad ibn Ishaq ibn Khuzaima*. From Nishapur (Persia). Scholar of hadith and law of the Shafi'i school; most known for his collection of hadith *Sahih ibn Khuzaima*. Died 311 A.H./923 A.D.

## Ibn Majah

أبو عبد الله محمد بن يزيد بن ماجه الربعي القزويني, *Abu Abdillah Muhammad ibn Yazid ibn Majah Al-Rab'i Al-Qazwini*. From Qazvin (Persia). Noted early scholar and prominent among the collectors of hadith; his collection (*Sunan*) is generally regarded as one of the leading works of Sunni hadith. Died 273 A.H./886 A.D.

## Ibn Nujaim

زين الدين بن ابراهيم إبن محمد, *Zayn Al-din Ibn Ibrahim ibn Muhammad*, known as إبن نجيم المصري الحنفي, *Ibn Nujaim Al-Misri Al-Hanafi*. Hanafi jurist from Egypt. Wrote *Al-bahr Al-ra'iq Sharh Kanz Al-daqa'iq* [The Tranquil Sea in Explanation of the Treasure of the Finer Points], a commentary on Al-Nasafi's *Kanz Al-daqa'iq* [Treasure of the Finer Points]. Died 970 A.H./1563 A.D.

## Ibn Qayyim

أبو عبدالله محمد بن ابي بكر بن أيوب بن سعد بن حرير الزرعي, *Abu Abdillah Muhammad ibn Abi Bakr ibn Ayyub ibn Sa'd bn Harir Al-Zur'i*, given the title شمس الدين, Sun of the *Deen* and primarily known as ابن قيّم الجوزية, *Ibn Qayyim Al-Jawziyya* [son of the principal of the Jawziya school]. From Damascus. Jurist, compiler of hadith, commentator, and important member of the Hanbali school; disciple of Ibn Taymiyyah. His works include *Al-tibb Al-nabawi* [Medicine of the Prophet] and *Bada'ia Al-fawa'id* [The Wonders of the Benefits]. Died 751 A.H./1350 A.D.

## Ibn Qudama

أبو محمد عبد الله بن أحمد بن قدامة بن مقدام المقدسي الجمّاعيلي, *Abu Muhammad Abdullah ibn Ahmad ibn Qudama ibn Miqdam Al-Maqdisi Al-Jama'ili*, given the title موفق الدين, Prosperous in the *Deen*. From Palestine, later Damascus. One of the most prominent figures of the Hanbali school; authored the highly regarded *Al-mughni* [The Enricher], one of the largest works of Islamic law, itself a commentary on *Al-Mukhtasar* by Al-Khiraqi. He also wrote *Al-kafi fi Fiqh Al-imam Ahmad ibn Hanbal* [Sufficiency in the Jurisprudence of Imam Ahmad ibn Hanbal]. Died 620 A.H./1223 A.D.

## Ibn Rushd

أبو الوليد محمد بن أحمد بن محمد بن أحمد بن أحمد بن رشد الأندلسي , *Abu Al-Walid Muhammad ibn Ahmad ibn Muhammad ibn Ahmad ibn Ahmad ibn Rushd Al-Andalusi,* known in Europe as Averroes. Judge, philosopher, physician, jurist, astronomer from Cordoba. Wrote a large number of works on many subjects, among these *Bidaya Al-mujtahid wa Nihaya Al-Muqtasid* [Primer for the Deducers and Resolution for the Moderate]. Died 595 A.H./1198 A.D.

## Ibn Taymiyyah

أبو العباس أحمد بن عبد الحليم بن عبد السلام بن عبدالله بن الخضر بن محمد بن الخضر بن علي بن عبدالله إبن تيمية الحراني, *Abu Al-'Abbas Ahmad ibn 'Abd Al-Halim ibn 'Abd Al-Salam ibn Abdillah ibn Al-Khidr ibn Muhammad ibn Al-Khidr ibn 'Ali ibn Abdillah Ibn Taymiyyah Al-Harrani,* given the title تقي الدين, Pious in the *Deen.* Theologian, jurist, commentator, and compiler of hadith; of the Hanbali school. From Harran (now Turkey) and later Damascus. Among his works are the *Majmu' Al-fatawa* [Collection of Fatwas], *Al-Tafsir Al-Kabir* [The Great Tafsir], and *Al-Sarim Al-Maslul 'ala Shatim Al-Rasoul* [Unsheathed Sword (or "Harshness Unsheathed") Against Those who Insult the Messenger]. Died 728 A.H./1328 A.D.

## Ibn Yahya

أبو نصر السموأل بن يحيى بن عباس المغربي, *Abu Nasr Al-Samaw'al ibn Yayha ibn 'Abbas Al-Maghrabi.* Jew from Morocco who embraced Islam; later lived in Baghdad and Persia; scholar of mathematics and physician. Among his works is *Nuzhat Al-ashab fi Mu'asharat Al-ahbab* [Stroll of the Companions in the Intimacy of Affections]. Died 562 A.H./1180 A.D.

## Malik

أبو عبدالله مالك بن أنس بن مالك بن ابي عامر الأصبحي الحميري المدني, *Abu Abdillah Malik ibn Anas ibn Malik ibn Abi 'Amir Al-Asbahi Al-Hamiri Al-Madini.* Jurist, theologian, and compiler of hadith from Medina, most known for the *Muwatta* [The Well-trodden Path], one of the earliest collections of Sunni hadith and therefore considered one of the most authentic. Founder of the Maliki school of law. Died 179 A.H./795 A.D.

## Muslim

مسلم بن الحجاج بن مسلم بن ورد بن كوشاذ القشيري النيسابوري, *Muslim ibn Al-Hajaj ibn Muslim ibn Ward ibn Kawshadh Al-Qushairi Al-Nisaburi.* From Nishapur (Persia). Compiled *Sahih Muslim,* one of the leading Sunni hadith collections and one of the two most highly regarded (along with *Sahih Al-Bukhari*). Died 261 A.H./875 A.D.